Moving Up in Academia

Moving Up in Academia
Essential Skills for Tenure and Promotion

ESAM EL-FAKAHANY

McFarland & Company, Inc., Publishers
Jefferson, North Carolina

ISBN (print) 978-1-4766-8805-3
ISBN (ebook) 978-1-4766-4625-1

LIBRARY OF CONGRESS AND BRITISH LIBRARY
CATALOGUING DATA ARE AVAILABLE

Library of Congress Control Number 2022005028

© 2022 Esam El-Fakahany. All rights reserved

No part of this book may be reproduced or transmitted in any form or by any means, electronic or mechanical, including photocopying or recording, or by any information storage and retrieval system, without permission in writing from the publisher.

Front cover images © Shutterstock

Printed in the United States of America

*McFarland & Company, Inc., Publishers
Box 611, Jefferson, North Carolina 28640
www.mcfarlandpub.com*

To my grandparents, Amin and Fida, who have been my guiding beacons and invaluable mentors

To my wife, Pamela, for her unwavering affection and support, and for emphasizing the role of relationships in career advancement

To my daughters, Sarah and Nora, for showering me with love

To my grandson, Ivan, for giving me hope for a bright future for the next generations

Acknowledgments

I sincerely acknowledge the valuable contributions to the content of this book made by many senior and junior colleagues. I would like to particularly thank Dr. Amanda Klein and Dr. Beshay Zordoky for their helpful comments on earlier drafts.

Table of Contents

Acknowledgments vi

Preface 1

Introduction 3

1. Understanding Your New Environment 9
2. Special Issues Facing Women and Minority Faculty 27
3. People Skills 45
4. Time and Energy Management 62
5. Advising and Mentoring Your Trainees 81
6. Team Management and Leadership 105
7. Benefiting from Mentoring 126
8. The Path to Promotion and Tenure 139
9. Maintaining the Vitality of Mid-Career and Senior Faculty 162
10. Preparing to Become a Future Academic Leader 189
11. Challenges to Academia 208

Bibliography 225

Index 229

Preface

Some time ago, years into a successful research career, I became involved in mentoring newly appointed junior faculty members who did not have a typical research training background. These were healthcare professionals who had in mind research questions that could potentially have a significant impact on human and animal health. Unfortunately, some lacked the skill of constructing proper research design or presenting their innovative ideas in a way that would be readily understood and appreciated by members of a diverse grant review panel. Helping these faculty members develop their research skills was quite rewarding. Many eventually succeeded in obtaining large federal research grants and became well published. Later, some even became leaders in their research fields. I felt tremendous joy and fulfillment watching their progress.

This experience made me reassess my motives in being a researcher, leading me to apply a wider lens in considering my approach to advancing scientific knowledge. The main questions that came to mind were: Do I have greater impact by continuing to do my own research or by helping others do theirs? Is it fair that I gain research money better spent on more clever ideas and questions proposed by the young and vigorous? The answer to both questions came to me by pure serendipity while I was watching a soccer game. As the camera focused on the coach sitting on the bench at the sideline, I saw an individual who was at one time a very talented player but decided at a certain juncture in their athletic career to move on to become a coach. This decision enabled them to enhance the talent of many others by sharing their experience on the field. Of course, some coaches had to quit playing as they aged and lost their agility. The wise ones, however, quit playing voluntarily while they were at the top of their game. These observations led me inexorably (if slowly) toward mentoring, my focus gradually shifting away from research to focusing on advancing the careers of others.

In 1999, I was appointed associate dean of the graduate school and assistant vice president for research at the University of Minnesota. I took advantage of being in such a position of power to develop formal programs to provide graduate students and postdoctoral fellows in all disciplines with soft skills that complement the scholarly training provided by their advisors. I also established a new Office for Postdoctoral Affairs to address the precarious situation of postdoctorals. Typically, they have a doctorate but are not ready yet to advance to the next step of becoming independent investigators. As a result, they often do not have a formal body to support their career advancement needs. Again, I found this experience most fulfilling. It stimulated me to pursue other administrative positions that would enable me to effect more change in the academic mentoring environment. In the period of 2011–2020, I served as associate dean for research, graduate studies and faculty affairs in the College of Pharmacy at the University of Minnesota. Since 2015, I have also been serving as co-director of mentoring in the Clinical and Translational Science Institute at the university. Together, these appointments allowed me to pursue my passion for mentoring faculty, postdoctorals and graduate students on a large scale. One area of emphasis has been "mentoring mentors on how to mentor"! In this regard, I have collaborated with others to develop online and in-person modules that focus on characteristics of good mentoring and how to deal with challenges that frequently test the mentoring relationship. The online course is available to graduate students, postdoctoral fellows and faculty from any college.

One central observation I have made is that junior faculty usually receive adequate advice on how to write successful grant applications or how to become a good teacher. There are actually many excellent books on these topics, in addition to specialized workshops organized by academic institutions. I have also sensed a common belief that being good at teaching and writing is mostly what an academic needs to establish a successful career. However, my long years of experience in this world have taught me otherwise. There is a long list of skills one must have in order to navigate the academic environment, without which success becomes rather uncertain. Examples include time and energy management; skills in advising, mentoring and leadership; and, most important, the ability to deal with people and difficult situations. There is also a lack of guidance for faculty at the midpoint of their careers (or later) regarding how to maintain their vigor and prepare for the possibility of becoming academic leaders. Together, these observations have stimulated me to write this book to fill in these important gaps.

Introduction

During my academic journey, as a result of much trial and error, I have learned a wide array of technical and soft skills necessary for success in my chosen career. The most pressing area of growth was learning how to navigate the academic arena and benefit from the environment. The need for many of these skills was not obvious to me when I started my journey, which led to my lack of preparedness. However, I still managed to succeed in spite of these deficiencies, simply because those were the good old days when jobs and research funding were plentiful. Competition was not as fierce as it is today. The picture is now quite different. One needs to have a very strong portfolio of both professional and personal skills to get a tenure-track job and, more important, succeed at it.

Through mentoring, it became apparent that there was a wide range of career development tools that some junior faculty members lacked more than others. Some needed to sharpen their writing and presentation skills. Others did not know how to successfully package and pitch a research question to make it appeal to different funding agencies. Like me when I started my academic career, most junior faculty perceive academicians as idealists and purists, thinking of them as people who have dedicated their lives to helping each other unravel the wonders of life and the universe, make an invention that facilitates industrial operations, or correct historical dogmas. These newcomers have a general impression that academic scholars are free of selfishness and territoriality and above making it ahead of others through unfair competition. They think these negative traits only afflict lay people! Of course, these assumptions are both naive and invalid. Scholars are people too! Furthermore, academia has its own share of politics that one must learn to navigate as early as possible to win allies and avoid making enemies.

When a junior faculty member starts their new job, they find themselves in a largely unfamiliar environment. They have to deal with new colleagues, especially a new boss. There is a very long list of committee and building acronyms, administrative titles and governing structures that do not mean much to them. Some junior faculty mistakenly believe that their success is mainly, or perhaps solely, based on the summation of their skills and hard work. They falsely presume that the only thing preventing them from achieving glory and fame was the lack of a starting faculty job, as they could succeed anywhere. As time goes on, they gradually realize the positive and negative impact that the prevailing culture of the department, college and institution can have on the advancement of their career. Many get hurt by saying or doing something with purely good intentions, only to find out that they rocked the boat the wrong way. Their words or actions may have been misinterpreted as aiming to minimize a superior or overstep the traditional administrative ladder in seeking consultation or making a complaint. Faculty of color may experience these challenges in a more magnified way. Many faculty members from underrepresented minority populations already suffer from feeling isolated and unappreciated. They may encounter a hostile environment that permits or encourages macro- and microaggressions. In addition, it is difficult for a minority faculty to maintain their cultural identity while they are trying to assimilate into an environment dominated by white people. Minority faculty are also often overtaxed by being required to serve on many committees as a voice of institutional diversity. At the same time, women faculty have their own share of challenges. They often have to cater to both work and family duties and therefore must assume multiple identities. Being in a predominantly white male environment makes women faculty vulnerable to being unfairly judged and compensated. This book offers advice and tools on how a junior faculty member can successfully navigate a complex academic environment and how to benefit from the positive aspects academia offers while avoiding invisible landmines.

One of the most serious stumbling blocks a junior faculty member may face is having to juggle so many types of responsibilities and activities. This is quite different from the limited responsibilities of doing research and taking courses while in graduate school. Junior faculty must deal with, and excel at, research, teaching and service. They must prepare for tomorrow's class while continuing to revise a grant proposal that is due the following week. Being busy preparing a grant application is not an acceptable excuse for delivering a lousy lecture to students. How does one fit so many things into their daily or weekly schedule without becoming burned out or sacrificing personal time with their families and friends? Are there tricks for better management of time, energy and projects? Do all the required responsibilities carry a comparable weight in the annual assessment of faculty performance and productivity? Do they matter equally in decisions on promotion and tenure? Should some responsibilities be delegated? How does one know when and to whom a given task should be delegated without sacrificing the quality of the outcome? How does a junior faculty member politely decline a request to serve on a new committee or teach additional lectures in a course without being labeled as uncooperative? These serious challenges (and methods for mitigating them) are the subject of some of the chapters in this book.

It is distressing for a junior faculty member to go it alone. Their journey will likely be full of painful and distressing trials and errors, needlessly consuming their time and energy, as well as harming their morale. More seriously, some of the mistakes made along the way may have long-lasting negative consequences that are difficult to reverse no matter how hard one may try. New faculty are often experts in their specific scholarly fields, but most lack experience in important life skills, such as dealing with rejection and taking control of their time despite the increasing demands of their jobs and families. Success in their academic mission also requires clear communication, both verbally and in writing. Even body language matters. In addition, they must be adept at winning over others, building trustworthiness, engaging in negotiation and conflict management, and dealing with difficult people. Multiple chapters in this book are dedicated to the importance of these skills.

Mentors provide knowledge about resources and how to get things done efficiently. They are well versed in navigating a political academic environment. If you are new to academia, you should benefit from their wisdom when you design a roadmap to achieve your goals. Seek their sage advice to further develop your strengths and overcome your shortcomings. Above all, mentors provide an important source of moral support. They are usually the first to celebrate a mentee's success and provide encouragement to get back in the saddle when he or she stumbles and falls.

At the start of a junior faculty career, one is not adequately familiar with many aspects pertaining to promotion and tenure. What type of documentation is needed? How should one select and cultivate external reviewers of the promotion dossier? What really matters in judging merit for promotion? What are the various steps in this lengthy process? Who is involved in making decisions at each step? Mentors are helpful in providing answers to these questions and more. They also serve as advocates when the junior faculty member comes up for promotion and tenure. Similar benefits may be derived from other types of collaborative connections within and outside one's institution.

This book instructs new faculty on how to benefit from the experience of mentors and professional networks. It also discusses criteria for a healthy and productive mentoring and networking relationship. Tools are provided for preparing junior faculty to become successful advisors and mentors to their students, postdoctoral fellows and other types of trainees.

Chapter 5 deals with fulfilling the needs of trainees in sharpening their skills and developing their professional independence. This chapter emphasizes the importance of the advisor's role in advocating for and marketing their trainees to help them move forward. Moreover, it includes advice on how to handle challenges to the advising and mentoring relationship as a result of misaligned expectations, miscommunication or lack of accountability. There is also discussion of the importance of catering to the specific needs of trainees from diverse populations and those who may have different career aspirations. In addition, this book provides important tools required for successful management of a research team, including tips on hiring, motivation and holding productive meetings at various levels.

A scholar's professional development does not stop at the time of being promoted to the rank of associate professor, with or without tenure. One should look at this important transition as only one of the milestones along their overall academic journey. They must maintain their momentum and remain productive in scholarly endeavors, teaching and service. Keeping up with the rapid advancement of research technology or methodology may require gaining additional training through courses or workshops. A faculty member may also benefit from taking a sabbatical at a different institution, perhaps even in a different country, to sharpen their skills. Chapter 9 is dedicated to maintaining the vitality and effecting professional growth of mid-career and senior faculty.

An associate or full professor may discover special aptitude in academic leadership. The academic world will always need leaders whose main drive is generating positive changes in the academic environment. One must avoid the misconception that a productive researcher would necessarily make an effective departmental, collegiate or institutional leader. First, there are vast differences between advising, management and leadership. Second, leadership at these higher levels is far more complicated than running a research laboratory or leading a group to excavate historical ruins somewhere on the other side of the world. A good leader must be consultative, decisive, transparent, visionary, practical, and bold, and they should excel at fiscal management. They should recognize the fine line between counseling and decisiveness and be ready to make difficult decisions for the good of the department, college or institution. The outcome of some of these decisions may not be optimal for all, which would obviously create personal clashes.

Faculty who at some point in their career contemplate moving to leadership positions must undergo careful self-reflection. They should take into consideration professional and personal strengths, future career goals and optimal life-work balance. She or he should also assess their readiness to make the move. Is it the right stage of their career? Does it fit the needs of their family? Are there missing skills a successful leader must acquire prior to pursuing leadership positions? How does one go about developing these skills? This book deals with these questions and more.

In sum, it is hoped that faculty who read this book will gain a variety of skills and learn about tools that complement their technical and professional talents and abilities. This book is also meant to serve as a guide to academic administrators in deciding curricula of institution-wide programs that aim to build the skills of postdoctoral fellows and faculty, particularly the junior members.

1

Understanding Your New Environment

There is so much joy associated with becoming a tenure-track assistant professor. It is a dream come true for any graduate student or a postdoctoral trainee who has hoped to pursue a career in academia. Peers and superiors in their new department are proud and thrilled to have recruited a junior colleague who pursues state-of-the-art scholarly endeavors. They are welcoming and willing to assist the new faculty in any way they can in getting settled and starting a successful career.

Triumph in landing a precious academic position, however, comes with significant responsibilities, in which one has a primary role in charting their own path. She or he has to do due diligence in understanding what is expected of them and what it takes to reach the next stage of their career—namely, the holy grail of becoming a tenured associate professor. They should be intentional in developing new personal skills that facilitate their assimilation into the new academic organization and in developing new relationships with colleagues, both within and outside their department, college or institution. Most important, a starting faculty member needs to understand the institutional administrative structure and figure out who to go to for help when challenging situations develop.

Moving to a New Environment

Change—any change in one's surroundings—can be quite unsettling. It certainly is for a new assistant professor who once thought that getting a tenure-track position would be the final answer to their worries. Surprise, surprise! He or she soon discovers that this is only one step on a very long and unpaved road. They feel like they are being watched by everybody with very high expectations for the new faculty member. This situation creates significant stress and internal turmoil, particularly due to fear of disappointing others. In addition, the tenure clock has started ticking from day one on the job. The junior faculty member knows exactly what the prize is but likely does not have a clear idea of how to qualify for it.

Moving to another city is also associated with marked anxiety. It takes time and effort to explore the new environment and make decisions about kids' schooling, daycare and healthcare. There are also many unknowns related to where one chooses to live. Numerous important questions come to mind: Should I live in the city or in the suburbs? How far am I willing to drive to work? How do I balance family safety, good education and commuting time? Which is the best grocery store in the neighborhood for ethnic foods? Where do I go for dry cleaning or veterinary care? How friendly are the neighbors? These and others are very important issues to ponder. One's surrounding community and resources could easily make the difference between social happiness and misery.

Skills You Did Not Learn in Graduate School

Becoming part of an academic faculty is both quite thrilling and overwhelming. It is indeed a long leap from being a graduate student or a postdoctoral fellow who was largely dependent on a research advisor who assumed multiple responsibilities to guide them through training. The advisor brought in grant money, designed projects and experiments, hired staff, assigned roles and responsibilities, and led group meetings. While in graduate school and during postdoctoral training, a trainee is mostly focused on taking courses and doing research. Expectations are clear. A junior faculty member, by contrast, must also develop skills to effectively juggle research, teaching, service and family responsibilities, ideally leaving sufficient time for relaxation, exercise, social connections and hobbies.

It is clear to graduate students that they can go to the director of the graduate program, the administrative assistants in the department or their research advisor when problems arise. This is essentially the limit of their required knowledge of college and institutional administrative structure. When they become assistant professors, they expand their communication circle to include the department head, dean, students, trainees, staff and peers. They have little or no knowledge of the roles and responsibilities of the many administrative offices in the department, let alone in the college and the university at large. There is a long list of administrative titles that do not mean much with regard to the impact these administrators have on the professional advancement of faculty. There is also a seemingly endless list of collegiate and institutional consultative and governance bodies to be

1. Understanding Your New Environment

introduced to. What is a college assembly or executive council? What is the role of the faculty senate? Why are there so many associate deans? What do they do with their time? What role do they play in assisting faculty to attain their career goals? What is a provost or a chancellor, and what responsibilities do they assume in leading the institution? What about the many vice presidents? Why have a university president since the provost and vice presidents do so much?

The extent of a junior faculty member's background skills and knowledge naturally depends on the quality of technical and career mentoring they received during their graduate and postdoctoral training. Some were solely "advised" about their research project and writing up research findings for publication. Others—the fortunate ones—were "mentored" on the many skills needed for success as independent investigators. Fortunate junior faculty are those who had advisors who allowed their students to shadow them or guided them to reading material or workshops to learn the principles of successfully operating an independent research program.

Many junior faculty did not have to worry about where research funding comes from while in graduate school, as long as they were getting paid and had the necessary equipment, reagents for their experiments or travel funds to study indigenous languages or customs in another part of the world. The lucky ones submitted proposals for independent fellowships that introduced them to grantsmanship. Getting internal and external research funding is quite a challenge for a novice. It requires iterative learning and growth that may take some time and involve many failed attempts.

While one might think that obtaining research funding is the most critical step in the career of junior faculty, what is more challenging (in my opinion) is using these funds effectively to build and manage a highly functional research team. One needs to develop expertise in interviewing, motivating, reprimanding and resolving conflicts. Some may wonder whether there is a crash course to quickly acquire these skills. Unfortunately, there isn't, but there are ways to gain these skills gradually over time. Senior colleagues and mentors could be an invaluable resource for providing tips on such people skills. However, balancing the desire of a junior faculty member to learn from others with the need to be perceived as independent is rather tricky.

When I was in graduate school in the late 1970s, I measured my value according to how many papers I read, my grades and my publication record. I had no idea what it takes to fund research, build a research team and, more seriously, manage a team to achieve harmony and high productivity. My advisor was world famous for his work and had multiple national research grants. I was never questioned when it came to requesting reagents for my research, no matter how expensive they were. The institution was committed to retaining my advisor against frequent lucrative offers from other prestigious institutions. He was guaranteed "full" bridge funding for two years for any grants he lost to allow him uninterrupted productivity. Every two years he received a large sum of money to upgrade laboratory equipment. He had more than a dozen technicians with assigned responsibilities for various services (e.g., laboratory safety surveys, ordering reagents, calling for equipment repair or calibration). It was a graduate student utopia that I took for granted.

Having such easy life and maintaining a narrow focus on my research project, however, came with a hefty price. I was not trained to do things or take on responsibilities that did not connect directly to progress toward my graduate degree. I still recall turning down offers from a senior laboratory technician to get involved in discussions comparing various brands and models of laboratory instruments or interviewing applicants for new positions in the laboratory. I thought that engaging in such activities was a waste of time I could use to read an article or do another experiment. I regretted this short-sighted vision when it was time for me to assume these responsibilities in building up my own laboratory and research team. I essentially learned the hard way, by trial and error!

Being spoiled with unlimited research funds and resources during graduate training also meant I had no idea how to handle a small startup budget and make sure to use every dollar wisely. Fortunately, I did my postdoctoral training in a laboratory that was significantly less funded than that of my doctoral advisor. It had only a couple of technicians who were assigned their own research projects, rather than being there to assist other researchers in the group. This arrangement gave me the opportunity to do many things on my own. I even had to learn how to synthesize an expensive research reagent from starting material in house. What a sharp contrast to the luxury I had enjoyed in my doctoral advisor's laboratory! I started realizing that perhaps my graduate training experience was the exception, rather than the norm.

When I assumed my first faculty position, my department chair made me an offer that I accepted without any hesitation. He asked me whether I would like to have two of his doctoral students join my laboratory to get me started. I thought this was a kind sentiment that really exceeded my expectations of generosity and unselfishness on his part. Reality, however, was quite painful and costly. These students turned out to be disastrous. One was easily distracted by his surroundings, to the extent of dropping crucial steps in experiments. The other student was hopelessly untrainable in maintaining a sterile environment for cell culture. I took it upon myself to help these students overcome their impediments. My attempts, however, were rather futile. It became apparent that my chair's seeming act of kindness was simply a bid to rid himself of these troublesome students. At this juncture, I wished I had been mentored in the people skills that would have helped me avoid such invisible traps. I also wished I had learned how to more effectively manage my time and decide on priorities to be able to successfully handle my diverse portfolio of responsibilities.

Understanding and Benefiting from the Academic Environment

While academic institutions share many characteristics and administrative structures, each has unique aspects. It is of utmost importance for a new junior faculty member to demystify and understand the academic culture of their institution. One must learn the nuances of how things operate in the department, college and institution. Who are the main players? Who has power to influence the directions of the college and institution? Who should the newcomer cultivate as an ally? The hierarchical nature of the power differential in academia grants faculty little clout and voice while they are in the probationary period of their employment. Things change dramatically when they are granted tenure.

It is essential for a junior faculty member to fully understand the criteria for promotion and tenure in their department. This must be done as soon as possible to direct their efforts toward what really counts when the time comes to prepare their promotion dossier. Newcomers should be aware of the types of journals that are valued in assessing scholarly productivity. They should also talk with recently promoted colleagues about their experience. It is wise to discover undocumented rules of the game. One should find candid answers to these commonly asked questions: How much weight is given to teaching compared to scholarship? Is it really mostly or all about research dollars? Will I get promoted mainly by being a good citizen who has not declined any requests to serve on various types of committees?!

Appreciation of the Role of Institutional Culture and Values in the Success of Junior Faculty

An institution's environment has tremendous influence on the productivity and job satisfaction of junior faculty. A talented individual will likely not succeed (or opt to stay) at an institution that does not provide necessary resources or one that allows practices that go against common academic values such as respect and integrity. Successful departments, colleges and universities live by their values with regard to diversity, inclusion, respect, trust, accountability and honesty. Collectively, these elements not only provide means for professional advancement but also ensure invaluable psychological support and comfort. Having mottos without corresponding actions causes mistrust, doubt, discouragement and dissatisfaction. A healthy environment also encourages individuals to speak up when they notice actions by individuals or groups that go against the expressed values. It holds perpetrators accountable.

Feeling cared for plays an important role in developing resilience when challenges arise. One will not feel alone or ashamed when they hear bad news about an unfunded grant application, a rejected research manuscript or negative teaching evaluations by students. A caring and supportive environment is quite conducive for establishing autonomy and self-confidence. Providing good mentoring is the best way to demonstrate that others genuinely care about the career trajectory and happiness of a junior faculty member. Unfortunately, junior faculty in a few institutions do not receive such support. Some may even feel like they are under a microscope, with colleagues waiting for them to make a mistake so as to point fingers. This type of hazing is utterly demeaning and demoralizing.

Another important element that contributes to psychological comfort and satisfaction is valuing junior faculty input in departmental and collegiate affairs. This includes being invited to contribute to strategic planning, recruitment of new faculty and graduate students, and so forth. A positive institutional professional environment also provides clear documentation of responsibilities and expectations, along with well-defined benchmarks for assessing the performance of all its members.

Understanding Institutional and Collegiate Governance Structure

When I became a tenure-track assistant professor, I was immediately faced with the task of deciphering dozens of terms, acronyms and policies. For some odd reason, some academics take joy in throwing out a bunch of acronyms that they know for sure do not mean anything to a new kid on the block. In my first week of employment my department head suggested I go to a seminar held by the CSFG of GPN in the PWH main classroom. I was too shy to ask what this jargon meant, but I was brave enough to consult with one of the department secretaries, who said, "He recommended you go to a seminar held by the Cognitive Science Focus Group in the Graduate Program in Neuroscience. The presentation is in the main classroom in the Philip Wangensteen Hall." As time went by, hundreds of acronyms became second nature to me. Eventually I even figured out the subtle differences between standing committees, focus groups, councils, task forces, boards and working groups.

Charter, Statutes, By-laws

The operation of each academic institution is governed by its charter. This is the document that defines the manner in which the university trustees or regents are selected and the authority they have in acting on the university's behalf. Institutional statutes detail the structure of the university in terms of constituent units and their mission. They also define the roles and responsibilities of officers, faculty and other key personnel who serve the university. In addition, statutes include policies that govern the terms of their appointment in each of these categories of employment. The most important academic institution statutes are the code of conduct and the policy on academic freedom and tenure (where tenure applies). All college and department administrative policies and by-laws must conform to the university charter and statutes. Each college develops its own constitution and by-laws, which must be approved by the higher university administration. These documents describe the administrative governing and consultative structures of the college, their membership and voting privileges.

Parliamentary Rules of Governance

When you start attending department and college meetings, you will hear a term that is likely totally foreign to you: "The Robert's Rules." This is a set of parliamentary rules to be adhered to in order to ensure that meetings are conducted in an orderly and democratic fashion. These procedures offer an environment that is conducive to providing justice and courtesy for all participants so that each side gets heard. They also provide guidelines for required quorum and the process of making motions and voting on issues.

After a fair discussion of an issue, the meeting chair will ask whether there is a motion with a proposal. The motion requires a second before discussing and voting on it. The seconded motion may be amended by striking or adding words or by substituting one paragraph for another. A vote is then taken, provided there is a quorum. For a motion to pass, it requires either two-thirds of the quorum or a simple majority, depending on the by-laws and the nature of the case at hand. College by-laws determine the specific faculty appointments that are associated with voting privileges. Practicing these privileges usually depends on the population of faculty affected by a given resolution. For example, contract (term) faculty on the non-tenure track are usually not allowed to vote on tenure-related matters.

Institutional Leadership Structure

The administrative structure of academic institutions varies dramatically, depending on their size and mission. Here is an example of the typical governance structure of a large research-intensive institution:

1. *Board of regents/trustees*: Governing board members in public institutions are usually appointed by the state governor, either directly or being subject to approval of the state legislature. They represent the citizens of the state. Boards of private universities are generally self-perpetuating, with new trustees chosen by the membership of the standing board. Others are recommended by university alums. The major responsibilities of boards of regents/trustees include preserving the university charter, conducting institutional performance evaluations, fund raising, and connecting with political bodies and external agencies. They are also responsible for institutional budget approval in addition to oversight of campus policies and investment strategies. Most important, it is these boards that hire university presidents and provosts and evaluate their performance. The university president serves ex officio on the board.

2. *President*: The president is the overall leader of an academic institution. He or she presides over its academic and administrative bureaus. One of the president's most important roles is fund raising. This task is particularly pivotal for the life of private institutions. Lately, however, fund raising has also become vital for public institutions due to the continually declining state support for higher education. Other presidential duties include delivering a positive image of the institution to the public in terms of contributions by the faculty to teaching, scholarship and community outreach.

3. *Senior executive vice president*: This person is assigned the responsibility of managing the budget and operations of various services in the university, such as the physical plant, public safety, human resources, institutional real estate, student services, and administrative support functions. This individual is often supported by a team of vice presidents (e.g., vice presidents for finances, facilities management, human resources, research, institutional compliance, procurement services, information technology).

4. *Provost*: The provost is the chief academic officer of the

institution who oversees all academic programs and their faculty to ensure the highest possible quality. She or he periodically evaluates colleges and programs, as well as their leadership, and makes final recommendations about faculty promotion and tenure to the board of regents. The provost also determines college budgets (in collaboration with the institution's senior financial officer) and approves modifications to college constitutions and by-laws. Moreover, the provost reviews and approves academic appointments and salaries, ensures salary equity and signs off on faculty developmental leaves (e.g., sabbaticals). The provost also reviews and acts on faculty grievances, including rebuttals in cases of denial of promotion or tenure, discrimination, or abuse. The provost is usually assisted by a group of vice provosts, the number and responsibilities of whom depend on the size of the institution, its mission and its needs. Examples include the vice provosts for faculty affairs, undergraduate education or graduate education. In some institutions, the latter two positions hold the title of "dean."

5. *University administrative units that matter to you the most*:

University senate: The formal governing body of the faculty at the institutional level is the academic senate, a group generally composed of tenured and tenure-track faculty from various disciplines and colleges. Depending on the institutional by-laws, this body may also include representatives of non-tenure-track faculty. The primary function of the senate is to represent the voice of the faculty in matters of university governance. It serves as a link connecting the faculty, the president and the board of regents. Thus, university senates are charged with reviewing educational policies and ensuring the welfare and academic freedom of faculty and students. They approve changes to the conditions for granting major degrees.

Vice president for research: This office develops and implements strategies for advancing research in the institution. It usually offers financial assistance for new research projects and collaborations, brings faculty together, and establishes partnerships with the community and the private sector. It is also responsible for maintaining the ethics and integrity of scholarly practices in the institution and monitoring the welfare of research animals and human subjects.

Vice provost for faculty affairs: The main function of this office is fostering a culture that enables faculty to achieve excellence in their various roles. It usually offers orientation programs for incoming faculty and new department heads. This office oversees the process of promotion and tenure and approves professional development leaves on behalf of the provost. It may also provide resources to support advances in teaching and learning skills.

Vice president for human resources: The office of human resources works with university administration, faculty and staff to provide the workforce and organizational capabilities that maintain excellence in the university. This office is a helpful source of information about healthcare and retirement benefits, well-being programs, work-life balance, hiring procedures, conflict resolution and grievances. It may also offer professional development opportunities for staff.

Office of the general counsel: Many (but not all) institutions have in-house law offices. When they exist, their main goal is to ensure the best possible outcomes in litigation between the university and external entities and to minimize legal problems by offering proactive services. In practice, this office represents the university in all legal matters and protects its interests. Most important, the office of the general counsel is responsible for guarding the principles of due process in how the university treats faculty, staff, students, and all other members of the institutional community.

6. *Common university consultative bodies:*
   - Council of collegiate deans
   - Council of associate deans for research
   - Council of associate deans for graduate education
   - Council of associate deans for undergraduate and professional education
   - Council of associate deans for faculty affairs
   - Council of academic professional and administrative staff
   - Council of graduate students

Collegiate Leadership Structure

The dean is the chief officer of a college. She or he is appointed by and reports to the university provost. The dean's responsibilities include oversight and making final decisions on academic planning, enhancing educational and research services, guiding preparation for professional and regional accreditation, recruiting faculty and students, maintaining faculty development and evaluation, advising, developing budgets, and allocating resources. The faculty evaluate the dean's performance, usually every three years. Assistant/associate deans, department chairs/unit heads and directors assist deans in running collegiate affairs. They are appointed by the dean, and their employment is usually renewable on an annual basis. Their performance is evaluated by the faculty, again about every three years. It is helpful to a new faculty member to understand the roles and responsibilities of each of these individuals and the extent of their authority—in other words, what influence they have on the faculty success and career advancement.

The department head or chair is responsible for assigning faculty duties and effort distribution. This individual also evaluates faculty performance and plays an important role in advocating for faculty at the time of promotion and tenure decisions. Department heads come in different forms, with varying degrees of management competence. More seriously, they differ in their ability to ensure the faculty and department continue moving not only forward but also upward. Most gravitate to such positions because of noble goals. Others do so to satisfy their thirst for power and control. The majority of department chairs serve as role models in maintaining their vigorous scholarship programs. Sadly, others decide to pursue department administration as a result of failing to remain competitive in a rapidly advancing research arena. Some chairs are selected on the basis of their glamorous research portfolio. However, the truth is that a successful researcher does not necessarily make a good leader, particularly if they decide to continue to pay more attention to their own research program at the expense of providing leadership to the department. It is very important that a department head possess excellent people skills. They should have a supportive personality that invites candid feedback from department faculty, students and staff. It is catastrophic to have a department chair who is difficult to get along with. Such a person will likely create a counterproductive culture that negatively influences the spirits of the faculty. Junior faculty suffer the most in these cases since the power differential and fear of retaliation makes them accept the status quo without complaining. (There will be more information to come on this issue in the chapters dedicated to leadership and people skills.)

Associate deans and directors could be quite helpful in advancing faculty careers. In particular, find out the responsibilities of the associate dean for research and what resources their office offers, especially with regard to seed funding. The office of the associate dean for faculty affairs is a useful resource for policies and procedures related to annual evaluation and promotion/tenure. Consult with the director of human resources in your college whenever you need to know more about the process of hiring, professional development opportunities for staff and disciplining underperformers.

Collegiate Governance and Consultative Bodies

College Executive Council

Members of this council usually include associate deans, department chairs, the chief financial officer and college directors (e.g., directors of communication, human resources, development, etc.). It is chaired by the dean. The executive council provides recommendations to the dean about strategic plans, college budget and investments, charges and membership on college committees. It also reviews the accomplishments and recommendations of various college committees. The executive council regularly provides reports to the college assembly.

College Assembly

This governing body is composed of the dean, faculty (tenured and tenure-track), and representatives of graduate, professional and undergraduate students. It also includes representatives of civil service/bargaining units and academic professional and administrative staff. Representatives of contract (non-tenure-track) faculty may also be members of the assembly, with or without voting rights. The college assembly serves as a forum for faculty, students, staff and administrators to discuss important college-wide issues. It is involved in making provisions, rules and regulations necessary for the governance of the college—most important, approval of the college constitution and by-laws, committee structures, charges and membership. It is also responsible for vetting proposals for programmatic modifications in the college.

College Faculty Consultative Committee

This committee usually includes faculty representatives from each collegiate department, plus the associate dean for faculty affairs (ex officio). It reviews department recommendations for promotion and tenure and advises the dean accordingly. It also handles various matters concerning faculty, including vetting requests for sabbatical leaves. In some colleges, this is the committee that initiates drafting and revising the college constitution and by-laws.

Collegiate Committees

Each college has its own set of committees that counsel the college administration on various aspects of the academic mission. Examples include committees on graduate education, curricula, research, safety and diversity. These committees are consultative rather than being a part of the governance structure.

Understanding and Dealing with Politics within and outside Your Academic Environment

Like any community, academic environments have a mixture of people with different personality traits and attitudes toward others. Fortunately, most are civil, respectful and cooperative. However, there are often a few difficult faculty or staff whom one cannot totally avoid interacting with (and perhaps become subjected to their uncivilized manners). These people include the selfish, sexist, antagonistic, alarming, hostile, pushy, arrogant, egotistic, obstinate, deceitful, manipulative, exploitative or overly critical. They are usually repeat offenders. Some even enjoy having the reputation of being a bully and justify their behavior by touting it as being frank with people and "telling it the way it is!" A lucky junior faculty member will discover early on who these folks are, watch for them and prepare to take precautions. No one should tolerate their negative and hurtful behaviors or let them interfere with their productivity and peace of mind. Their behavior should be reported to the department head and mentors, who are usually capable of providing good advice on how to handle these people—and sometimes even tame them and transform them into allies. They most certainly have had past experience in watching these difficult people in action over the years. Chapter 3 offers tools for handling different types of difficult individuals.

Academic institutions vary widely in walking their talk when it comes to living and practicing their proclaimed values. Exemplary universities enforce civility, respect and cooperation. They reward those who practice these core values and curtail the ones who don't. Others are at fault for giving a free reign to some influential faculty who feel free to insult and harass students, staff and other faculty. Those people are usually prima donnas or primo uomos who are endowed with large amounts of research funding. Institutions sometimes look the other way to avoid having high-ranking faculty walk out.

Acknowledging the Dark Side of Academia

There is a prevailing dogma that academicians choose this taxing career only for the purpose of seeking new knowledge or producing inventions that improve the lives of all living creatures on Planet Earth. Therefore, they are thought to be above suffering from negative personality traits that afflict "the commoners." They are expected to rise above feelings of envy and possessiveness. They derive joy from watching a colleague solve a complicated mathematical problem or discover a biological phenomenon or a social relationship before they did, since advancement of knowledge is their main drive, regardless of who gets the credit.

The truth, however, is that academic scholars are people too. They come with a mixed bag of personality traits, some of which are not ones to be proud of. A number of these traits are part of individuals' genetic makeup or the result of the way they were brought up by their families or trained by their advisors. Others become reinforced during the pursuit of their academic career. Over time, they gradually develop emotions and biases that influence their decision making. Fierce and sometimes unfair or unethical competition comes to the top of the list. There is often a race between scholars working on similar projects. While a large majority of academics recognize the benefits of collaborating with others to expedite discoveries, others make a personal decision to pursue the journey alone and are determined to get to the finish line first, no matter how or at what cost to others. A famous example is the competition between two groups seeking to decode the human genome. Each group applied a different approach, and both succeeded, completing the genome sequencing at about the same time. However, the project would have been completed much sooner if they had worked together. Some investigators put a stop to their collaboration with others and may actually become personal and professional enemies due to fighting over credit for a major discovery. There are numerous similar examples in all fields of scholarship.

In academia, resources are scarce, especially research funding. This situation leads some to guard their turf by shunning newcomers to the field, especially those whose line of research does not support their favored dogma. Such selfish behaviors may be reflected in the manner of training graduate students and postdoctoral fellows—for example, not sharing important trade secrets with them or forbidding them to pursue their projects once they leave the group. I even know of a senior faculty member who decided not to train graduate students for fear of creating competitors! Such unfair (and sometimes unethical) competition comes in many forms and has different roots. One of these is having personal conflicts of interest interfere with one's ability to make fair decisions in evaluating scholarly manuscripts or grant proposals. A journal reviewer, for instance, may be tempted to reject a manuscript simply to allow themselves time to finish and publish similar work. Worse yet, there is a history of unethical scholars who stole research ideas and ran with them as if they were their own creation.

Fortunately, there are measures to curb and punish such immoral behaviors. Many institutions offer obligatory training in the principles of ethical research conduct to their faculty, staff, graduate students and post-doctoral fellows. Moreover, there are mechanisms in place to report and investigate unethical practices in research, at both the institutional and the national level. A junior faculty member should take advantage of these resources to protect their intellectual property and the integrity of their research program.

Issues Specific to Adjunct and Contract Faculty

Many higher education institutions hire a large proportion of adjunct faculty, mainly to help with the educational mission. This arrangement permits tenured and tenure-track faculty to dedicate more time and effort to the scholarly endeavors that bring both money and fame to the institution. It is also common knowledge that adjunct faculty are paid much less and do not accrue the same benefits as regular faculty, especially in earning contributions to retirement plans by the institution. Adjunct appointments are usually part time, depending on the teaching needs. Therefore, adjunct faculty may have positions at more than one university, or they may hold another position in their professional specialty in the non-academic sector. Some prefer the flexibility provided by an adjunct appointment since it allows more time for taking care of family and personal affairs. Furthermore, adjunct faculty have the major advantage of not being required to go through the pain of writing proposals for research funding and not having to attend the many types of lengthy, frequent, and sometimes wasteful departmental and college meetings. These appointments generally work well for those who love teaching more than any other academic activity. Many adjunct faculty, however, suffer from unfair compensation. They do not get paid enough to cover their financial needs, and they also do not get paid at all during non-teaching periods of the year.

Contract faculty are usually hired to fill in temporary teaching needs or because they are more knowledgeable on certain contemporary or applied topics than regular faculty. For example, a clinical pharmacist may be hired part time on an annually renewable basis to teach applied therapeutics courses. Clinical contract faculty may be needed to both teach and contribute to clinical services in a medical, dental or veterinary college. Alternatively, contract faculty may pursue research as their main academic mission. Their positions are renewable on an annual, biannual or triannual basis. However, despite their valuable contributions to academic life, contract faculty who specialize in teaching or service are sometimes treated as second-class citizens. In many cases, they do not even have voting rights in college matters. This situation is quite demeaning and discouraging, especially since many contract faculty provide higher-quality teaching than tenured or tenure-track faculty. In my own college, it is contract faculty who are regularly voted by students as teachers of the year.

Role of Individual Professional Experience and Soft Skills in the Success of Junior Faculty

There are many professional and soft skills that are required for success in an academic environment. Entry-level competencies in these skills vary according to one's training background and personal traits. Professional skills include familiarity with literature (both old and new) in one's scholarly field, training in information-searching tools, knowledge of proper experimental design, the ability to identify critical gaps in knowledge, proficiency in data analysis, research ethics, writing and presentation skills, grantsmanship and teaching skills (designing courses and curricula, presentation skills, team-based learning, active learning and problem-solving methods). It is equally important to have or gain competence in many soft skills, including conflict resolution, setting priorities, time and energy management, people management and leadership skills, project management, delegation, networking and socializing, building productive collaborative relationships, balancing life and work and developing resilience.

Success in one's career depends on both professional and personal abilities. One does not work without the other. This fact goes against the belief held by some junior faculty that possessing technical skills, asking impactful research questions and being productive are sufficient for advancement and success. This may be true in an ideal world. In real life, however, an individual must be or become skillful in dealing with people who play different roles in determining their success.

Role of Mentors in Assimilating Junior Faculty in the New Academic Environment

Mentoring is essential in guiding new faculty to the nuances of their academic environment. It is also important for filling in gaps in the

1. Understanding Your New Environment

experience and skills of starting junior faculty. A chairperson is often considered the strongest advocate for new faculty, particularly junior faculty. They are supposed to shepherd newcomers to unique opportunities, protect their time and celebrate their success. Unfortunately, some department chairs play more of a manager's role than that of a leader, or they may not have sufficient time to offer effective mentoring. It is therefore customary for the department head to appoint a mentor or two for each new faculty member to help them navigate the unfamiliar environment. Most often, the match will be made on the basis of common research interests. Ideally, however, selection of the mentors should take into consideration the special needs of the mentee and the expertise of each mentor. While having common scholarly interests matters, a junior faculty member is usually more in need of institutional knowledge and social skills that fall outside the scholastic realm. It cannot be assumed that all senior faculty who are successful in research are equally talented in social skills (especially how to provide effective mentoring). Senior faculty are usually very busy people. They may not touch base with their junior faculty mentees as frequently as they should. It is therefore important for junior faculty to engage their mentors and be proactive in seeking their advice.

Mentors play an important role in familiarizing junior faculty with technical and intellectual resources provided by the institution. These include core facilities (e.g., gene sequencing, historical archives) or centers that include clusters of investigators of potential interest to the junior faculty. Mentors may also inform their mentees about graduate programs they may wish to join or seminar series in other departments or colleges they may wish to attend. In addition, mentors are a good source of knowledge regarding internal funding and career development opportunities available through the department, college or university. They likewise act as a sounding board in making important decisions, such as hiring personnel to meet specific research needs and accepting invitations to speak or serve as a grant reviewer. They know what it takes to get tenured and promoted and whether engaging in new opportunities would be beneficial or detrimental in this regard.

Mentors also serve as advocates for the junior faculty at the time of annual evaluation or promotion and tenure. They usually attend some of their mentee's lectures to provide advice on improving delivery and modernizing teaching methods. Watching the junior faculty teach also gives mentors a chance to serve as peer evaluators of teaching, which is usually required in support of promotion. (More details on the characteristics of good mentoring and how to mitigate challenges to the mentoring relationship are provided in chapter 5.)

Summary

Being a new junior faculty member is both exciting and anxiety-provoking. Getting a tenure-track academic position places them on the road to fulfill their dreams and ambitions. There are, however, significant challenges that come with being in a new environment and having to perform unfamiliar roles and responsibilities. There is also much to learn about the culture, administrative structure and technical and intellectual resources in the new institution. It is therefore essential for junior faculty to be aware of these challenges and work with their mentors to chart a path to change these challenges into opportunities that further their careers.

Self-Reflection Exercises

- Draft lists of exciting and challenging aspects of your new faculty appointment. Prioritize the items in each list regarding their impact on having a successful academic career.
- List your technical and soft competencies and take note of the ones that require improvement.
- Think of strategies to improve existing skills and gain new ones.

2

Special Issues Facing Women and Minority Faculty

Women and minority faculty face additional challenges when compared to their white male counterparts. Most of these issues stem from unfair implicit or explicit bias that these individuals are not fit for the academic profession, likely because they are relative newcomers to an environment that has been dominated by white males for quite a long time. These false beliefs often result in the accomplishments of women and minority faculty being undermined, which consequently slows their career advancement. Moreover, women faculty have to cater to the needs of their families. Both categories of faculty are also assigned extra duties related to their gender or minority status. These additional responsibilities distract them from focusing on their research productivity, which is still the gold standard for promotion and tenure.

Challenges to Women Faculty

Representation of women at higher education institutions has been on a steady rise. Most women faculty have excelled in scholarship, teaching and service. There is ample evidence that women are quite able and highly driven to succeed in academia. Since the days of Madame Marie Curie, women have continued to be major contributors to many fields of scholarship. Many have been honored with prestigious awards for their seminal contributions to advancing knowledge. For example, at the time of writing this book, there have been two women Nobel Prize laureates in economic sciences, sixteen in literature, four in physics, seven in chemistry and twelve in medicine. Given the right environment, therefore, women can be as successful as (or even more successful than) their male peers. In my academic career I have personally known numerous female faculty who have outperformed their male colleagues at similar career stages. This is in spite of being taxed with significant gender-specific roles outside work. Many women have had to swim upstream and get around hurdles that their male peers do not have to tackle.

Gender-Related Stereotypes

Significant barriers continue to face women faculty as a result of the white male–dominated academic environment. Women in general suffer from implicit bias that comes in various forms. While this bias is not as rampant in academic institutions, academicians are not fully immune to such tendencies. Women faculty usually experience more pressure to perform than their male colleagues. Some of this pressure is self-perpetrated. Women faculty feel obliged to work hard to prove that females are as capable as males (or even more so) in accomplishing their academic duties. They realize that their performance reflects on the image of women faculty in general. Women faculty have to continue to disprove some prevalent stereotypes (e.g., they are less intelligent or competent in certain fields such as mathematics). Women faculty are also thought of as more subjective and emotional in making judgments and decisions than men. Supposedly, this quality hinders their ability to objectively interpret research data. In addition, women faculty have to contend with suspicion regarding their capabilities and their commitment to the demands of academic life. The success and prestige of many women in their scholarly fields is not guaranteed to silence these nagging whispers of doubt. Furthermore, women scholars are usually not given due credit in collaborative projects with men. There is an unfortunate tendency to attribute credit to male team members by default, unless proven otherwise.

Being in such a degrading and demoralizing environment, and suffering from many other aspects of gender bias, has persuaded some women faculty to leave academia. More seriously, it has led them to dissuade female graduate students from pursuing academic careers. Many women who showed initial interest in enrolling in these fields in graduate school have ended up deciding to do their graduate work in other fields. The obvious result is significant successive attrition of the number of women in academia, especially in the science and engineering fields.

The Gender Gap

While the gender gap in compensation has narrowed over time, there is evidence that women faculty still get paid less than their male colleagues at similar career stages. This disparity continues at all levels of professorship. There is also a marked difference between female and male academicians in the speed of climbing the academic ladder. Women faculty frequently have multiple identities, including being a scholar, a spouse and a mother. They must juggle the myriad of responsibilities associated with each of these identities in the hope of maintaining a harmonious balance between them. This task, however, is much easier said than done. Family responsibilities are often associated with frequent unplanned surprises that are usually delegated by default to wives or female partners. Most of these problems are quite urgent in nature—for example, picking up a sick child from school in the middle of the day. Unfortunately, some women get bad looks from colleagues for leaving work early due to family emergencies. Colleagues or superiors may also become critical if a woman brings her toddlers or young teenagers to work once in a while during school breaks. This reaction stands in sharp contrast to the way colleagues would voice their accolades at times when I brought my two daughters to work during the summer. I was touted as being an exemplary father who was doing a good job in introducing his daughters to what it takes to become a successful scholar.

Additionally, being responsible for children or elderly family members in the evening deprives female faculty of the chance to participate in important social and business functions that connect them with others, such as large college or institutional celebrations or dinner interviews of faculty and leaders. The result is diminished visibility and lost opportunities for networking. These challenges are naturally increased for single mothers with young children. Women faculty have also been disproportionately disadvantaged during the COVID-19 pandemic. Many lost work hours in order to take care of children who stayed home due to school and daycare closures.

One of the most serious and painful experiences of women in academia is having to disguise their multiple identities as faculty, spouses and mothers. They feel compelled to keep plans to have children a secret out of fear of being perceived as preparing to slow down. Many women postpone having children because they are explicitly or implicitly discouraged from doing so while in training. However, deciding on how long to wait to bear children is limited by natural biological clocks. Therefore, both men and women must recognize that women who want families do not have the luxury of waiting to have children until they have fully established their independent careers.

Paradoxically, one important element that leads to the slow progress of women faculty in advancing their career goals is having positive personal traits that are generally more prevalent among women than men. Women are commonly more generous in sharing their precious time with others. Many will sacrifice their own pressing needs for the sake of helping someone who is in dire straits. In academia, women faculty often become more engaged in mentoring graduate students and junior faculty than their male peers. This situation is reflected not only in the number of mentees women faculty take on but also in the quality of mentoring and the time dedicated to each mentee. Unfortunately, there are no significant rewards for such activities that are of paramount importance for preparing the next generation of scholars and teachers in a prevailing academic environment where more emphasis is placed on the number of publications and amounts of external funding a faculty member brings. Men, in contrast, are more aware of and focused on what really matters regarding promotion and tenure, and they therefore keep their eyes exclusively focused on the prize. Some use the criterion "what's in it for me?" to decide whether to help someone else. Men also excel at marketing themselves in so many ways, which contributes to increasing their visibility and therefore advancing their careers. In some cases, this practice reaches the extreme of shameless self-promotion. In sharp contrast, many women have a hard time advocating for themselves or bragging about their accomplishments. Some are advised to let performance speak for itself to avoid accusations of being arrogant.

Here is what my dear colleague, Professor Dorothy Hatsukami, has shared with me to describe her triumphs and tribulations in being a female academician:

> Related to being a woman in an academic institution, earlier in my career I may have been perceived as a helper rather than having a career of my own. Others claimed some of my ideas as theirs. I had no mentors to guide my career. Even though my husband was very helpful, juggling home and academic life was sometimes challenging. However, being left alone to carve my own career path, having a can-do attitude and having marvelous and supportive collaborators who respected me helped my professional life. Furthermore, I think a woman's career trajectory, perhaps especially those of the older generation, might have been a bit different than of a man. Once the children are independent and out of the home, women have greater freedom to focus on their careers. I have heard from other women that they are busier than ever in their career now they have the freedom to focus on it.

Role of Institutions in Promoting Careers of Women Faculty

Every effort should be made to remove impediments to women's careers in academia. Institutional policies and procedures should be closely examined to eliminate sources of overt and covert gender bias. The magnitude and systemic nature of these biases mandate continuous attention and evaluation. Top administrators in academic institutions should provide strong leadership in changing the culture to encourage recruiting, training, promoting and retaining women faculty. Mere mantras in institutional strategic plans are not enough in the absence of corresponding well-designed tactics and ways to gauge progress. Top university administrators should monitor signs of gender inequities and take immediate and just actions to remedy them. They should provide training in equity to deans and department chairs and hold them accountable for creating and nourishing a fair, gender-neutral system in recruitment and in evaluating and rewarding faculty effort. Moreover, the tenure process and timeline should take into consideration interruptions in the careers of women faculty as a result of having children. It would be helpful for institutions to establish high-quality on-campus childcare facilities and provide paid parental leave for new parents.

One positive aspect of the COVID-19 pandemic is that we have embraced options for virtual meetings and teaching. This approach has provided much flexibility to faculty to work remotely and save on travel time to campus. It is hoped that institutions will continue to provide this type of flexibility to accommodate the special needs of mothers with children in particular. Continuing to offer scholars virtual speaking opportunities at other institutions would alleviate some of the burden of travel on parents of young children and enable them to accept more speaking engagements.

Some aspects of the academic environment, like many other male-dominated arenas, are hostile to women. Sometimes women faculty suffer from harassment and bullying by their male colleagues. More effective interventions are needed to take concrete steps toward eradicating harassment, starting with establishing explicit policies to guard against these hostile behaviors—most important, to ensure that a victim of such terrible treatment can report her painful experience, be it with a peer or a superior, without fear of stigma or retaliation. Institutional leaders should also ensure that there are supportive processes and a healing environment available for women who experience sexual and gender-based harassment. They should deliver a loud and clear message that mistreatment of women—or anyone, for that matter—will not be tolerated. Training programs should be designed to educate faculty, students and staff on the types of behaviors that muddy collegiality and the consequences of committing such actions against women and others.

Challenges to Women Academic Leaders

There is much to be done in the arena of furthering the role of women in institutional leadership. There is a need to mentor women in leadership skills, perhaps best accomplished by pairing them with role model women leaders within or outside the institution. A positive sign in the evolution of the academy is the increased representation of women faculty on leadership teams. I was thrilled when my institution, the University of Minnesota, decided to hire its first female president a couple of years ago. I am proud to say she has outshined many of her male predecessors. Still, there are multiple factors that prevent or discourage women from assuming leadership positions in academic institutions. First, there is both explicit and implicit gender bias that gives preference to male leaders. Second, and more important, women leaders usually have to handle more hecklers and have fewer cheerleaders than male leaders. They are often criticized for their "soft" style of leadership, no matter how much proof there is regarding its effectiveness. Women generally lead through collaboration and consultation and use transformational leadership styles in persuasion to effect change. Many male leaders, in contrast, do not hesitate to make major decisions singlehandedly or with very limited consultation. They are cheered for their boldness and decisiveness, whereas women academic leaders are criticized if they use similar masculine approaches to problem solving.

Role of Mentors and Support Groups

Mentors have an important role in empowering women faculty to become more proactive and assertive in closing the gender gap. They should train their mentees in negotiation skills, both to secure higher initial pay when they get hired and to gain maximal annual merit raises commensurate with their performance. The same applies to negotiating startup packages, additional research funds, equipment, research space, and access to support staff and graduate students, and it also pertains to proposing being considered for promotion. Support groups led by parents (men and women) who have successfully navigated the current academic structures while raising children would also be helpful in providing valuable guidance. One example at my institution is the "Mothers Leading Science" initiative. It is a year-long leadership development program designed to support female faculty who are taking care of school-age and/or young children. The purpose of this group is to foster professional and personal growth, provide peer mentoring, integrate the dual roles of scholars and mothers, and build a network of peers for ongoing support throughout participants' careers.

Needed Change at the National Level

Much change is also needed at the national level. Professional societies, for example, should ensure that women are invited as keynote speakers at society-sponsored events to reflect the diverse membership. Journals should increase women representation on editorial boards. Granting agencies should allow women scholars to extend the lifetime of a grant when they go on leave due to family or other caregiving responsibilities. Academic institutions' compliance with gender-blind policies should be monitored at the federal level, with serious reprimands for universities that repeatedly fail to adhere to these policies.

The National Science Foundation's ADVANCE program is one example of efforts at the national level to close the gender gap in academia. Its goal is to increase the representation, contribution and advancement of women in academic science and engineering careers. It also provides collaborative opportunities with academic institutions and associated communities and organizations to address various aspects of academic culture and institutional structure that may disproportionately affect women faculty and academic administrators.

Challenges Faced by Minority Faculty

Changes in faculty demographics are lagging behind the overall demographics of the country. Dominance by white men is reflected more in the racial makeup of senior faculty. Of special note, the majority of those in top academic leadership positions are unfortunately the ones who have the least experience with faculty diversity and its related opportunities and challenges. This deficiency clouds their vision of how to effectively create a truly inclusive environment. Most leaders, therefore, do better in recruiting than retaining minority faculty. Hopefully the future will bring about enrichment of academic leadership with individuals from underrepresented minority groups. There is evidence that things are moving in that healthy direction. There are ample examples of women who have broken the glass ceiling to become deans, provosts and presidents in premier academic institutions. It is hoped the same will be true for faculty of color, but it may be a long road to get to this laudable target.

The vision statements of almost all academic institutions in the United States include increasing diversity as one of their top targets. Most universities, and sometimes individual colleges, have offices that deal with issues of diversity and inclusion. One of the important functions of these offices is helping to recruit minority faculty and students and providing guidance in advancing their careers. They also aim to maintain a culture that is respectful and fair for all, regardless of color, race, religion or sexual orientation, through holding workshops to discuss matters of equity and mutual respect among people from different walks of life. The main stumbling block that hinders the effectiveness of such endeavors is that most faculty subscribe to the false belief that they are "color blind" or "color neutral," which is a trend similar to that prevailing in the mainstream U.S. society. The main danger here is that people become blind to discrimination based on color or any other aspect of diversity. This perspective naturally leads one to comfortably put aside discussions of the origins and consequences of systemic racism and how to find solutions to combat it.

Recruiting faculty of color is one thing; retaining them is another. When faculty of color are hired, they are often expected to take on more responsibilities than their white colleagues. This tendency has been coined "cultural taxation." Faculty members of color or those from underrepresented minority populations are usually thought of as the diversity expert representatives on hiring committees or the ideal mentors to assign to students of color in the department or college at large. This challenge is further exacerbated in the case of dual appointments, in which each of the hiring departments would ask for this type of contribution from the minority faculty. While the intellectual contribution of minority faculty to these tasks is quite valuable to the mission of their institution, such costly, time-consuming engagement is rarely incentivized and rewarded. When it is time to decide on promotion or tenure, a faculty member of color or one from other underrepresented minority groups will be held to the same criteria and standards of high volume of seminal publications and outstanding teaching and service as their white counterparts who were not distracted by these extra chores. This double standard limits their success and accelerates their departure.

One of the proclaimed goals of having minority faculty serve on so many committees is to have them voice opinions that represent those of minority faculty from their ethnic or racial background. This belief is both unrealistic and unfair. Nobody envisions that a single white person could speak fairly on behalf of all white people. Why should it be different for people of color? A faculty member of color in this situation feels tremendous pressure and responsibility in representing all. Individual faculty from any race or ethnic group have their own beliefs and stances about any subject, similar to their white counterparts.

White faculty gain significant power and influence on the direction of their department, college and institution upon gaining tenure. Being tenured gives them freedom to debate and disagree with others, including department, college and institutional leaders, without being subjected to losing their jobs. Tenured minority faculty, by contrast, are still constrained about what they say or do. Their opinions may not be as respected or valued as those of white faculty.

Racially based double standards are rampant in academia. Faculty of color may not get nominated as frequently as their white colleagues for well-deserved awards or prestigious leadership positions. There may be a tendency for evaluation committees to focus on negative aspects of the performance of a minority faculty member while speaking at length about the great accomplishments of white faculty and finding excuses for their shortcomings. A white faculty member who publishes with other independent scholars is usually deemed "collaborative," while a minority faculty member doing the same thing may be judged as "not independent." While having a white faculty member branch off to new areas of scholarship may be seen as "innovative," the same behavior by a faculty member of color could be classified as "lacking focus." In essence, getting tenure does not shield minority faculty from implicit bias by their peers, superiors and students. Their status in society as being "different" does not change on demonstrating they are worthy of promotion to associate professor with indefinite tenure.

Other challenges facing faculty of color include having significant difficulty in their assimilation into the academic community while maintaining their own cultural identity. Some may adopt "go along to get along" as an approach to blending in, which creates internal conflicts between appearances and beliefs. Other psychological stressors that impact the productivity and well-being of faculty of color include feeling overly scrutinized and stereotyped as a potential failure. As a result, they always try to go the extra mile to prove their competence. Experiencing minor failures on the way may cause them to lose self-confidence and eventually develop "imposter syndrome." Faculty from certain minority groups must also be particularly careful about what they say or do to avoid being misunderstood. They feel that their behavior and performance will impact recruiting other faculty of color, especially from their particular ethnic group. This belief makes them become extra self-aware and holds them back from initiating relationships for fear of making mistakes that would further affirm existing stereotypes of their culture.

Some academic environments are particularly racist and therefore hostile to minority faculty. Signs of such racism are seen frequently despite the good intentions by institutions to create a diversity-welcoming environment. Minority faculty often face marginalization and disrespectful interactions, mostly reflected as microaggressions. These hurtful behaviors are categorized as microassaults, microinsults and microinvalidations and are exemplified by derogatory comments about certain ethnic groups or stereotyping minority faculty, students or staff according to their racial background. Microaggressions may also be nonverbal; for example, a faculty member from a minority religious group may be mandated to attend a college function during one of their important religious holidays. Regardless of being intentional or unintentional, microaggressions of all kinds deliver hostile and demeaning messages that target people based solely on their marginalized group membership. Left uncontrolled, they cause persistent pain, humiliation and discouragement to minority faculty that will eventually lead to their departure to other institutions or even leaving academia all together.

Similarly, faculty of color frequently face unintended but implicitly based insults. The disproportionality between black faculty and black service employees on most campuses, for example, leads some people to mistake a black professor for a janitor or a food delivery person. Sometimes students make demeaning remarks to faculty of color, such as "do you have a doctorate?" or "have you taught this class before?" As a result, minority professors work harder than others to prove their proficiency in the lecture topic. They are conscious that any mistakes along the way will awaken those doubting voices among the students.

One of the deceptive features of racism in general is that a minority faculty member may think they are individually targeted. The truth is that racism is systemic and rampant in all sectors of our society, including academia. Such misconception weakens arguments against the widespread nature of discrimination. It tempts perpetrators to falsely accuse the victim of their abusive behavior of being "overly sensitive" or "playing the race card." A minority faculty member who is subjected to microaggression represents the first line of defense against the aggressors in order to stop this negative behavior before it goes too far.

Here are recommended approaches extracted from the literature on how to proceed with difficult conversations following an incident of racially driven microaggression: The victim should ask for elaboration of the meaning of what was just said or done. This request helps them understand the perpetrator's perspective and gives them a chance to correct possible misunderstanding or unintended misspoken words. "Why"-type questions during the conversation should be avoided since they tend to elicit defensiveness. The minority faculty member should reflect, paraphrase and reframe to demonstrate understanding of what was said and, more important, what they heard. They should explain to the microaggressor the harmful impact of their words or actions without blaming them or categorizing their behavior with adjectives. Moreover, they should clearly state their preference for how things should have been said or done to reach the intended goal of the conversation or relationship. It often helps when these dialogues are held a day or two after the incident to avoid overreacting while being emotionally charged and agitated. However, one should not wait longer than that since effective resolutions to any problem require dealing with the underlying issue while the experience is still fresh in one's mind.

Minority scholars are often the only person of their racial, cultural or religious background in their department, or even in their college, which causes feelings of separation from their familiar environment. This negative effect may be compounded by the possible lack of diversity of the community outside work. A small college town, for example, may not have as diverse a population as a large metropolis. Together, this unfamiliar setting deprives one of essential emotional support and leads to feelings of isolation.

Many minority faculty intentionally select fields of scholarship that address issues related to their cultural background. Their research projects may focus on community diversity issues or tackle challenges facing underrepresented communities or people in under-developed countries. Some feel the need to justify and defend the legitimacy of such projects in terms of their expected impact, especially to administrators and leaders who tend to judge the importance of research, in part, by the amount of funding it brings to the institution. There is usually some concern that this type of "off the map" research may not be flashy enough to qualify for generous funding by external agencies. As a result, such areas of scholarly inquiry may be devalued in comparison to mainstream research topics. Furthermore, many of the research projects that involve investigating social problems seem to be qualitative in nature. Unfortunately, there is evidence that grant reviewers often deem this type of research "pedestrian" or "descriptive." Together, these factors culminate in the existing lower rate of federal research funding granted to faculty of color. This differential rate of success in garnering funding represents a glaring example of systemic racism in the academic world, which is also reflected in negatively biased student assessment of minority faculty's teaching skills.

Suggested Solutions

Of course, a faculty member of color must perform due diligence before deciding to join an institution. They should deeply research the institutional environment regarding diversity, especially how the department and college leaders walk their talk. It is always wise to interview existing faculty of color, and those who left, about their experience with the environment. A minority faculty member who is considering moving to a given university should also research the track record of the institution, not only in recruitment of faculty from underrepresented populations but also, and more important, in their cultivation and retention.

Minority faculty should also recognize their responsibility in becoming proactive in creating their own path, starting with paying special attention to understanding the culture of the department, college and institution to avoid uncomfortable surprises. A new minority faculty member should explore institutional resources and find out who makes decisions that have significant bearing on the progress of their career. They should promote themselves and network to cultivate advocates. This networking will also help establish new teaching or scholarly collaborations. Proper mentoring is key in helping one gain control of commitments and achieve ideal work-life balance. Like all other faculty, a minority faculty member should become less defensive when given advice. They should learn to benefit from constructive criticism and avoid knee-jerk reactions in interpreting negative comments on their performance as being mainly based on racial prejudice or implicit bias. They should use these comments and recommendations to better their abilities. Meanwhile, they should keep track of whether following recommendations and improving performance results in progressively more positive evaluations over time. Lack of such change, especially when it is associated with moving targets, should raise red flags.

Taking Full Advantage of Available Resources

Minority faculty should benefit from internal resources designed to assist them in succeeding in their academic career. Many institutions have mentoring programs specifically designed for minority students and faculty or institutional offices of equity and diversity whose staff are well trained in guiding minority faculty and students to various types of technical, intellectual and career development resources. These offices also provide guidance for establishing various kinds of professional and social networks. A new minority faculty member should also benefit from external organizations. Notable examples include the National Research Mentoring Foundation and the National Center for Faculty Development & Diversity. MentorNet.org is a nonprofit organization that pairs mentees with mentors in higher education.

Self-Marketing

A junior faculty member from an underrepresented group should take the initiative in familiarizing colleagues, especially leaders, with the unique skills they bring to the institution. They should discuss their research area with the department chair/head, especially if it falls outside the mainstream, to get their buy-in and seek their advice on how to convey the importance of their research to other faculty. It is very important to share this knowledge with senior colleagues who will be voting on promotion and tenure. Similarly, a minority faculty member should take advantage of available opportunities to present their research, both within and outside the department and college. A department head or a mentor may offer guidance regarding where to publish scholarly findings. This issue is particularly relevant in case journals that specialize in publishing certain types of culturally-oriented or community-engaged scholarship are not included in the department's list of most esteemed venues of publishing. In case the scholarship of a faculty of color is qualtitative in nature, senior faculty at the same or other institutions who do similar research may provide sage advice on how to deal with associated challenges.

It is advisable for senior colleagues or mentors to attend lectures by a minority faculty member and give feedback on their teaching style and effectiveness. This approach will familiarize the senior faculty with their junior colleague's teaching skills and the unique aspects he or she brings to the classroom. It will also negate conscious or unconscious assumptions that faculty of color, or minority faculty in general, are less effective as teachers than white faculty. These biases are usually based on unsubstantiated stereotyping. Ideally, the practice of this type of peer evaluation of teaching should extend to all junior faculty, regardless of race and gender. Otherwise, students may develop a false perception that a specific minority faculty member is being monitored because of a reputation for poor teaching skills.

Guarding One's Time against Cultural Taxation

Success of a minority faculty member in obtaining promotion and tenure depends largely on maintaining a good balance among research, teaching and service. Therefore, they should be aware of the danger of being sucked into performing services on many committees at the expense of scholarly work, teaching or personal time dedicated to self, family and friends. She or he should critically assess every new request to serve on a committee, task force or work group in terms of how this service will be weighed in terms of evaluating their progress and productivity. They should learn upfront and take into consideration the amount of time involved.

I recommend that minority faculty follow their passion, social mission and personal values in selecting which committees to serve on and prioritize service that specifically benefits from their unique background and would enhance their connection with key colleagues or administrators. For example, serving on a student recruitment committee may allow them to have a unique impact on changing the recruitment and admission process and criteria to use holistic evaluation of applicants rather than simply relying on grades and national test scores. Sharing their personal experience on a task force for providing better mentoring to graduate students and postdoctoral fellows from underrepresented populations may ensure their retention. Another example is becoming a member of a group that is charged with defining institutional values, mission and strategic priorities. A minority faculty member likely has much to contribute in this regard to ensure the creation of an academic environment that is welcoming for all. Low priority and preference should be given to serving on committees or focus groups where ethnic background does not contribute much (for example, a task force that looks into where to place a new lunchroom in the department). It is advisable for a starting minority faculty member to consult with their department head and mentors before they commit to service requests from outside the department or college. Using the department head or mentor's advice against accepting the service appointment as an excuse to decline the invitation provides a safe way out, thereby avoiding coercion from powerful colleagues.

Building a Community

A new minority faculty member should force themselves not to remain isolated from the surrounding academic community. She or he should not sit alone in their office feeling sorry that their colleagues are not knocking on the door to introduce themselves and ask how they may be of assistance. A new faculty member, especially one from a minority group, should be proactive in mixing with other faculty—for example, by inviting them to have lunch together. Such an informal environment is conducive to having people share their experiences, both positive and negative. One could learn from peers how to successfully navigate the administrative structure of the department, college and university. Relaxed conversations outside the work environment are also helpful in discovering fun things to do around town (e.g., favorite restaurants, theaters, hiking and biking trails, etc.). Networking with other faculty of color helps with understanding institutional values and culture, particularly pertaining to circumventing challenges associated with diversity. Most are willing to share their experiences and the lessons learned along the way to make a new faculty member aware of how to avoid or deactivate potential landmines. However, minority faculty should not limit their interactions to colleagues with similar cultural or racial backgrounds. One must get to understand the nature and dimensions of the majority culture of the institution to help them acclimate in a way that does not compromise their cultural identity or core values. Sharing feelings of isolation, prejudice and inequality with white faculty makes them aware of the problems experienced by a minority faculty member. This is the first step in establishing collaborative efforts between minority and majority faculty to identify the deep roots of these challenges and design effective solutions. In sharing such negative experiences, one should also highlight what is working well. Nobody wants to be labeled an "eternal complainer"! A new minority faculty member should also explore possibilities for creating scholarly collaborations that would be mutually beneficial to all parties involved, such as research that enables asking impactful questions that cannot be addressed adequately through individual efforts. They should identify and cultivate strong advocates who will speak to their productivity and contributions at the time of promotion and tenure. Minority faculty also need to find ways to get members of the dominant culture to understand and appreciate who they are, what they are capable of offering, and the value of added diversity of thoughts, experiences and approaches they may provide.

Benefiting from Mentoring

I highly recommend that a minority faculty member seek proper mentors as soon as they start. Being mentored by senior faculty has many advantages. A mentoring relationship will facilitate orientation. Mentors help troubleshoot looming challenges and can teach their mentees about institutional power channels, hidden resources and unwritten rules. One of the most common concerns expressed by underrepresented faculty is the lack of mentors with a similar racial or ethnic background. Most firmly believe in the value of being mentored by someone from one's own cultural/ethnic group to ensure the understanding of special challenges that may not be shared by white faculty. I strongly advise that one choose a mentor who is genuinely interested in exploring and appreciating cultural differences, regardless of their gender or racial makeup. A mentor who comes highly recommended by other minority faculty would be an excellent choice. There is marked benefit in having a diverse mentoring team, in which each member would offer support commensurate with their professional and personal experiences and strengths.

Institutional mentors should provide a safe space for mentees to share any concerns they may have. This process involves ensuring confidentiality and avoiding judgment. Meanwhile, a minority faculty member should maintain their external network with contacts in other institutions. These include former classmates from graduate school, members of scholarly societies and special interest groups.

Some minority faculty may be hesitant to either seek or accept mentoring. They may worry about the stigma of appearing to need "remedial" or "special" help. For the same reason, they may even hesitate to participate in institutional programs that have been specifically established to provide career assistance to faculty of color. Pride may lead some to decide to go it alone to prove they are independent and capable of succeeding on their own. I recommend that one work hard to conquer these concerns. There is no shame in seeking support. Having a mentor or a mentoring team will not only assist in developing your professional skills but also provide the psychological comfort of being emotionally supported. One's mentors are usually one's strongest and most vocal advocates.

Like any mentoring relationship, a minority faculty mentee should resist efforts by the mentor to make them a clone of themselves—to create someone who thinks, walks and talks like them. It takes special skills to become aware of this flaw in a given mentor's approach to providing guidance. This issue is particularly important in cases of interracial mentoring, as a white mentor may try, with good intentions, to change the minority mentee's personality or approach to decision making to mimic their own. Also watch for power differential games, especially in mixed-race or mixed-gender mentoring relationships. Develop an understanding early on in the relationship that you are the final arbitrator in deciding whether to follow or decline recommendations by the mentor. Always be courteous in expressing your appreciation for the advice and in explaining the rationale of your decision to take it or leave it.

Most mentors in academia have little or no cross-gender or cross-cultural mentoring experience. Moreover, not all those who have had this experience were successful at it due to the special challenges inherent in such a mentoring relationship. A mentor must constantly work hard to recognize and overcome their fears, stereotypes and biases. They must tread gently and extra carefully to gain the trust of their mentees. On the other side of the coin, some women faculty or faculty of color may hesitate to share some of their weaknesses or challenges with mentors who are white men. They may think twice before they bring up failure in balancing work and family life, for example. They worry that a person who is not subjected to similar career barriers would not understand, empathize or be able to provide support.

Your mentor may also try, with purely good intentions, to help you assimilate in the white male–dominated culture to a point that would suppress or eliminate your cultural identity. Do not succumb to this temptation. It is wiser to maintain who you are while making every effort to understand who you are dealing with and the environment that surrounds you. Early negotiations of the terms of a mentoring relationship should address these issues with candidness and openness.

* * *

Cultural differences may also make some mentors hesitant to interact frequently with a mentee of a different color. They worry about unintentionally doing or saying something that would hurt the feelings of their mentee or even result in negative consequences that would end the mentoring relationship. Political correctness has made professional relationships, including mentoring, more precarious and sometimes awkward. It is almost inevitable that one may utter words out of sheer ignorance that would be perceived as hostile, discriminatory or demeaning to someone from a different culture. In such cases, the mentee owes it to the mentor to explain why what he or she said or did is hurtful. This is a good example of much-needed reciprocal mentoring. A healthy mentoring relationship is conducive to this invaluable exchange.

Summary

While assuming a tenure-track academic position is quite challenging in its own right, women and minority faculty face significant additional obstacles that interfere with their progress. Challenges that afflict both groups include having to serve on more committees than white male faculty to represent their gender or race. There is a dominant bias that women and minority faculty are not capable of performing at the same level as their white male counterparts. This situation makes them go the extra mile to prove their competence. They also face a glass ceiling that slows down their promotion and assumption of leadership positions. Women faculty are sometimes the target of sexual harassment, while faculty of color are often subjected to inappropriate discriminatory remarks and actions. Together, these serious obstacles lead to their early departure, either to other academic institutions or outside academia altogether. What a waste of valuable talent that is! Institutions have so much work to do to ameliorate this serious situation.

Self-Reflection Exercises

- In what ways has your gender or racial identity enabled you to provide unique contributions to the academic mission of your department, college and institution?
- List the challenges you have faced as a result of being a woman or a minority faculty member. Which ones have you succeeded in circumventing? How did you accomplish this? How do you plan to address the remaining challenges?
- If you are a white male, think of the obstacles your women and

minority colleagues have faced. What role have you played or should you have played in helping them chart their path in spite of these challenges? What role have you played or should you have played in changing the academic environment to become more hospitable and equitable to all?

3

People Skills

Good people skills are as crucial for success in academia as professional and technical competencies. This is a fact that often escapes the minds of junior scholars who have confidence in their professional abilities and deeply believe there is nothing else they need to achieve their goals. This belief is utterly misleading. I liken it to thinking that a piece of meat on its own makes a delicious dish, which is obviously incorrect; what makes this meal delicious is a mix of spices and perhaps a side salad with a tasty dressing. Similarly, there is a long list of elements that contribute to the success of a faculty member other than their professional abilities. People skills come to the top of the list. A junior faculty member lives in a community where others contribute to their progress. Their productivity is assessed by colleagues and superiors. The quality of their work, be it a manuscript or a grant proposal, is evaluated by others from outside their institutional community. Therefore, establishing productive and healthy relationships with others is key to advancement in an academic career. These relationships also contribute to one's happiness and comfort within the professional environment. This chapter deals with various strategies a junior faculty member needs to practice to establish new connections and maintain or expand existing ones. It also addresses other essential people skills such as communication, negotiation, conflict resolution, and dealing with difficult people and challenging situations.

Importance of Networking

Relationships cultivate possibilities for sharing, planning and creating. The academic community we belong to has an important role in shaping our path. You need others to guide you to unique resources in your department, college and institution (financial, technical and intellectual). Senior colleagues are especially helpful in this regard. They have created connections with many individuals and groups within and outside the institution during their many years of service. They have done their homework to find information that is likely similar to what you may be seeking. Such "institutional memory" represents an invaluable source of knowledge.

One may erroneously think that people are not needed to gain such information at a time when the answer to almost any question is a click away through the internet. This is an incorrect assumption. Some important resources are not well advertised or are posted on very crowded or poorly designed websites. Past scholarly interests of colleagues may not be included on their current professional or social web pages. It may happen that finding a collaborator in these areas is exactly what a junior faculty member needs. A senior colleague may be aware of pertinent unpublished data that support a hypothesis underlying a new scholarly project. Networking may also guide you to highly qualified persons to add to your scholarly team—for example, a skilled technician who lost their job due to lack of funding or other reasons, or a highly competent graduate student who is about to finish their degree and is looking for a postdoctoral position in the same institution to avoid moving their family.

It is becoming apparent that research is quickly moving away from individual investigators to teams of scientists with varied research expertise. Collaborations (especially interdisciplinary ones) are more likely to develop novel scholarship questions that have high significance and impact. You may be surprised at how many productive research relationships have been sparked by pure serendipity—namely, by unexpectedly having two scholars not personally acquainted with each other in the same room at the same time. Take advantage of any gatherings to connect with others. Invite colleagues to coffee or dinner at professional conferences to learn of each other's research interests and professional plans. Do the same when you serve on grant review panels. Socialize with seminar speakers in your department. I am usually surprised by the lack of interest displayed by my colleagues in getting a free dinner at a fancy place that is accompanied by intellectual conversation with a guest of the department.

Social events at work are important for making connections and establishing new relationships. I truly believe it is a mistake for a junior faculty member to skip these gatherings in favor of reading an article or writing a manuscript. Make time to socialize and discover common ground and interests with others, both professionally and socially. Going with colleagues for coffee or lunch provides an optimal relaxed ambiance for this type of exchange. Socializing will also provide you with great comfort as a result of creating a sense of a community in the workplace. One approach I have adopted is to create social groups, such as a culinary club in which my wife and I invite other couples from our workplaces to come to our home to share cooking and eating a meal with us. This activity rotates among the homes of the club members on a monthly basis. We have greatly enjoyed getting to know the "people side" of our professional colleagues.

Winning People Over

First impressions are priceless. As the saying goes, "you never get a second chance to make a first impression." Create opportunities to have everybody in your work environment warm up to you from day one on the job. One of my favorite past presidents at my institution was a master at relating to people. Soon after his arrival on campus, he publicly shared his passion for pancakes. He asked faculty, staff and students to recommend good places to have pancakes and to send him their favorite pancake recipes. He then put these recipes together in a booklet that he gifted to visitors to the university. He also used it for fund raising and even distributed the booklet to legislators when negotiating state support to the university to get them to warm up to the cause. This president was often seen riding golf carts with facilities management staff to tour the campus and shake hands with students, faculty and staff. These personal touches made him one of the most beloved and approachable university presidents in the history of the institution.

One of my most cherished skills is making amazing baklava. When I started my first faculty job several decades ago, I made a large sheet of baklava and took it to work. I walked around the department, introduced myself and offered a piece of baklava to each person I met. I made sure to ask everyone a couple of questions about themselves and what they did on the job. I soon started receiving requests for the recipe and was asked later to hold baklava-making workshops. Student organizations proposed that I offer such baklava-baking demonstrations as one of the items in their fund-raising auctions. I agreed to all of these requests. These simple efforts paid great dividends in building relationships and making people friendly and welcoming. Over time I became known in the college as "Professor Baklava Sam"! It is a title I am quite proud of!

Create your own personal touches. Make yourself visible. Keep your office door open whenever possible. When you need a break, walk around the corridors and greet those you run into. Make a special stop in the department office to say hello to the administrative and secretarial staff. They are usually undervalued and used to hearing more complaints than gratitude or cheerful remarks. Show up early at department seminars and intentionally sit next to different people each time and initiate conversations if they do not. Mix with colleagues from other departments during college-wide seminars and social events. Prepare short statements to introduce yourself when you briefly run into people. These "elevator speeches" may have different degrees of depth and technical language, depending on the audience and how much time you have. Here are examples:

- Brief: I work on anticancer drugs.
- Medium: In my lab, we synthesize and test anticancer drugs.
- Full: In my lab, we synthesize and test drugs for the treatment of sarcoma.
- Extra full: In my lab, we synthesize and test anticancer drugs for sarcoma. These drugs are derivatives of vinblastine.

I do realize that my advice herein is easier said than done if you are an introvert, in which case doing too much of what I have recommended may leave you drained of energy. A good solution is to fight your comfort level in being alone and go about socializing in brief stints.

Elements of Healthy Relationships

Relationships are most effective when their benefits are reciprocal. Be proactive in exploring the needs of your colleagues and offer your assistance whenever you think you may make a difference in their lives. Share resources you recently learned about, such as new funding mechanisms or interesting workshops. Offer help if you sense a colleague is under stress in meeting a deadline. Express your genuine interest in the success and well-being of your colleagues and avoid waiting until you need them to start initiating connections. Recognize and express your respect for the experience and accomplishments of your colleagues and seek their assistance in areas that are important for your professional development. Acknowledge the role they play in your success by thanking them in public and nominating them for mentoring awards.

Practice confidentiality and make sure your behavior establishes reliability and trust. Don't be a tattletale who runs to the boss to complain when problems with coworkers arise. This negative attitude will lead you to lose their trust and possibly be shunned. It is best to deal with problems on your own first, and then go to the boss if your initial attempts fail.

Avoid being perceived as arrogant. One thing that kindles feelings of envy and animosity is overconfidence displayed by a new junior faculty member, one who shamelessly boasts about their uninterrupted series of successes and glories. This behavior may invite some colleagues, especially seniors, to do whatever it takes to show this person where their place really is in the academic hierarchy. However, there are lessons to be learned from those who excel at making others aware of their special talents and accomplishments without blatantly appearing to be tooting their own horn. Here is an example of how one may put it in words: "I recently received an invite from *Nature* to serve as an editor, but I am really busy with so many other things! I would like to seek your advice about deciding whether to accept invitations to serve on editorial boards in general at this stage of my career." Here is another: "When I recently attended the meeting of the International Conference on Arts and Humanities, I was approached by a guy from X University who was trying to recruit me by convincing me it is time for me to move up to tier 1 institutions. I immediately told him to take a hike. I am so happy where I am now."

Communication Skills

Good communication builds relationships; miscommunication kills them. This principle applies to all relationships, whether with your boss, peers, staff, trainees, family or friends. Communication is a wide umbrella that includes conversational skills, clear expectations of roles and responsibilities and alignment of goals.

Active listening is the main element of productive conversations. Do not just hear, but really listen to what somebody is trying to communicate to you. Pay attention to both their words and body language. Focusing on comprehension will allow you an opportunity to learn not only what the other person is saying but also what they mean to say but haven't. You will understand where they are coming from and what their goals are, as well as their reservations and what they need from you. This valuable opportunity is lost during a conversation if you focus on planning your response to what they are saying instead of actively listening. Do not interrupt but indicate your attentiveness to the conversation by using verbal cues such as "I see" or "yes" or nonverbal gestures like nodding your head. Maintain eye contact without necessarily gazing at your conversation partner, and avoid body language that implies disagreement or puzzlement, such as rolling your eyes or shrugging your shoulders. Other types of behavior convey lack of interest or boredom (for example, scrolling through your cell phone, shuffling stacks of paper, or looking at your watch or out the window). Summarize what you understood from the conversation when you sense a lull. Ask open-ended follow-up questions to probe deeper into the background and goals behind the spoken words. Sidestep making judgments by calling what you just heard wrong, false, ridiculous or inaccurate. Start by responding to the part of the conversation with which you concur. This practice will suppress spontaneous defensive reactions. Be succinct; avoid lengthy digression.

Believe me, I do know how difficult it is to fight the temptation to interrupt or respond to somebody who goes on and on to relay a point of view. Patience and self-restraint are worth it, though. They enable you to develop an educated response strategy. They also show your conversation partner that you genuinely care about clearly understanding the message they intend to convey and that you respect their point of view even if it differs from yours. Of course, there are people who thrive on dominating conversations without allowing others to chime in. This controlling behavior may go to extremes so that an entire meeting may be consumed in having them talk without any pauses or invitations to hear your response. One solution is to acknowledge this fact at the end of the meeting and communicate your wish to schedule a follow-up meeting in which you have a chance to respond. Another is to send an email right away to state your point of view without being interrupted or dominated. Using this approach has the added advantage of giving you a chance to weigh your words carefully and express yourself clearly. It also provides documentation of difficult conversations.

Maintaining civility is essential for productive conversations. Heated arguments trigger angry emotions and invite defensiveness and aggression. They result in everybody pointing fingers at others and people shouting uncontrollably without actually listening to what others are saying. Think carefully before you speak. Sometimes we say things that we may regret later. Even when one apologizes for having said something hurtful, the negative effects of bad words may be long lasting. I recall many examples of things I wanted to say during conversations that, fortunately, I refrained from saying. I also remember instances when I said things I should not have, which I still and will always regret.

Conflict Resolution Skills

As long as there are humans, there are and will be conflicts. Conflicts vary in seriousness and ease of resolution. When I first attended a workshop on conflict resolution skills, I was quite surprised to hear the speaker say, "Conflicts are a good thing to have." This statement felt counterintuitive. Surprisingly, however, I found this point to be true as I became more adept in people skills. Conflicts are indeed helpful in that they bring points of disagreement into the light, ideally in their early stages. Ignoring small conflicts at work or at home will not make them evaporate and disappear. Instead, they will build up on top of each other to create bigger conflicts that are harder to control.

* * *

3. People Skills

Mishandling of conflicts will result in new ones. The main roadblock to resolving conflicts is the desire of both parties to get what they want, without paying attention to the needs of the other person or group. Each is looking for absolute victory. Rigid positions make them inflexible and blind to solutions that may work well for all. Imagine two people on opposite sides of a swinging door. Each is trying to push the door at the same time to go through. As a result, neither will get to where they want to be.

There is so much homework you must do prior to engaging in a conversation to resolve a conflict. Of course, it would be ideal if the person you are in conflict with does the same. Remember, however, you only have control over changing your own attitude. Step back and look at the situation from a distance. These wide-lens optics will make you envision the situation more objectively. Start by assessing your own position. Become aware of the full negative impact of the conflict on you. Recall how the conflict started and why. Contemplate what you and your opponent hope to accomplish during the process of resolving the conflict. Do you expect your opponent to be cooperative, or do they just want to win, no matter how or at what price? What are your and your opponent's needs and fears? How far are you willing to give in? Most important, is meeting halfway the best option in solving the problem? Sometimes taking this easy approach does not fulfill the needs of either party.

Identify and prioritize your interests in attempting to resolve a conflict so that you do not end up trading a critical goal or need for another that is less meaningful to you. For example, you may deem retaining a good relationship with somebody your highest priority in a given conflict. Having identified this priority could then lead you to sacrifice a specific gain you were after at the beginning of negotiation. This does not mean you should always succumb to pressure to please others. If you yield simply to get out of an uncomfortable conversation, you may expose yourself to future exploitation and domination. In addition, you may get burned if you allow your opponent to have it their way in the expectation that they will allow you to have it your way when another conflict arises. First, this approach may set you back in your career development in case your need is urgent. Second, your stakes in the next conflict may not be as important as those in the current encounter. Third, there is no guarantee that your opponent will actually act as you expect, especially if they are in a position of greater power. They may continue to want to win everything, all the time. It is therefore best to contemplate numerous potential solutions that will allow you to achieve your objectives prior to meeting to discuss a challenging situation. Doing so will guide you to satisfy your interests and reach your goals without necessarily fighting to maintain the initial position you assumed at the beginning of the conversation.

* * *

Plan to moderate the conflict resolution meeting to ensure that logic and reason prevail over emotions and kneejerk responses. Natural reactions to conflicts include striking back. This practice naturally elevates hostility and defensiveness. You must suppress your fight-or-flight reflexes in response to what appears to be aggression, hostility or domination. Being lured to respond in the same way will direct you to reject, argue and intentionally escalate. Be ready to provide facts and information your opponent may not be aware of. Explore common goals and approaches to reach end points that meet everybody's needs. Make it clear this is your main target in resolving the conflict. Most important, put yourself and your opponent on the same side of the table in confronting the problem. This arrangement works much better than having the two of you face each other in a fighting mode. It will drastically shift the prevailing spirit from confrontation to collaboration.

When you meet to discuss a conflict, start by asking your opponent about their needs and explore their initial understanding of yours. Ask what they think may work best to reach both your and their desired end point, and build on their suggestions. Inviting your opponent to speak is a strong indication of your desire to learn what they have to say and understand their perspective of the problem. It contributes to creating a cooperative attitude and will steer the rest of the conversation into a healthier and more productive direction. Do not interrupt, except to rephrase what they said to reflect correct understanding. Differentiate acknowledgment from agreement. Distinguish giving way from giving in.

It takes practice and building additional skills in conflict resolution when you negotiate with individuals who are not willing to consider anything but their initial position regarding the conflicted issue. Their rigidity may be based on fear or distrust created by a painful background history of being taken advantage of. You may also deal with someone who is too proud to give in or feels powerful as a result of turning down any suggestions brought up by others. Sometimes it is helpful to acknowledge the other person's authority and experience. Emphasize that you are committed to maintaining a healthy relationship and finding a win-win solution. Ask questions aimed at clarification. Explore issues hidden behind the main issues. Identify real sources of problems. Again, do all you can to shift positional bargaining to joint problem solving.

Bargaining and Negotiation Skills

I was born and raised in the Middle East, living there until I was twenty-seven. I grew up accustomed to bargaining as a way of life. My mother was a pro at it. When I came to the United States for my education,

I was surprised that people shied away from this practice. I often felt they considered bargaining impolite or useless. I decided to give it a try anyhow! I was pleasantly surprised that I was successful in getting many price discounts and additional complimentary perks. I have also applied my haggling skills at work, which led me to negotiate and receive a job offer for my first academic position with a higher starting salary and more generous startup package than was the norm at that time. I was also able to reduce my proposed teaching load during the first few years of employment as a faculty member. Later on, I negotiated higher annual salary raises than those initially proposed by my department head. My secret in approaching these and similar cases was to be reasonable in my requests. I also entered the bargaining arena prepared to offer logical justification based on my accomplishments, rather than my personal financial needs. I armed myself with data whenever possible to steer discussions in an objective direction.

Suppose you plan to negotiate a salary raise with your department chair. I recommend that you do not preface the conversation by stating that you deserve a raise or that you need increased pay to meet the needs of your family. Start by asking your chair how she or he values your performance and contributions to the department, and then follow up with your self-assessment. Be clear that money is not your main drive to perform; rather, it reflects how the department values your efforts. Watch for a clever ploy, though. There are many associate professors around the country who may be paid just a few thousand dollars more than a starting assistant professor. This is because annual raises have been minimal during recent times, barely keeping up with inflation. In addition, salary freezes have been enforced in many institutions periodically due to a struggling economy. However, the market value of junior faculty hires has been steadily rising. Your department chair may be clever enough to try to convince you that you should be satisfied with already being paid close to what an associate professor takes home. Do not buy into this argument. Rely on data pertaining to those at the same stage of their career in your college and university and nationally in similar departments.

You may also wish to negotiate coming up earlier than regularly scheduled for promotion and tenure. You may believe you have accomplished enough (or even more) to warrant an early promotion. I have been puzzled to witness some department chairs trying to convince faculty in this situation to wait for a year or two before they apply for promotion with tenure. Their argument is usually that the promotion dossier will become even more convincing and impressive if the junior faculty member publishes a couple more papers or gets another big research grant. I believe most chairs adopt this approach with the noble intention of protecting their junior faculty from any potential disappointment. They want to ensure a slam dunk that nobody could argue against. The result for the junior faculty member, however, is disappointment. She or he has worked so hard and produced so much, while their chair is treating the probation period for tenure as an inflexible prison sentence. Be prepared for similar arguments when you approach your department chair regarding early promotion. Compare your accomplishments to the documented criteria for promotion. Share your vitae with senior faculty, especially those who currently serve or have served on college or institution promotion committees, to get a sense of how your accomplishments compare with those of others who have recently made it. At the meeting with your chair, acknowledge their good intentions in trying to protect you. Explain your desire to gain the peace of mind and academic freedom associated with tenure as soon as possible. Come across as self-confident without slipping into entitlement or arrogance.

There are a few golden rules I advise you to adopt when you plan a meeting to negotiate on a serious matter that requires a thoughtful discussion. First, I recommend that you dedicate the entire meeting to this topic. Inform your conversation partner of the agenda to give them a chance to think about it ahead of the meeting. Avoid scheduling meetings close to major events or busy academic seasons. You may also want to refrain from scheduling meetings on Mondays, when most people are stressed by what they have on their plate for the rest of the week, or on Fridays, when they are likely anxious over having to finish tasks that fell through the cracks during the week.

Dealing with Difficult People at Work

Any workplace has its share of people with a variety of personality traits, both good and bad. Academia is not immune to this rule, even though the majority of academics are reasonable, fair and civil people. The worst type of a problematic person is a tyrant who believes they have utmost authority and wisdom. Tyrants truly believe they can ask anybody to jump, and they will or should perform, no questions asked. They often do that in a disrespectful and abusive way by being harsh, dictatorial and abrasive. They take pleasure in demeaning others. Bullies, by contrast, use outrage and intimidation to get people to do what they want. They scream, yell and pound on their desks. One may also encounter sadists at work, those who enjoy seeing others suffer while facing serious problems. These folks are willing to go out of their way to create new problems for others or make existing issues even worse. They rule arbitrarily, constantly moving the target so that people around them cannot claim success in meeting their goals.

This inflicted misery gives such individuals the pleasure of blaming and demeaning others when they make the slightest mistake.

Some of your bosses or peers may engage in one or more of these negative and abusive behaviors. They act this way to show their power, authority and dominance and to create a culture of intimidation and fear that satisfies their hunger for power and control. Their behavior usually reflects lack of self-confidence and esteem. I recall a favorite proverb from my home country, Egypt: "the hollower the drum, the louder it sounds!" I truly believe that this concept applies perfectly to such abusive bosses. All of these types of people behave worse if they sense weakness or fragility. They actively try to get their coworkers angry and worked up to create a situation that permits them to get even louder and more out of control. Do not succumb to such abusive behaviors if you are the victim, even if the offender is your department head or dean. Avoid reacting in the moment. Calm down and give yourself a chance to develop a strategy to respond. Schedule a meeting and give the other person a heads-up regarding what you intend to discuss. Difficult people generally do not like to be ambushed. Do not start with accusations or naming their terrible behavior. Instead, describe the situation and your feelings when you were bullied or treated with disrespect. State the negative impact on your state of mind and performance. Acknowledge that while they may mean well in getting the job done to their satisfaction, you respond better to calm, respectful and collaborative discussion. Leave the meeting if the abuser becomes volatile and starts screaming at you, and then resume the discussion at a later time. The more they realize that you will not respond to their terrible behavior, the more reasonable and cooperative they will eventually become, even though this change may take some time to occur.

Other problematic people believe nothing could be done without their personal contribution and supervision. They end up being annoying micromanagers. Gently let them know that you appreciate their willingness to help with every step on the way, but you need to try things out on your own and learn from your mistakes, and you will seek their input and contribution whenever you feel you need it. Others may discredit your ideas simply to advance theirs or try to claim credit for your work and initiatives. After all, it isn't possible that anybody but them would come up with such brilliant ideas! Fight to maintain the credit you deserve.

Some of your colleagues may simply be too difficult to deal with. They may exhibit persistent patterns that combine many of the personality flaws mentioned above, and perhaps even more. These people drain energy from colleagues and create a miserable work environment. They are therefore damaging to the organization if left unmanaged. Their behavior lowers morale and causes high employee turnover. Luckily, these "certified difficult people" are rare in academia. Limit your exposure to and interaction with such individuals but realize that they will go out of their way to find you and try to make your life miserable. Stand up for yourself and object to their behavior. Meanwhile, try not to take their demeaning language or actions personally. Gradually build an invisible psychological wall that will allow you not to hear them barking at you.

Watch out for back stabbers. Avoid sharing sensitive personal or professional information they may seek to use against you. Do the same with smooth operators and manipulators who seek to convince you to do their bidding on controversial issues. Some colleagues may become envious of your success. It makes them resentful and may lead them to create obstacles to slow you down by derailing your progress. They may try to find a way to somehow make you look bad in the eyes of your peers and superiors. Regardless of whether their attempts are successful, it is emotionally taxing to constantly deal with potential sabotage. Being surrounded by such people will consume much of your precious time in designing preemptive protective approaches instead of focusing on planning and executing your work. Try to understand the basis of their fears and assure them that you do not aim to overshine them by keeping a highly productive profile. Acknowledge their accomplishments and any role they may have played in your own success. Whenever applicable, discuss potential collaborations that would advance their career as well as yours. This approach will change the optics they use to judge you.

Your boss or one of your colleagues may be arrogant, egotistical or self-centered. These people believe they are uncontested giants in their fields or styles of leadership. Their feelings of superiority may sometimes be based on past history that has faded over time. Fight the temptation to bring them down to reality. Avoid creating enemies if a certain negative behavior is annoying rather than harmful. Focus your energy on increasing your productivity.

You may have a department head or dean who frequently fails to deliver on their pledges. Any time they promise you something verbally, respond with an email to thank them for their support and document your understanding of it. Politely ask for their commitment to a timeline for delivery. Written documentation is particularly valuable in cases of changing guards. A new department chair or dean may choose not to abide by undocumented promises made by their predecessors. Similarly, written performance evaluations become especially important when you deal with such superiors. These documents protect you from the danger of having your silent chair surprise you by not supporting your tenure or promotion later on without giving you due early warnings.

* * *

Lack of accountability and dependability by some is a serious problem in any workplace. It may be reflected in having colleagues or staff who do not meet deadlines or own their mistakes. This irresponsible behavior often hurts progress and curtails the productivity of the entire team. Precious opportunities may be lost as a result. Others may have to do extra work to compensate and fill in the gap, especially in the case of a looming deadline that must be met. It is not uncommon for some people to consider accountability a one-way road. They hold others, but not themselves, accountable. A person who lacks active responsibility may be aware of this defect and may be trying to find a cure. It is best to acknowledge their attempts to improve and guide them to self-help literature, workshops or appropriate mentors to assist them in effecting the desired change. Others may not be fully aware of the negative consequences of their behavior and would benefit from candid feedback. The most dangerous folks, however, are those who may recognize that they do not respect or adhere to principles of accountability but do not care what detrimental effects their irresponsible behavior may have on others. Therefore, they do not intend to change. A difficult conversation must be had with such problematic people. It may involve a mediator or moderator. The conversation may also involve intervention by the perpetrator's superiors. The main advice I have for you is to protect yourself against those who are not accountable or dependable. Once you know who they are, avoid collaborating with them if you have a choice. If you must work with them on a common project, make them commit in writing to a timeline for deliverables, ideally for each stage of the project. This step will prevent a disappointing surprise close to the final project deadline.

There are a few uncommunicative or aloof department heads who do not let faculty in on what they think of them or how they judge their work. Their behavior may be due to a preference for avoiding confrontations or pleasure in being elusive. If your department head is one of those individuals, take the initiative of starting a dialogue. Make an active effort to ask them about how they value your progress and what suggestions they may have for you to better your performance. Email them work plans and ask for feedback. If you receive nothing, let them know in writing that you interpret their silence as approval of your plans.

You may also have colleagues who are eternal skeptics. They discourage new initiatives and delay starting projects because they see only potential problems, not benefits. They are essentially "chronic rejectors" who end up becoming spiritual downers. If your boss is one, keep working on building preliminary evidence to support your proposed plans and preempt any concerns. Highlight the potential benefits of the project and its value to the department and college. Invite your superior's contribution to ensure that risks are calculated and mitigation plans are in place if things do not work out as planned. This approach will make them feel like partners toward achieving a common goal. Sometimes one has to be clever by making a chronic doubter and objector gradually and subliminally believe that the proposed idea was theirs. This approach of trading credit for the sake of the common good has a high chance of success, since it satisfies someone's ego and love of power and control.

Temporary versus Chronically Difficult Colleagues

As you get to know your colleagues better, you will be able to differentiate between temporary and chronic types of difficult people. A colleague who is usually cheerful and polite may one day explode at you for no apparent reason. While this behavior is inexcusable, you may realize it is due to a passing stressor in this person's life. Soon after, you should approach him or her to discuss the incident and its basis. Offer your assistance in solving the problem they have at hand, even if only by becoming a sounding board. This sporadic behavior is quite distinct from dealing with another colleague who regularly exhibits high temper, one who often shouts and throws objects across the room. These nasty behaviors are deeply embedded in this person's psychological makeup. They may reflect a history of dysfunctional family dynamics, psychological disorders (depression or anxiety), or perhaps drug addiction problems. You therefore need a different strategy to handle such chronically difficult people.

Your approach depends on the nature of your professional and personal relationship with this person. If you have a candid relationship, ask probing questions to guide them to discover the basis of their destructive behavior and the resulting harm. Discuss healthier alternatives. If you are not close to this person, work with a colleague who is, or you may choose to work with their superior. However, do not be overly optimistic in expecting difficult people to be totally cured. Ideally, you want to change the specific behaviors that affect you. In reality, however, the only power you have is to adjust your cognitive reaction to these behaviors. Do not get sucked into their negative energy tunnels, and do not retaliate by treating problematic people in a similar manner. Remain true to yourself and be an example of how people should treat each other.

Dealing with Harassment and Discrimination

Harassment in the workplace comes in many forms (for example, sexual or verbal). All types of harassment result in suppressing morale and productivity and create an environment dominated by fear and mistrust. They must therefore be controlled as early and effectively as possible. All of these types of harassment may be associated with discrimination in evaluations, promotion, assignments, inclusion or career development opportunities in case the person who is being harassed objects to these behaviors.

A victim may experience harassment because of their skin color, ancestry, country of origin or citizenship status. A person may also be harassed or discriminated against based on their biological gender, sexual orientation or preferred gender pronouns. Harassment may be expressed in the form of slurs, insults, stereotypes, jokes, intolerance or indifference. Other related expressions of harassment may not be as overt, such as hurtful comments about having an accent, curly hair or preference for certain music genres. Other examples include derogatory comments about customs, practices or clothing related to religious beliefs.

Sexual harassment generally includes unwanted romantic advances, conduct or behavior. For instance, someone at work may share pornographic photos with colleagues or subordinates, post obscene content on the walls of their office or make sexual comments and jokes. This behavior may escalate to inappropriate touching and sexual gestures. The harasser, who is often a senior-level employee, may offer deals in return for sexual favors (for example, positive performance evaluations, raises, promotions or lighter assignments). There were days when men were allowed to speak to women colleagues in a demeaning and disrespectful manner. Some looked at women as sex objects and downplayed their contributions to the work environment. While there has been a dramatic change in policies and behaviors, there are still many incidents of men using their powerful positions to coerce women colleagues, staff or students into various types of sexual relationships. This type of exploitative behavior happens less frequently between female bosses and male employees.

General microaggressions, whether overt or covert, represent the most frequent type of harassment. They include recurrent belittling, trivializing, ignoring, isolating and discrediting. Microaggressions are sometimes difficult to analyze and assign blame for. Each individual incident of microaggression may be too small to be noticed. It is the cumulative effect that becomes devastating to the victim. There is sometimes a sharp contrast between the intent of the perpetrator and the negative impact on the recipient of a given act of microaggression. One, for instance, may say something without realizing it is related to a deeply rooted and painful social problem or a history of exploitation of a certain population of people. The perpetrator may even mean well but use inappropriate language to express the message they want to deliver. In a healthy working environment, there is space for deep exploration of intentions and negative consequences of a given behavior. The recipient and the perpetrator would work it out through a respectful dialogue that results in having the culprit apologize and express willingness to alter their behavior to avoid a repetition of the incident in the future. In other cases, resolution may necessitate intervention by a superior or a moderator. I recommend that junior faculty familiarize themselves with guidelines for proper interactions with colleagues. It is also helpful to attend training aimed at avoiding committing microaggressions against others and explaining how to deal with being harassed.

If you feel that you have been harassed or discriminated against for any reason, you should spend time reflecting on the patterns, frequency and severity of the associated actions. Document each incident—its date, time, place—and describe the specific behavior. List the names of witnesses present at the time. Read institutional policies and guidelines on defining and dealing with harassment. As a first step, meet with the harasser to let them know how you perceive their behavior and what negative effects it has had on you. Remain calm. Describe the behavior rather than assigning adjectives. Emphasize your desire to maintain a mutually respectful professional relationship. The perpetrator may appreciate you bringing the matter to their attention and declare their intention to immediately change their ways. If this is the case, give them a chance to demonstrate the change and do acknowledge it, but watch for a possible relapse over time. However, the perpetrator may remain in denial and accuse you of imagining things or being unnecessarily sensitive. In this case, you should bring the issue to your department chair, who may refer you to the dean or to the office of human resources. Going directly to the dean or the director of human resources would be your only choice if your department chair is the culprit. If these bodies do not resolve the issue at hand to your satisfaction, file a formal grievance with the office of equal opportunities and affirmative action in your university. Make sure you document any attempts by the perpetrator to intimidate, threaten or retaliate against you.

Summary

It is necessary for a junior faculty member to interact with others in the workplace in accomplishing their work. These people include peer faculty, the department head, the dean, staff, trainees and students. This is their village. Junior faculty must also interact with people outside their institutions, such as journal editors, suppliers of research material and equipment, and officers in grant-awarding agencies. In these situations, one's personal skills in dealing with people will determine success or failure. A junior faculty member is not likely to succeed on the sole basis of their professional abilities (for example, excelling in scholarly productivity or teaching). It is the people in their community who will facilitate their journey and judge their performance. One's work usually benefits from collaborating with others who add their own special expertise and skills. A junior faculty member needs to develop strategies to proactively seek out and connect with potential collaborators and mentors.

It is fortunate that people generally choose an academic employment track as a result of an innate desire to help others and guide them to achieve their career goals. Consequently, most people in an academic environment are civil, kind and cooperative. However, there are a few who suffer from one or more of a large number of personality problems that make them difficult to deal with. A junior faculty member must learn how to handle such problematic persons to stop these individuals from decelerating their progress or depriving them of happiness in the workplace. Other important people skills include negotiation and conflict resolution.

Self-Reflection Exercises

- What are your three strongest and three weakest people skills?
- Reflect on the effectiveness of your approach to creating new networks, and list the benefits you have gained through networking.
- What are your main challenges in starting healthy and productive relationships?
- Recall success stories in dealing with difficult people in a healthy and productive way.
- Recall situations in which relationships went sour. What are the lessons learned from these experiences?

4

Time and Energy Management

Time and energy are two finite resources; therefore, they should be consumed judiciously to make the best use of them. A tenure-track junior faculty member is in a race to qualify for tenure and promotion after a specified number of years. They must work hard to demonstrate high productivity and prove themselves worthy of this highly coveted status. Meanwhile, being in a marathon, they cannot (and should not) expend all of their energy in the first few stages along the long and exhausting journey. What makes it even more complicated for a tenure-track faculty member is that they must perform a variety of tasks at the same time, and they must learn how to fit all these tasks within a confined time frame. A junior faculty member will crash and burn if they lack the skills necessary to handle this complicated and demanding lifestyle.

Time Management

Time management is mainly about coordinating tasks and finding ways to do them faster without sacrificing quality. You are in the driver's seat when it comes to making choices in utilizing and prioritizing your time. The most successful people are usually aware of the whole picture of their life and work priorities. They are clear about the goals they aim to achieve, in both the short run and the long run. They use this unique vision to decide on agendas for every day, week and month, while leaving spare time for urgent surprises. Successful individuals realize that time is not expandable; rather, it is a limited commodity in which adding a new task necessitates taking another out of the playing field. Therefore, they assess the importance of each new assignment in terms of the overall perspective rather than dealing with each task in isolation. The central element of skillful time management is assigning specific times for accomplishing

4. Time and Energy Management 63

individual tasks and abiding by the regimen. Without this type of discipline, a given task may get displaced by others that appear more urgent or more important.

First, decide on priorities and what exactly you plan to do with your day. If you find there is not enough time to accomplish all that you have in your bucket to your level of satisfaction, you must apply the "4 Ds" principle: delete, delegate, delay or diminish (divide large projects into small pieces). Make fast but educated decisions regarding whether a certain task fits in your priority bucket. Delete it if it does not. When I was a junior assistant professor, like many, I did not have the skills to properly assess the relative importance of different tasks and how much time was really needed to accomplish each one. This deficiency in my judgment led to the gradual buildup of a high stack of paper at the corner of my desk that was labeled "to read or act upon when there is time." In reality, of course, there was never time to get to read any of this material, let alone act on it. At the end of each year, I gave the department janitor a generous tip and asked him to please make this pile disappear while I was away. He obliged by tossing the pile into the recycling bin. For heaven's sake, I was not even brave enough to do this myself!!! Fortunately, I received a valuable advice from a senior colleague at a time when we all received large volumes of postal and campus mail on a daily basis. She taught me to hold up each piece of mail and then either place it in my to-do box or toss it into the recycling bin—nothing in between, and no buts or ifs. Her advice was game changing for me. The psychologically draining "maybe" pile disappeared from my desk thanks to this clever "deletion" technique.

In setting priorities, you may discover a pattern in the nature of chores you decide to delay. We often tend to prioritize things we enjoy doing and escape from reality by putting off tasks that are complex, unfamiliar or unenjoyable. The latter category usually includes responsibilities that are assigned by others—for example, by your department head or the chair of a committee you are serving on. Your enthusiasm for tackling some of these items may be dampened by your lack of belief in their relevance. They may not conform perfectly to your personal values and what you deem important. Here is a wakeup call: postponing these tasks will not make them disappear from the battle plan. You need to learn how to deal with them too. Remove these tasks from your time bucket if you have a choice. However, there are some tasks that are not much fun to tackle but contribute to the bigger picture in helping you reach your career goals. Bite the bullet and get them done.

A major problem in prioritizing tasks is tackling those labeled by others as "urgent" or "time sensitive." You may receive requests to handle more than one of these on a given day. Of course, this will throw your thoughtful planning out of balance. I recall a time early in my career when my secretary walked into my office with a pile of paperwork and a grumpy look on her face and said, "All of these assignments you asked me to do today have ASAP stickers on them. Would you please tell me which should be my ASAP1, ASAP2, ASAP3 and ASAP infinity?" I felt terrible on both her behalf and mine. I realized not only that I had been unfair in not giving her helpful directions on which tasks were most critical but also that I was unable to assign priorities to what I needed done. Everything seemed of the highest priority and urgency. Houston, we have a problem!

Apply the following urgency index inventory in classifying and prioritizing tasks in a descending rank order:

- Urgent and important
- Important but not urgent
- Urgent but not important
- Not urgent, not important

Assign lower priority to tasks that a colleague deems urgent, starting with ones originally assigned to somebody else who did not get the job done on time. Having said that, I must clarify that I am not suggesting you become self-centered. I am only advising you to guard yourself against repeat offenders who may see you as an easy target in the future. Erring on the side of repeating myself, remember that any new task has to displace another that is already in your time bucket. Learn how to gracefully say no. (See details on that process later in this chapter.)

Do not anticipate achieving perfect management of your time once you start your job, no matter how much you might learn from others, books or podcasts about such an important skill. Time management is something that one learns with experience. Furthermore, there is too much to handle when you move to your new institution. Transitions cause significant disturbance of one's life equilibrium, both at work and at home. Getting settled somewhere new requires dealing with an astronomical number of chores, most of which will diminish or dissipate after the first couple of months. Do not take failure to manage your time well during this period of the "big bang" as a negative reflection on your future handling of time and efforts.

Energy Management

Time management is a generic concept. Energy management, by contrast, connects us to our distinct strengths, daily habits and personal preferences. Managing energy helps individuals perform at their best. An important component of managing one's energy is prioritizing one's goals.

Start every day by recalling what really matters to you in your life in general. Your list may include family, friends, health, wealth management and professional success. Count your blessings. This exercise sets a positive mood for the day. It also helps you to handle setbacks you may encounter. One of my early graduate students shared with me a great piece of wisdom that I still apply now. Whenever something bad took place, she immediately thought of ten worse things that could have happened instead. Most likely, some of these items would be irreversible, such as the passing of a pet or losing a precious plant as a result of unanticipated killer frost. Not finishing a task you planned to get done today isn't a catastrophe! Having a paper or a grant get rejected isn't either!

We all differ in how we distribute our energy and attention during the day. Some of us are early risers; others, like me, are night owls. Some feel more comfortable getting rid of easy tasks in the beginning of the day and then tackling more problematic or time-consuming ones later on. This approach boosts their energy by allowing them to conquer a large number of obstacles in a short time and significantly decreasing the number of items on their to-do list, leaving them ready to deal with the big gorillas. Others prefer the opposite routine. To them, the presence of a monster in the background may obscure their ability to concentrate. In this case, preference must be given to starting the day with managing the more challenging tasks. Whichever approach you feel more comfortable with, make sure that each planned task on a given day has its own protected time slot. Do not let one bleed into the time allotted for another.

People also differ in their preference for being around or away from others while working, especially on tasks that require concentration. Introverts favor staying in their offices, likely with the door closed. Extroverts, however, get a boost from being with others; their energy will quickly dissipate if they remain alone for a long time. I am an extreme extrovert. I also have a rather short span of attention and concentration. Walking down to the department office to get coffee in between tasks allows me the chance of running into and greeting colleagues, staff and students. Such simple encounters with people recharge my battery. However, while I need people to maintain my own energy, I am fully aware of boundaries and do my best to avoid interrupting them or wasting their time. I am also aware that introverts become exhausted by lengthy interactions with people, especially when they try to appear gregarious. I therefore do not overtax them with unnecessary lengthy chats.

Changing my working space throughout the day also helps me avoid boredom. I often walk to the local coffee shop in the afternoon and do my work there. Switching scenery and being in the middle of a crowd lifts my spirit, even though I may not know a single person there. I use headphones or ear plugs to block noise and avoid distraction. Sometimes my private space gets invaded by a colleague who stops by to pick up a drink or a snack. He or she may invite themselves to my table and start a conversation. I have prepared this boiler-plate speech that I often use to defend my space and time in anticipation of these likely invasive and disruptive situations: "Hey, it is so good to see you. Unfortunately, I am not able to chat right now since I have a very pressing deadline to meet. Let's schedule time to get together soon. See ya."

Develop habits that boost your positive energy during the day, whether going for a short walk, stretching, or visiting the gym. I do not recommend using downtime to surf social media or news sites. Your brain is busy enough processing the information it already has, let alone adding more information of a completely different type. Effective mental relaxation during work hours requires engaging brain areas different from those involved in cognitive tasks.

A proper physical environment is essential for providing positive energy. A desk and a room free of major clutter helps one focus on the tasks at hand. A good filing system, be it electronic or an old-fashioned file cabinet, allows you to easily locate information and avoid significant interruptions of the flow of your thoughts. Our brains bear some resemblance to manual stick-shift cars. Every time you stop, you must go back to a slow low gear. In doing so, you waste time and exhaust mental energy. Imagine your daily calendar as a closet that has limited dimensions and envision your tasks as "stuff" to be stored in it. You can place things in an organized manner to maximize space utilization and easily find necessary items, or you can simply toss objects in and then dive into the piles every time you need to locate something in this inefficient mess. The same analogy applies to storing information in a way that facilitates its retrieval and, more important, deciding on which information to keep and which to toss away.

We also differ in our proficiency and preference for handling more than one thing simultaneously (multitasking) as opposed to going back and forth between different tasks (switch tasking). It is easy for the human brain to handle doing simple and familiar things at the same time (for example, sipping on coffee while talking on the phone). There is a large body of research, however, that suggests there is a high psychological cost to simultaneously performing more than one task that requires attention. There is also risk in possibly lowering the quality of each task's outcome. A good example is texting while driving, in which case you will be sacrificing your safety and the safety of others. Another is replying to email while attending a seminar, as you are not giving either task your full mental attention. I hope by now you realize that when academics tout the value of multitasking, they actually mean the ability to switch tasks and to be skilled at balancing and keeping track of multiple projects that are at different stages of completion and urgency. (More information on project management is available later in this chapter.)

An honest self-study and assessment of what is not working well will let you know how to adjust your actions to achieve more energy efficiency. Take a look at how much you have accomplished on a given day out of what you had planned to do. Identify tasks that took longer than expected and ones that had to be delayed until the next day because you ran out of time, and use this information to assign more realistic time slots to individual tasks. Pay special attention to big projects that you have been delaying from one day to the next for the past few weeks. Consider breaking them down into manageable pieces. Reflect frequently to revise and improve efficiency in your utilization of both time and energy.

The 80/20 Rule of Time Management

The 80/20 rule, also known as the Pareto Principle, is an aphorism asserting that 80 percent of outcomes (or outputs) result from 20 percent of all inputs for any given event or action. This principle applies to the proportion of one's time that results in significant accomplishments. Learning to recognize and then focus on that 20 percent is the key to making the most effective use of your time and to boosting your productivity. We all know many people who appear super busy all the time but do not have much to show for it at the end of the day. This result is usually due to their paying attention to less important tasks and ignoring major ones.

There are general indicators as to whether you are spending your time in the most productive 20 percent zone—most significantly, whether you are mostly engaged in activities that advance your career and that you are enjoying. Another indicator is whether you are reaching milestones in a timely manner without feeling stressed or squeezed for time. Similarly, there are warning signs that tell you loud and clear that you need to use your time and energy more judiciously. Examples include realizing that you are not really invested in certain tasks that other people want you to take care of, or frequently dealing with tasks categorized as "urgent," or having a hard time juggling deadlines or being involved in complicated tasks that you truly believe others may be more qualified to take on.

The 80/20 rule also applies to your interactions with others at work. When you take a more realistic look at the help you receive from staff, for example, you may well find that only a few of these individuals provide the majority of administrative assistance you need. Focus your energy on interacting with these helpers to benefit from their reliable service. Be sure to express your appreciation to those folks to establish a good working relationship and do your best to help them back. More important, do not overtax them. Save them for complicated or urgent tasks, and give the less important ones to others.

Pay enough attention to steps in each project that are rate-limiting to progress (i.e., bottlenecks). Figuring out how to alleviate these constraints will speed up progress for subsequent parts of the project. Identify other roadblocks to achieving your goals and work on eliminating them. It is possible that you do not have optimal experience or skills to handle a given task, in which case you should seek assistance. It is also plausible that your progress is being halted by others who are not pulling their weight. In such cases, a civil conversation about roles, responsibilities and mutual expectations is in order.

Barriers to Effective Time Management

When confronted with a new task, it is rather difficult to estimate the time needed to accomplish it properly. One may not be aware of hidden nuances—for instance, perhaps they did not estimate how long it would take to get feedback from others or approval of research protocols by institutional regulatory bodies. I highly recommend that you consult with more senior faculty to benefit from their experience in estimating time needed for big projects. Moreover, unfortunate situations that halt progress may arise, not the least of which is an unexpected internet malfunction or having to pick up a sick child from school. Allow cushion time for these unavoidable setbacks. You should also allocate more time than you think for completing unfamiliar tasks. It is always better to finish earlier than planned than to have an incomplete product due to running out of time.

Procrastination is one of the major enemies of effective time management. There are many reasons why people procrastinate. Some may be fearful of tackling a big project or one with which they have little experience. Others may put things off until the eleventh hour because they enjoy working in crisis mode. Procrastination leads not only to heightened anxiety close to a deadline but also to lower product quality because the work is done in a rush without having an adequate chance to review, revise and improve.

Much of what academics produce is reflected in writing. Like any other art form, writing is a process that mandates deep reflection and editing for better clarity and flow. This naturally takes time and many iterations. We are all familiar with a common scene in movies and TV shows where a writer crumbles a document they just crafted and tosses it in the trash because they do not like what they produced. Hasty writing ends up generating grant proposals that are unclear and unfocused and full of grammatical and typographical errors. This is wasteful of time and energy, since such a poorly crafted document will be likely rejected by reviewers and therefore require multiple rounds of revision and resubmission. I will never forget an example of a grant proposal I reviewed a couple of decades ago, in which the author left many notes to his graduate students to search the literature for published references that supported various assertions he made. Of course, these notes were taken by the assigned reviewers and other members of the review panel as an indication that this was a last-minute job. More seriously, it demonstrated that the applicant was dishonest in making up important statements that were not valid. These errors were just the tip of the iceberg that revealed a diffuse proposal built on a poor experimental design. Needless to say, the application was rejected flat out.

Procrastination is also dangerous in the case of tasks that unexpectedly expand and branch out. They develop malignancies that are hard to contain. Anytime one thinks they are done, important remaining details or newly developed nuances may come to light. Starting early on these projects would enable the responsible party to tackle them calmly and allow themselves a chance to slow down, breathe and reflect.

Another problem is perfectionism. A perfectionist is never satisfied with what they (or others) have achieved or produced. There is always a better way to say or do things. Let's work on another draft. Let's wordsmith a document ad nauseum. How about using this font? Isn't it more impressive and eye catching? Perfectionists do this with every task, regardless of its nature or importance. Successful people, by contrast, have the ability to size up every project and assign it a degree of relevance and time for completion. They dedicate more time to projects that require exactness and thoughtfulness as compared to less impactful, run-of-the-mill projects.

Please note that I am by no means advising you to lower your standards by sacrificing quality for the sake of saving time. I am simply recommending that you give each task the attention it needs according to where it lies on the "scale of desired or requited perfection." Imagine you work for an aircraft manufacturing company. Checking the setup of the toilet paper dispensary in the lavatory obviously does not require the same level of accuracy as certifying the optimal dynamics of jets.

The most important external factor that interferes with time management is interruptions by others—namely, walk-ins or new urgent tasks imposed on you by others. You need to allow time for some degree of interruption. In an interruption-rich environment, however, such intrusions could easily eat up most of your day, every day of the week. You may frequently find yourself going home with many of the items on your to-do list left unfinished. The "not-done-yet" list will grow from one day to the next to form a formidable mountain. Whenever someone asks whether you have "a minute" to discuss something that has just come up, I assure you the conversation will take much longer than that. You have to be upfront in telling this person how much time you have available and end the conversation politely at that time. People love to hear themselves talk. Some have difficulty relaying their story in a linear and coherent fashion. It takes them what seems to be forever to get to the point. Nobody should be the victim of such time-wasting exercises. Others have difficulty ending a conversation. While discussing the main topic of a meeting agenda may only take a few minutes, closing remarks or switching to other topics that are not relevant may drag on. Similarly, many people have a hard time ending phone conversations. You must develop vocal cues or body language in different situations to bring a conversation to an end. Be in the driver's seat to guard your time.

Electronic calendars that are visible to all open the door to "calendar predators." Having people request or schedule meetings on short notice during open times on your calendar may come to you as a surprise that interferes with the plans you have in mind. Block out as many time slots as needed on your calendar for you to focus on projects that require seamless attention, continuity and concentration. I have been applying this practice for a long time and have found it vital in reserving quality time for writing in particular. Of course I bend these rules if a request for a meeting to work on an urgent, time-sensitive issue comes along. As stated above, however, I do not place all urgent requests at the same level of importance.

Your time may also be wasted by having to deal with others' chaos. A colleague may stay in the office late in the evening to draft large sections of a grant proposal, which suddenly appears to be practically impossible to finish by the designated deadline. This person walks around the department corridors and discovers that your office lights are on. They dash in and ask whether you would help with part of the task (for example, proofreading or searching the literature for key information). You are frustrated by this "work dumping" attitude, especially since you were about to leave the office to spend some time with your family. Similarly, your boss may suddenly ask you to gather complicated information for a report he or she must submit to the dean in a few hours. Power dynamics or kindness may prevent you from declining these and similar requests. I advise you to do your best not be the one who pays the price for others' negative traits and behaviors. You must develop proactive tactics to politely and firmly deal with work dumping by others. Take responsibility for protecting your time and work plans in order to maintain sanity and allow for a reasonable work-life balance.

Project Management

Careful long-term planning is key to success. As Benjamin Franklin said, "If you fail to plan, you are planning to fail." Any academic must learn how to juggle a myriad of simultaneous projects that are at different stages of completion or have different submission deadlines. The first step in efficient project management is creating a document that includes a comprehensive list of all the tasks, as well as their goals, strategies and tactics to achieve them. A goal is a broad primary outcome (for example, building your research or teaching portfolio to support your future application for promotion with tenure). A strategy is the approach you adopt to achieve a goal. Increasing the number of publications in reputable journals and being well funded are strategies for demonstrating outstanding research productivity. A tactic is an actionable step you take to achieve a strategy (for instance, bringing the long list of "manuscripts in preparation" to fruition so that they may be submitted and published). Some objectives are short-term ones, such as submitting a grant proposal. Others, like building up preliminary data for your next grant application or having your doctoral students receive their degrees, are long term. Note the status of each objective and its anticipated (or required) date of completion.

Be realistic in planning timelines. A submitted manuscript may take a couple of months for the first cycle of reviews, a couple more if you need to perform additional experiments to respond to reviewers' concerns, and another month or so to receive a final decision from the editorial office. Of course, there are exceptions and extremes on both sides of the time spectrum. In my entire career, I have had only a single manuscript accepted as is on first submission, and a few that required minor revisions, but the majority required one or two lengthy revision and resubmission cycles. The same rule applies to grant applications, with an even more expanded time scale. It usually takes about four to six months to receive reviews of the first submission, another few months to revise the application to respond to reviewers' concerns (and often doing extra work to support the aims of the proposal), and then four to six more months to receive the reviews of the second submission. A very small percentage of proposals get funded on the first try. The good news is that such instant success is often granted to applications by junior faculty. They put so much effort into writing, editing and perfecting their applications. They also usually run their proposals by a few faculty members with vast experience in serving on grant review panels.

In essence, the project management document described above represents your own vision, strategic plan and how/when to accomplish individual goals that fall under this wide umbrella. You must review this document and update it frequently as circumstances change. You may want to save the document on an internet drive to make it accessible wherever you are. I also suggest sharing it with your department head and mentors to keep them abreast of your progress and benefit from their comments and suggestions.

Delegation of Responsibilities

New tasks and responsibilities will most certainly continue to pile up. There will come a time when you sense that you can no longer keep up with accomplishing all the work you have at the high standard you desire. One option is to delegate some of your responsibilities to others. Delegation may relate to specific short-term tasks or significant chunks of work. There are many factors to consider that will make delegation effective and time saving. Consider these important questions: Is there somebody you trust with the task? If not, is there somebody who could easily and quickly be trained to perform it? Will adding this assignment to this person's existing duties hurt the progress of their other projects? Do you expect the task to appeal to this person and perhaps contribute to their professional growth? Are you overtaxing a certain individual who has a good track record in getting things done? Most important, will delegation end up costing you more time rather than saving it if you have to closely supervise the person to whom you are delegating and troubleshoot at every step of the way?

Look at the big picture when you consider to whom to delegate a given task. Depending on the skills of people around you, you may delegate responsibilities to staff, trainees, colleagues or outside services. Be mindful when you delegate time-consuming tasks to graduate students or postdoctoral trainees. Their main effort must be dedicated to their research and finishing their training in a reasonable time. However, asking them to assist with some responsibilities may be helpful in developing their career (for example, facilitating classroom discussion). The best strategy in delegating to colleagues is to approach the process from a collaborative angle. This way they do not look at you as someone who is trying to take advantage of their generosity by asking them to do your work for you without sharing the credit. Odd though it may sound, you may also choose to approach your boss to ask whether he or she would be willing to collaborate on a project to reduce your workload. Your boss may have special expertise or skills that pertain to a portion of the work that is pivotal to success of the entire project.

Whenever you delegate, you should start by presenting the nature of the job, its background and anticipated outcome. Make time to answer questions, both during initial planning and throughout execution of the project. Clear expectations are required for successful delegation. Share the timeline and expected quality of deliverables. Communicate accountability and delegated level of authority and check for understanding. Provide necessary resources, training and information. Trust the person or group you delegate a responsibility to, but gauge the outcome at various stages of progress and provide periodic advice while avoiding micromanaging. Share feedback and positive reinforcement. Avoid the blame-and-shame game if the project does not succeed for reasons beyond the other person or group's control. If things are not moving along, consider giving the project to someone else or taking care of it yourself. Contemplate the possibility of farming out the project to professionals within or outside your institution. In certain situations (particularly in accomplishing highly technical tasks), this approach may actually end up saving you money and time.

One of the main obstacles to delegation is fear of giving up control. Remember, however, that delegation actually gives you more control over your time. It permits you to focus on projects that require your higher level of expertise. Another roadblock to delegation is the concern that others may not handle the assigned project to your satisfaction. One solution is to delegate the task at hand for a limited duration of time—a test period—after which you can judge the quality of the outcome and adjust your plan accordingly. Remember that delegation empowers members of a group through involving them in a project of common benefit. It creates self-confidence, professional growth and commitment to the common cause. It is also effective in team building. You may be pleasantly surprised if the outcome turns out even better than if you had done the work yourself. People have diverse experiences and approach problem solving differently. Some may see possibilities or solutions that were not readily obvious to you.

When and How to Say "No"

As a junior faculty member, you are likely allowed protected time to enable you to get your research program off the ground. Having protection, however, may not necessarily stop superiors and colleagues from asking you to take on additional chores in teaching or service. This situation creates a dilemma. You are eager to please and prove that you are a good citizen and a team player, or you may fear creating adversaries by declining these requests, especially when they come from your department chair. Meanwhile, you are constantly reminded by your colleagues and mentors that research accomplishments are the main criteria for promotion and tenure, regardless of what is stated in institutional policies about equally valuing research, teaching and service. Carefully analyze your motivation if you find yourself readily accepting new tasks that interfere with your overall productivity. You may be a very kind person who gets satisfaction from helping others. This is a good quality, provided it is harnessed in a way that does not halt or slow down your own progress. Deeper analysis, however, may reveal that you are a workaholic who experiences guilt for having downtime, one who probably unconsciously finds comfort in adding time fillers. This is a harmful trait that you should strive to change both to protect your progress toward promotion and to keep a healthy balance in your overall work-life portfolio.

Consider these questions whenever you are asked to take on an additional duty: How does it fit with your goals for the year and multi-year plan? Are there potential benefits such as generating publications, establishing new connections, and gaining enhanced visibility (local, national, international)? What is the "actual" workload? Is this project short or long term? What exactly is required of you? What must you give up in order to accommodate the new task? Could you assume the new responsibility without sacrificing free time dedicated to yourself and your family? What compensation will you acquire (financial gains, experience, networking opportunities)? How much do you know about the specific task (or the entire project)? Do you have sufficient experience, or do you need to gain more? Is this a once-in-a-lifetime chance, or will there be similar opportunities at a more opportune time in the future?

You should also consider whether you are the right person to do the task. You have two main options if you feel you are not adequately qualified to handle it. The best option is to discuss your concerns with the person who is requesting your contribution. Share your overcommitment and lack of experience, if this is the case. The less optimal choice (which I actually do not recommend) is to bite the bullet and give it a try. Once you have started on this road, it will be difficult for you to change course. Your pride and reputation are at stake; you do not want to admit failure or appear incompetent. You either keep trying until you eventually give up or somehow succeed in getting the task done, though not necessarily to your or others' satisfaction. This is a no-win situation.

If your analysis indicates that accepting the new task is associated with more costs than benefits, you must find a way to gracefully decline. If the request came from a colleague, discuss it with your department chair and mentors to get their take. Use their objection (if that is their reaction) as a polite way out. Things get more complicated if you need to decline a request made by your chair. However, there are ways to do that politely and safely. It is always wise to acknowledge the authority of your boss and that they have the final say in your effort distribution. Emphasize that the two of you share the same goal of having you succeed on your path to promotion and tenure. Empathize by stating your understanding of the importance of getting the task done for the common good. This approach is effective in avoiding or minimizing power struggles. Share your answers to the questions stated above. Gently remind your boss of your need for the promised time protection during the early years of your employment. Engage your boss in the analysis of benefits and costs involved in taking on the new assignment. Better yet, share with your boss the project management scheme mentioned above and ask for their guidance regarding what to give up in order to accommodate the new task. This request certainly puts things into perspective.

Email Management

I consider email the modern "Cookie Monster" that constantly eats up our time. I miss the days when postal or campus mail used to be the main venue for professional communication. It took many days for a letter to be delivered, plus a similar length of time to receive a response. Email, by contrast, reaches its destination anywhere in the world in a matter of seconds. Moreover, it takes only a click on a computer keyboard to attach a very large document that may take significant time to read. Often a number of recipients are copied on email messages, some of whom choose to respond by selecting "reply all." A molehill suddenly becomes a mountain. What initially started as a simple message crafted by someone in a couple of minutes has somehow led to having numerous people invest significant time preparing an educated response. By the time any of these people finishes this task, it is highly likely they will find dozens of messages residing in their inbox. The end result is that while communication technology has certainly enabled us to do things much faster, it has not necessarily saved us time that we can use for leisure. In fact, the opposite may be true. Yes, we get things done faster using the internet, but we have many more things to do compared to the good old days. Accessibility of information at any time, in any place, has made it difficult to step away from your work environment. One simply cannot escape or hide!

Checking email every time you hear a chime announcing that "you've got mail" is a major source of interruption and distraction. It will diminish your productivity by interfering with your mental concentration. It is a good idea to deactivate audible and visual email alerts or, better yet, adjust your email settings to check for and download new messages only at specific times. Communicate this practice and the reasoning behind it to your department chair and colleagues. Sometimes you may need to stay away from email for most of a given day, or for the entire day, for instance, to allow you to focus on a project with a pressing deadline. In these cases, I recommend that you create an auto-reply message to let people know to expect a delayed response. Include the name and contact information of a person you have designated to coordinate incoming requests in case of an emergency.

It is recommended that one set aside specific times every day for checking and responding to email—for example, at the beginning of the day or after lunch. Allocate a certain amount of time to take care of email. I highly advise against checking for new email as you are getting ready to depart your office late in the afternoon. You may be tempted to stay longer to respond to a few messages.

You need to develop efficient strategies for reading and responding to email. It helps to classify messages into "to read" and "to respond to" categories, and then divide them further by their priority and urgency. Be succinct when you respond. This practice will save you and the recipients significant time. Create templates or canned messages, such as "will do" or "will get back to you ASAP." Create macros. In prioritizing responding to email, I prefer to start with messages that need less than a couple of minutes to respond to. I find it psychologically comforting to reduce the number of messages in my inbox. Furthermore, I copy only those who must stay timely informed of progress on a given issue. In my experience, the more people I copy on email, the more comments I receive that require further action on my part.

File original emails and your responses under designated labels and sublabels that enable you to locate individual messages with ease. Create folders for specific projects or recurring meetings. Some email services (for example, Outlook and Gmail) can be set up to automatically file new messages into specific folders. However, I do not favor this approach. I would rather keep emails visible in my inbox until I delete, read or respond to them and then archive them in appropriate folders. This way I maintain control of my email and also have a constant visual reminder of the need for action on messages in my inbox.

Work with your colleagues and members of your scholarly team to establish mutual understanding and expectations of when they need to copy you on emails. This is really a matter of personal preference and management style. I prefer to be copied whenever the sender feels I should be kept in the loop. This practice keeps me informed and gives me the option to respond or comment if need be. Otherwise I glance at the message for information only. Being copied also assures me that a task I assigned to someone else is being taken care of in a timely manner. Others prefer to be copied only in cases when their immediate involvement in the matter is required or when there is an emergency.

4. Time and Energy Management

Work-Life Balance

You need to give your family their share of your time. You should step away from work to allow yourself a chance to reflect, regain your full mental energy and avoid burnout. It is essential to maintain an active social circle and to keep up with your hobbies. I have known so many academics who dedicated every minute of their days to work. Their lives became a seamless cycle of activities related to their professional career. They felt strange, and perhaps guilty, for having any downtime. In essence, they became addicted to work. Whenever they stepped away from the work environment, they experienced withdrawal episodes that were usually manifested as being anxious and feeling lost. Many ended up losing their friends or becoming estranged from their spouses and children. They lost touch with things they once immensely enjoyed doing outside the work environment. I have witnessed some of my friends with such unbalanced distribution of their life and work activities slide through a spiral of depression and hopelessness as soon as they retired. They did not know what to do with their free time. It was too late for some to reconnect with old friends or regain the affection of their family.

Contemplate how you envision a favorable balance between work and other life activities. Determine what works best for you, since one size does not fit all. Take into consideration your priorities for various professional and social goals. Realize that an ideal balance may shift from one day to another depending on circumstances. There have been countless occasions when my calendar for a given day was completely free, but requests for meetings and urgent work that had to be dealt with started crawling out of nowhere and ended up consuming a good part of the day. Moreover, watch carefully for work responsibilities that tend to expand and reclaim their dominance in your daily activities. Periodically assess how successful you have been in implementing your plans for time distribution. Consult with specialists if needed. Institutions may have counselors who provide advice on optimizing the investment of one's time.

Consider your overall mental and physical wellness in planning for a favorable work-life balance. Include time for daily exercise. Allow yourself enough hours of sleep. Make sure you schedule annual medical and dental examinations on time. Invest time and energy in keeping a healthy diet. Do not feel guilty about unplugging when you are home, especially over weekends and holidays. Set expectations and make people at work aware of these boundaries. Schedule weekly or more frequent gatherings with friends and extended family. These human connections are vital for good mental health. They will decrease your level of stress and provide much-needed emotional support. Avoid talking shop when you get together socially with colleagues and their families. First, this will defeat the purpose of getting away from the work environment. Second, talking about your work will exclude spouses and others who do not have a direct stake or interest in these topics. Whenever my wife and I go out to a restaurant with friends, I impose the "El-Fakahany rule of talking shop"—namely, the first person who starts a work conversation pays for drinks! It is amazing how effective such a simple preemptive intervention has proven to be.

You need to enjoy your children at every stage of their development. They grow so fast. Before you know it, they will develop wings and fly away. At an early stage of my career, I was a poor example of practicing what I am preaching now. I used to be in my office early every morning and often did not get home until late in the evening. I was at work on weekends and during holidays. Even when I was home, I often called my students or postdoctoral fellows to inquire about the results of their experiments. Having my wife work evening shifts and on weekends made this practice possible. Unfortunately, I did not change this pattern when we had children, and I spent very little time with them. The cure to my work addiction came about in the most serendipitous and providential way. On my drive back from work one evening, I was listening to the song "Cat's in the Cradle" by Harry Chapin. The song is about a father who was too busy with work to get to know his son when he was little. It was not until his son became an adult and left home that he recognized the need to establish a father-son relationship, but it was too late by then. His son brushed off repeated attempts by his dad to get together to punish his dad for not being available when he needed him. As he said while growing up, "I'm gonna be like you, Dad, you know I'm gonna be like you." I still vividly recall pulling over and starting to cry uncontrollably. The song was about me! It opened my eyes to the need to change, immediately. I am so glad I did when I had a chance.

Enjoy the benefits provided by your institution that allow you the time you need to cater to family demands. These include parental leaves for both parents when a child is born or adopted. Moreover, it has become the norm in the academy to extend the tenure clock by one year upon the birth of each child. You may request a similar extension if you are caring for a family member who has serious health issues. These extensions will be noted in your promotion file and communicated to external reviewers of your dossier to explain resulting gaps in your vitae, particularly in publications. Take your full allotted vacation. Resist temptations to connect with members of your laboratory or even think of work while you are away. The more refreshed you become during your vacation, the more productive you will be when you get back to work.

Handling Job-Related Stress

Stress at work builds up slowly. It remains unnoticed until it surpasses a certain threshold the body cannot tolerate. Sources of stress include being in a new environment, facing an unfamiliar assignment, taking on too many responsibilities, and failing to maintain good time and energy management. A junior faculty member is suddenly required to successfully juggle many responsibilities in a limited amount of time. They deal mostly with delightful and helpful colleagues, but perhaps also with some who may not be as nice or welcoming. Excelling at people skills and at time/energy management is the best prophylactic for stressors. Prevent stress by being on top of your tasks. Do not take on too much at once. Stagger projects. Start working early on each project or assignment.

Do not let your stressors take you away from your family. Do not bring your stress home. Families may not understand the gravity of your current stressful situation or other long-term challenges in your academic life. They measure successes and failures using different optics. I still vividly recall the day I learned my very first grant application had been rejected. I went home devastated. I expected my family to understand the gravity of the situation and shower me with all kinds of emotional support. To give them credit, they asked many probing questions to understand why I looked so miserable: Did somebody die? Were you in an accident? Did you get injured in a fight? I answered "no" to all of these and many similar questions and then told them about my grant application being rejected. My youngest daughter (then four years old) said, "I hate 'Uncle Grant' who made you so upset!" The older (seven years) asked, "Will you be fired because you did not get this grant?" When I answered in the negative, she responded with a voice of authority and wisdom, "There is no reason to worry, then!!!"

Importance of Reflection

Stepping back gives one a unique opportunity to see the forest instead of being knee deep in the weeds. I get my most creative ideas related to work when I am far removed from the work environment. Many interesting research projects were conceived while I was watering or weeding my flower garden or taking a walk in the woods. Another helpful habit I have developed is scheduling regular time at the end of each week to evaluate the quality and volume of my accomplishments during the week. I take note of lessons learned and how to do better moving forward. Reflection has been most helpful in setting and recalibrating my priorities and in using my time efficiently. I strongly advise you to make time for this kind of deep reflection.

Summary

Time is the most valuable commodity available to all of us, but only the wise realize its limited nature and our inability to stretch it. All one can do is to budget their time to get things done and still have opportunities left for fun. This feat is accomplished by carefully sizing up and prioritizing tasks and assigning them a specific length of time. It also requires building skills in delegating responsibilities to others and optimizing energy expenditure.

Self-Reflection Exercises

- When are your highest and lowest energy patterns during a day?
- What are the main barriers to having full command of your time? Come up with mitigation plans for each.
- Recall a time when you delegated a project to somebody. Evaluate the outcome and how to do better in the future.
- Think of situations when you felt pressured to accept responsibilities that contributed little to the progress of your career. Using such examples, how do you plan to sharpen your skills in saying no in the future?
- What do you plan to do to better manage your email?

5

Advising and Mentoring Your Trainees

Contributing to the growth and development of undergraduates, graduate students and postdoctoral fellows is one of the most important tasks performed by faculty. It represents their way to pay back by preparing the next generation of highly qualified and successful scholars. I liken the experience to taking care of a thin seedling by watering it, fertilizing it, and making sure it gets enough sunlight during the day. Many of the skills of advising and mentoring are derived from personal experience. When being trained, one learns what is helpful and what is not. Trainees observe behaviors on the part of their advisors that make them more motivated and others that lead them to lose self-confidence. You may have noticed that your advisor and members of your dissertation committee went beyond designing your thesis project or discussing research findings. They cared about your career trajectory and therefore guided you to best practices in soft skills such as writing, public speaking and healthy ways to resolve conflicts. In addition to personal experience gained from watching others, there are many resources for improving the mentoring and advising abilities of a junior faculty member.

Advising versus Mentoring

Some confuse the terms "advising" and "mentoring." Advising graduate students, for instance, is mostly limited to providing them with information on degree requirements, helping in their academic progress by monitoring their performance in coursework and guiding them toward degree completion. As they start their dissertation research, the advisor is responsible for helping graduate students plan projects, design experiments, and interpret data. The advisor also guides students and postdoctoral fellows to pertinent literature and assists in critiquing drafts of manuscripts. She or he provides performance assessment and plans interventions to improve the quality and quantity of the trainee's work.

An advisor who is also a mentor goes far beyond mere technical supervision. He or she actively engages in the overall development of their graduate students and postdoctoral trainees as independent scholars and educators. They guide trainees in successfully transitioning into the next stage of their career and thereafter. Successful mentors usually apply a Socratic method in training. They do not dictate directions (e.g., how a given experiment should be designed). Instead, they collaborate with the trainees to construct a plan. The mentor asks guiding and probing questions that lead the mentee to find their own answer. Sometimes trainees supplement guidance from their advisor related to the subject matter of their studies by seeking mentoring from other senior faculty or peers at a more advanced stage of their training.

Mentoring should be deliberate and thoughtful. Its main goal is to provide adequate support, challenge and vision. The success associated with good mentoring and guidance naturally enhances retention and degree completion. Your reputation as a caring mentor will pay dividends by attracting top trainees to your group. Most important, adequate preparation of the next generation of scholars is both a duty and a pleasure. This fact makes mentoring a moral responsibility, especially in the academic world. As your career advances toward retirement, you will find yourself gauging your overall contribution to the scholarly world by the number of mentees you have served and how successful they have been in their careers. You will take comfort in trusting that they will continue your mission in advancing the creation of knowledge and mentoring others. This legacy will continue long past the span of your lifetime on this planet.

Good mentoring and apprenticeship are the reason why many Nobel laureates have been trained by past winners of this prestigious distinction. For example, MIT professor Dan Kleppner trained David Pritchard, who, in turn, trained five Nobel laureates in physics. There are numerous other examples that offer strong proof that scholarly success is a product of both innate talent and nurturing.

Elements of Effective Mentoring

Like parents, research advisors and career mentors tend to apply approaches that their own advisors used to train them, even though they may have loathed some of these practices or found them counterproductive, demeaning or demoralizing. People in general tend to forget some negative aspects of personal experience and therefore repeat them

5. Advising and Mentoring Your Trainees

unconsciously. While I was growing up, I faithfully kept a daily diary until I was twenty-five years old. Every now and then I randomly open pages in the diary, and I get a chuckle when I notice that it is full of complaints about the way my parents raised me. Oddly enough, I realized that I repeated some of the hated actions embedded in this parenting style, which led me to correct my path accordingly. A healthy approach to mentoring, therefore, mandates thoughtful and intentional reflection on one's past experience to learn what to adopt and what to avoid, in addition to identifying resources to sharpen one's mentoring skills. These resources include books, review articles, podcasts and workshops. There are even many journals dedicated to mentoring practices. Benefit from these resources to develop a healthier approach to mentoring.

Experts in the pedagogy of mentoring recommend a systematic approach to learning about the characteristics of good mentoring and applying them. They prefer this method over winging it and then dealing with challenges to the mentoring relationship as they come. While benefiting from one's mistakes is the best way to learn, there is a good reason not to subject trainees to poor advising and mentoring if there is a way to avoid that problem from the very start. Furthermore, it may not be easy for an advisor to recognize that they are either hurtful or discouraging since trainees may not be forthcoming in complaining or asking for change.

Mentoring philosophies and practices may differ depending on the mentor and the mentee. However, there are main principles that are agreed upon. The most critical element that should never be lost is the feeling of mutual trust, as it is difficult to regain fully. Open and respectful communication is the most essential ingredient for establishing rapport. All parties involved must feel secure and safe in their communication with each other. Such a healthy climate is conducive to learning. A good mentor realizes that mentoring must be customized according to the specialized career goals of each mentee. This approach naturally requires proactive planning and consideration. A mentor should be accessible, responsible and accountable. They should be on time for meetings and meet deadlines for promised deliverables. Good listeners who invite diverse views and value bidirectional constructive feedback make excellent mentors. Helpful mentors, similar to career coaches, avoid providing immediate answers to arising challenges. They encourage trainees to develop alternative approaches and have an open and calm conversation about the pros and cons of each approach. What a great active learning experience that is!

Most mentees prefer candid and specific feedback on what they need to change and improve, instead of vague, sugarcoated advice. It is quite comforting to mentees to hear about not only their mentors' triumphs but also their failures. These revelations give a junior mentee hope that they will eventually make it in spite of potential challenges and failures at the outset of their journey. Finally, a mentor should demonstrate respect, honesty, integrity, empathy, consistency, fairness and impeccable ethical conduct. Mastering optimal mentoring skills may take a lifetime. Like any relationship, mentoring requires maintenance and nourishment. It is important to periodically evaluate what works and what doesn't, as well as opportunities for improvement.

Some junior mentors use their own work styles and accomplishments during their training period as a yardstick to assess a mentee's potential to succeed in their future career. After all, these are the qualities that have contributed to their success so far. I truly believe, however, that trying to make students and postdoctoral fellows clones of their mentors is rather unwise. Needless to say, there is always more than one way to achieve a given goal. How one approaches problem solving, for example, varies as a result of differences in past training, cultural background and personal traits. A good mentor should therefore invite and appreciate diversity of thoughts and approaches rather than trying to place all trainees in the same mold. Furthermore, there is a better chance to effect a paradigm shift in knowledge and practices when two people who are not alike work collaboratively together.

A mentor should also not be rigid in their expectations regarding how trainees go about getting their work done. It is not helpful for a mentor to compare how they used to run their lives earlier in their career to how students and postdocs conduct theirs. These are different times, and there is a wide generational gap that results in significant differences in attitudes, expectations and resources. Young trainees have skills, tools, needs and preferences their mentors did not have back in graduate school.

In addition, mentors should not aim to train everybody to be a successful academic. They should take into consideration the many exciting alternate careers trainees have available to them nowadays. Many current advisors and mentors were trained at a time when the dream of every graduate student or postdoctoral fellow was to become an assistant professor, ideally in a research-intensive institution. Those who "did not make it" sought employment in big or small firms or businesses. Nowadays, trainees may instead actively pursue employment in biotechnology, journalism, broadcasting, consulting, regulatory affairs, research project management, and so forth. Each of these careers requires different skill sets that necessitate tailored training.

 Allow for an independent work style, but encourage collaborations at the expense of competition. Delineate project leaders (especially in the case of graduate students). Each student eventually needs to claim ownership of their dissertation project. They also need a coherent project with well-connected components to produce a thesis. It is easier for postdoctoral trainees than graduate students to mix and match in pursuing different directions of scholarship.

Maintain harmony in your research group. Do not permit actions that demean or insult others. Share with the entire group the roles and responsibilities of every member and how they fit in the big picture. Encourage sharing knowledge and expertise. Reward those who excel at mentoring and go out of their way to help in developing the skills of others. These strategies are necessary for creating team spirit and rewarding good deeds.

Roles and Responsibilities of a Mentor

There are numerous roles a mentor plays in guiding mentees toward a successful career. The most important responsibility is serving as a role model to emulate, particularly with regard to ethical conduct of research. A mentor stimulates self-reflection by the mentee and provides psychological support in the form of motivation and encouragement. He or she challenges mentees to improve their skills and learn new ones and coaches them to explore and discover hidden strengths and competencies. They share experience and knowledge with mentees and guide them through goal setting and designing a path to get there. Of paramount relevance is mentoring trainees in people skills and critical approaches to problem solving. One of the most important roles a mentor plays in the life of a mentee is being their advocate and sponsor in brokering career advancement opportunities.

It is a good idea for you to draft a mentoring philosophy statement. This statement should include the main features of your mentoring style. Offer details of the services you are able and willing to offer, along with your expectations of mentees who work under your tutelage. This document represents the first step in establishing clear communication about mutual expectations. New trainees will know up front what they will be getting into and whether your research group suits their career goals and work style preferences.

Roles and Responsibilities of a Mentee

A mentoring relationship cannot succeed without contributions from mentees. The most critical trait a mentee must exhibit is a willingness to learn new skills and to commit the time and effort required for that process. Likewise, they must be open to opportunities that build their professional independence and advance their career. A dependable mentee takes ownership of their general education and career goals, is engaged and passionate about their work, and frequently reflects on career advancement plans and progress toward achieving those goals. They keep track of advice and follow through with actions. Mentees should also be proactive in setting up meetings to ask questions and seek feedback and clarification in a timely manner.

Individual Development Plans

Working with trainees to produce a customized career development plan provides a helpful roadmap. It adds structure, clear expectations and accountability. It also makes it easier to track progress toward individual career goals and maintain an optimal balance in achieving them. Individual development plans should provide a timeline for completing courses and exams, as well as writing manuscripts and fellowship applications and conference presentations. In addition, they should address approaches to improving soft skills. As mentioned previously, mastering these skills is necessary for scholastic success. This rule generally applies to any type of career a trainee decides to pursue in the future, though different careers require more emphasis on certain sets of skills than others.

For each goal, there should be a statement of the anticipated date of completion. Such dates should be reasonable in a practical sense and should be mutually agreed upon rather than being imposed on the trainee. There should also be a timeline for each step involved (for example, the expected dates for providing a first draft of a manuscript to the advisor and for submitting the completed manuscript to a journal). Discussion of a trainee's progress should be based on these expectations and commitments. Timelines for individual projects should be recalibrated to accommodate challenges that may arise. The master plan should be revisited at least every six months. Changes in the trainee's goals or circumstances would require modifying the plan to make it more realistic and achievable.

Communicating and Aligning Expectations

> "The single biggest problem in communication is the illusion that it has taken place."—George Bernard Shaw

Ask your mentees to share their expectations of themselves and of you. Give them your full attention during these conversations. Listen carefully to understand both overt and covert messages they wish to deliver to you.

Outline specific benchmarks of independence along the mentee's training trajectory. Acknowledge and respect their communication styles and preferences. Convey your expectations of behaviors and attitudes toward others in the research group. Discuss guidelines you use for determining authorship on scientific publications. Expectations change over time as a mentee further develops to the point of being able to perform higher-level tasks such as advising undergraduate students who join the research team for the summer or producing better-quality manuscript drafts. This development necessitates revisiting expectations from both sides. As trainees gain more experience, they may need more challenges and independence with less guidance.

Discuss career goals and plans to achieve them with advanced trainees. Do they hope to continue working in your area of scholarship, or will they take an entirely new direction? It is important to discuss and agree on a plan for your mentees' future independent research projects. Most beneficial strategies would distinguish their future research from yours so that they establish a unique niche in the field. Allow some flexibility and be benevolent. Do not be one of those selfish advisors who forbid their trainees to pursue anything related to your mainstream direction of research when they leave your group. I know of one elite laboratory where applicants for postdoctoral training must sign an agreement to this effect before they are offered a position and accepted in the group.

Some experts in the mentoring world recommend detailing expectations in a written document, generally known as a mentoring compact. I recommend this approach as well, even though it may appear daunting and somewhat bureaucratic. The main content of a mentoring compact includes roles and responsibilities of the mentor and the mentee, overall training goals, and type and frequency of meetings. There should also be agreements about ground rules for communication, including confidentiality, candor, and boundaries.

Establishing Trust

Trust is the most important element necessary for success in any relationship. There are many ways for you to build trust with your mentees. Acknowledge each person's strengths and unique qualities. Help them self-identify their challenges and promise to work with them to devise remedies. Share your own story, including both successes and failures at various stages of career development. Provide a secure, respectful and safe environment that is conducive to candid conversations and bidirectional exchange of views. Demonstrate in both words and actions that you truly care about your mentees' professional success and happiness in their lives. Maintain strict confidence regarding any personal information a mentee shares with you and avoid gossiping and talking badly about any members of the group in their absence. Engaging in such practices is a surefire way to lose trust, as mentees will realize that you likely gossip about them in their absence as well.

Boundary Setting

It is important to set boundaries in the mentoring relationship and communicate with your trainees regarding those ground rules as early as possible. For instance, be clear about when is it appropriate to contact each other by or email after work hours, especially on weekends or during holidays. Is it all right for you or them to share personal problems outside the work environment? Are your trainees allowed to walk into your office when they have urgent questions? Do they have to go through a gatekeeper to schedule meetings with you? These boundaries should be designed in collaboration between the mentor and the mentee and must be applied and respected bidirectionally. It is important to realize, however, that rigid ground rules may stifle the mentoring relationship. There should be space for flexibility and exceptions (for example, in case of emergencies or when timely interventions are needed to avoid time-wasting derailment of a project).

Mentors are generally discouraged from getting involved in providing advice related to their trainees' personal or family problems. Such conversations take time away from discussions of work-related issues. They also place the advisor in an awkward situation, as he or she may feel obligated to provide advice without having necessary training as a therapist or a counselor.

Identifying proper boundaries in a mentoring relationship is rather tricky. Some actions or behaviors based on purely good intentions may be misinterpreted by the involved mentee or by others in the group. Should the mentor ask how things are going for the mentee outside the work environment? Should they propose meeting for lunch or coffee to create a more relaxed and friendly environment that would be conducive to mutual understanding and trust? Should one invite a mentee who does not have family in the area for a holiday at the mentor's home? How does the mentor approach extending such opportunities in a way that does not make the mentee feel coerced in accepting the invitation or fear negative consequences if they don't? How should a mentor respond to an invitation by a mentee to share a drink at happy hour or go for a walk during lunch time?

I am by nature an extrovert. I enjoy knowing the personal side of my trainees and colleagues. I like to learn about their hobbies and take pleasure in exchanging recommendations about restaurants, movies, theater performances and recipes. I have found that mixing with trainees outside the work environment is a major element in building warmth and trust in my professional relationship with them. My wife and I usually hold an annual holiday gathering for the entire team and their families at our home. Not enjoying having lunch alone at work, I extend an invitation to join me to everyone in my group. I also accept invitations from individuals to go to lunch to discuss work-related matters away from the office environment. However, I make it clear to all that I am open to such invitations from any of them. When the group goes out together to lunch or happy hour, I make sure to avoid the appearance of preferring to hold conversations with certain individuals in the group more than others. I also try to balance who I spend time with outside the workplace.

I generally find it is wiser for a mentor to be friendly than to be a friend. Be easygoing and create mutual rapport and respect. Establishing a close friendship with select mentees is difficult to navigate due to the power differential. There is also the danger of having a close friendship slip gradually into becoming a romantic one. In addition, friendship may make it difficult for you to remain objective in evaluating performance. Even if you succeed in being neutral, others in your group may suspect you aren't. You may therefore be accused of favoritism, which will likely create jealousy and diminish team morale. There is also great risk if your friendship with a mentee ends on a bad note, making it difficult to continue your professional relationship with that person. You will no longer feel safe about any secrets or private information you may have shared with your mentee. Some sensitive information may come back to haunt you.

Effective Feedback and Difficult Conversations

Design a way to give and receive regular feedback from your mentees from the very start. Be candid and specific in giving feedback; use examples of recent behaviors or actions by the mentee. Avoid being judgmental or shaming. Explore the basis of the action at hand by asking questions rather than making accusations or delivering verdicts. Invite your trainees to participate in exploring solutions and deciding on a remedial action plan. Steer the conversation toward a positive outcome. Early interventions make it easier to redirect the mentee's path toward success before a bad habit gets deeply engrained. You should seek aid from others if the conversation encounters a dead end; your department head or director of the graduate program would be obvious choices. You may engage them in joining your meetings with the trainee or ask them to talk with you or the mentee individually. Serious conflicts may require the participation of an impartial party, such as the institutional ombudsman or representatives from the office of human resources.

You should provide your trainees with standards to use in gauging their aptitude for a given career path. I have found it helpful for graduate students and postdoctoral fellows who intend to pursue future academic jobs to read exemplary curricula vitae of star individuals who apply for faculty positions in my college. This insight makes them realize what it takes to achieve their career goal. One of the most difficult roles of a mentor is to help a trainee align their career ambitions with the reality of their accomplishments and abilities. I truly believe it is unethical to lead a trainee on if you believe they may well be on the wrong career path. It is your responsibility to give trainees a clear picture of what it takes to get to a certain point of a given career. You should tell an underperforming trainee that they may have difficulty finding or succeeding in a tenure-track job in a research-intensive university in case this is their expressed goal. Make it clear this assessment does not mean they should consider themselves a total failure and quit their training altogether. You are simply opening their eyes to reality. The final choice is theirs to make.

Guide your trainees to books on alternative careers for doctorates. They may discover a passion for a career opportunity that never crossed their mind. Life is full of examples of people who are very successful in a career that was not their first choice or intention. These people are thankful that someone helped them reassess their professional goals based on their particular abilities and the work-life balance that best suits them. Encourage entrepreneurship in those who gravitate toward it. The founders of the internet giant Google often publicly acknowledge their dissertation advisors who, when they were computer science doctoral students at Stanford University in the late 1990s, encouraged them to pursue commercial applications for the algorithm they had developed. It goes without saying that such sage advice not only changed their lives but also has impacted how we all search the worldwide web for information and allowed us to benefit from the many amazing free services Google has provided and continues to develop.

Fostering Independence

The performance of a graduate student or a postdoctoral fellow is mainly based on their innate intellectual abilities and dedication. It may

5. Advising and Mentoring Your Trainees

be accentuated, however, by encouragement, instilling confidence and giving them the opportunity to learn new tools and skills. These tools may include knowledge of important literature or being connected with another research group to learn new methodology. More important, it is essential to realize that academic training is based on apprenticeship. Trainees develop their professional skills not only according to what you tell them but also by watching you perform your duties. In his book *Apprentice to Genius: The Making of a Scientific Dynasty*, Robert Kanigel demonstrates various styles of research apprenticeship provided by very famous biomedical scientists who trained equally successful scholars. Some of these scholars watched their trainees from a distance, reserving their input for discussions of experimental results and their interpretation. Others preferred to stay close. Dr. Robert Furchgott, for example, chose to place his desk inside the main laboratory space. He sat by the chemical scale. This strategic position allowed him to chat with individuals about their plans for the day as they were weighing chemicals for their experimental solutions. He would occasionally walk around the laboratory to observe how students and technicians were going about performing their experiments. He taught his trainees the power of keen observation. It was this skill, in addition to serendipity, that led him to a groundbreaking research finding, which came out of a series of failed experiments performed by a new laboratory technician. Instead of firing this technician, Dr. Furchgott followed her one day from the beginning to the end of her experiment. He noticed that she went out of her way in cleaning the experimental tissue compared to others. He wondered whether this meticulous tissue cleaning procedure removed a component essential for the response of the tissue to drugs, therefore explaining why her results were at variance with everybody else's. Dr. Furchgott designed experiments to test his speculation. Eventually, this line of inquiry led him to identify a new cell signaling molecule (nitric oxide) and gained him the Nobel Prize in Biomedical Sciences in 1998. I often use this example with graduate students and postdoctoral scholars in my research group to teach them not to dismiss the results of experiments that did not turn out as expected.

    One of the major roles of a mentor/advisor is developing their trainees to become independent thinkers and planners. There are important milestones to achieving these central goals. The most important milestone is being able to properly plan and design individual experiments or projects. This process includes careful consideration of necessary positive and negative controls. In the case of clinical or community based trial studies, one should be able to determine appropriate recruitment strategies, inclusion criteria, experimental protocols and measures. If your research focuses on studying the migration patterns of monarch butterflies, advanced trainees should be able to decide on optimal locations and ensure availability of proper personnel and equipment. Other benchmarks include being able to interpret data correctly and troubleshoot unsuccessful experiments. Furthermore, your trainees should gradually become more competent in writing manuscripts for submission to peer-reviewed journals, including selection of appropriate journals and responding to criticisms raised by the reviewers. Other skills include learning how to work successfully with a research team—for example, how to engage collaborators, advise students, supervise technicians and design future major projects in preparation for submission of grant applications to fund these projects.

Some faculty apply the concept of "sink or swim" to their training of students and postdoctoral associates. They give their trainees ample space to prove they can stand on their own feet and then decide whether to keep them or ask them to leave the group at the end of the test period. Other advisors lean toward the opposite extreme by being caretakers and micromanagers. Neither approach is healthy. It is always wise to hold hands in the beginning and then let go gradually. Teach your trainees how to make educated decisions and troubleshoot on their own. One approach is to start by providing specific information regarding the design of the intended work. When the trainee develops further, ask her or him to design their own approach before bringing it to you for critique. Some advisors prefer allowing the trainee to do the work as they designed it independently and then bring up the missing or incorrect elements later when they share their findings. Both Socratic methods have their pros and cons. You may choose one over the other depending on the abilities of the trainee and the extent of loss incurred by letting him or her pursue a segment of research that you know ahead of time is faulty in one aspect or another. Analysis of loss should include considerations of time, financial cost and, of course, safety.

When editing drafts of manuscripts prepared by your trainees, use these documents as an opportunity to advance their skills as independent writers. You will not be helpful at all if you simply provide them with a revised manuscript without indicating what you have changed and, more important, why. Use tracking to highlight changes you made. Add comments on specific rules of good writing in regard to repetitive errors in wording, grammar or style. Meet with your trainees to explain why specific changes needed to be made and respond to their queries. In some cases, you may opt for an even higher level of learning. Comment on the parts that need editing and indicate your reasoning, but let the trainee figure out how to go about making the necessary changes. Of course, these learning and professional development experiences are more time consuming than making changes yourself while offering little or no explanation. However, this additional investment in proper training of future independent scholars is exactly what differentiates a research advisor from a career mentor.

Provide appropriate challenge levels. Set high expectations, allowing for growth. Ask questions that stimulate reflection. Help your mentees learn the ropes of making educated decisions and choices, some of which may involve calculated risk. Guide them through how you approach problem solving and evaluating options. Share how you explore and determine all necessary elements needed for designing and conducting a successful research protocol. Effective mentoring toward establishing independence requires an optimal balance of both challenge and support. Too much of either element could stunt progress. Repeated failures due to unreasonably hard challenges at a given developmental stage of one's career may be discouraging enough to make a trainee develop imposter's syndrome and quit. Excessive handholding and protection of a mentee, however, will deprive them of the chance to grow on their own. Try to find a sweet spot for each of your trainees depending on their personal abilities and the stage of their career.

Promoting Professional Development

A complete package of effective training includes both research and career mentoring. There are many ways a mentor could contribute to planning successful career paths for their trainees. These plans are more helpful if they are customized to fit the goals and skills of each trainee. However, many of their elements are common and apply across many types of careers. These include providing training on productive social and professional networking and collaboration, public speaking, scientific writing, grantsmanship, time management, exploring unique funding mechanisms, management, mentoring and leadership skills. There are many approaches to deliver such training. First, refer your mentees to specialized workshops and literature. Second, allow them to shadow you. Third, you may arrange to have your trainees work with one or more other faculty members as their career mentors while you focus on assisting them with sharpening their research skills. You should also play an active role in marketing your trainees and increasing their visibility in the scientific community. Include them in social events at national and international meetings. Introduce them to key figures in your field. Recommend them to give seminars at other institutions. Invite them to coauthor invited review articles and book chapters.

Mentoring Diverse Trainees

The academic world has become more enriched by the presence of diverse graduate students, postdoctoral trainees and faculty. Diversity in academia has numerous merits. It offers breadth of ideas and approaches in pursuing unique scholarly projects, teaching methodology and problem solving. When one considers diversity, however, they should not limit their thoughts to race or color. These differences extend to age, gender identity, sexual orientation, physical and intellectual abilities, nationality/ethnicity and immigration status. There are also many layers of individual diversity that produce the overall unique personality of any given person. These include learning styles (by doing, by watching, by listening, by reading), communication styles (thinking before speaking, thinking while speaking, being comfortable with interruptions), conflict-handling modes (competing, collaborating, compromising, combative, avoiding, accommodating) and Myers-Briggs personality types (extroversion/introversion, sensing/intuition, thinking/feeling, judging/perceiving). Added to this list are external elements of diversity, which include socio-economic class, personal habits, hobbies, religion/spirituality, education, life experience or marital and parental status. Taken together, there are more differences than similarities in individuals from a given culture or race. In other words, there is diversity within diversity. Making a diverse mentoring relationship work well requires understanding and appreciating these differences. A successful mentor strives to learn about the background of each trainee and tailor their mentoring plan accordingly. One model does not fit all. Good mentors avoid the danger of making stereotypical assumptions that may lead them to unnecessarily lower or raise their expectations.

Familiarize yourself with literature on the nuances of supervising and advising people from each layer of diversity. Understand how you should adapt your style to fit the specific needs of each person in your group. Deal with individuals by acknowledging that their behaviors and preferences are the result of a myriad of diverse factors. Understand and respect cultural and religious customs and habits of members of your groups.

Mentoring International Trainees

International trainees may face language barriers, isolation and culture shock. Knowledge of differences in cultural background will help you understand the source of some behaviors and habits of your international trainees that may appear odd at first glance. Many of these are related to personal interactions and communication. For instance, people from certain

5. Advising and Mentoring Your Trainees

cultures are taught not to look a more senior person in the eye during a conversation. Others were raised to believe they should never question a superior or doubt their wisdom in making decisions. More seriously, some trainees come from academic cultures in which laboratory technicians and administrative staff are considered inferior to other team members with a higher level of education and training.

A wise mentor recognizes the need to handle various challenges arising from the cultural background of international trainees in different ways. In case of lack of eye contact, the mentor should "advise" the trainee to express their point of view while avoiding looking down while speaking. They should explain to their trainee that lack of eye contact may be misinterpreted the American culture as a reflection of lack of confidence or dishonesty. Not being guided to change these habits would be detrimental to the mentee during job interviews. In contrast, the mentor should "mandate" a change in the behavior of one who does not show respect for other members of the group or has habits that make others uncomfortable. A mentor should think of an approach to effect this change that will inflict minimal damage on the pride of the perpetrator. Once I received several complaints from my trainees that a certain member of the group did not maintain good personal hygiene. I wrote a short memo addressed to all members of the group stressing the importance of personal cleanliness but placed it only in the mailbox of this person. It worked. However, the jury is still out on whether my approach was ethical.

I had difficulty adjusting to the new culture when I came to the United States from Egypt in the late 1970s for graduate training. I was surprised—actually, shocked—to hear all lab members call my advisor by his first name. Furthermore, I was puzzled by the way people in elevators silently looked up at floor numbers instead of initiating a conversation as Middle Easterners would do. Many idioms were very hard for me to comprehend, such as "on a wild goose chase," "out in the boondocks" or "once in a blue moon." Also, some commonly used statements did not make any sense to me. I heard a fellow student say, for example, "I was late coming to the meeting because my alarm did not go off." Did he actually mean the alarm did not go "on"?! And what does the expression "quite a few" really mean? Is it too much? Is it too little? Moreover, I could not perceive why someone in my department would ask me on a Monday how my weekend was and then walk away without waiting to hear details about what I did over the weekend. I was fortunate that one of the department faculty members took me under his wing and introduced me to understanding and appreciating the American culture. He referred me to books on specific cultural issues. One of the most helpful books was *American Ways: A Guide for Foreigners in the United States* by Gary Althen. My mentor also invited me to gatherings at his home to observe how people communicate and connected me with many American friends.

Most institutions have offices that assist international scholars and trainees with their entry visas and housing. Graduate programs similarly pay special attention to the unique needs of international students. Unfortunately, international postdoctoral scholars often do not have analogous program advocates. You therefore need to help them get settled and pay attention to their needs. Tailor your mentoring style and approach to provide both international graduate students and postdoctoral fellows with social tools and people skills necessary the American society. Doing so will facilitate their assimilation into the local culture, both in and outside the work environment. Encourage them to read local and national newspapers and to watch news programs. This practice will make them familiar with important happenings, so that they will be able to be a part of a conversation when their American colleagues chat about latest sports or political events. It will also improve their English reading and speaking skills. Make your international trainees aware of entertainment opportunities—for examples, plays, musical or dance performances, movies, sports events, festivals, and parades. Recommend good restaurants, especially those that specialize in local cuisine. Provide resources for outdoor activities such as maps of biking or skiing trails, camping sites, and canoe rentals. In the process, make it clear that you are encouraging them to benefit from what the society has to offer, rather than forcing them to undergo a cultural transformation. In fact, you should connect your foreign trainees with international groups on or off campus to maintain their connection with their native culture. However, encourage them to use English in communicating with their country mates. I actually discourage foreign trainees in my laboratory from sharing housing with people who speak their mother tongue. I can easily tell the difference in English proficiency between those who did and those who did not follow my advice. My international trainees have found it helpful to attend "English as a second language" classes and use mobile phone applications that improve one's pronunciation (for example, Duolingo). Others participated in meetings of Toastmasters International, a nonprofit educational organization that teaches public speaking and leadership skills through a worldwide network of clubs.

Mentoring Across Races

An interracial mentoring relationship has its special merits and challenges. This arrangement benefits from varied cultural backgrounds and differences in life experiences. It also provides trainees with a wider selection of mentors since there are usually only a few minority faculty members (who most likely already have more than their fair share of minority mentees). I have seen many examples of a faculty member of color successfully mentoring a white student and vice versa. It is very important to realize, however, that many good people with the best intentions have blind spots when it comes to interacting with others who are not like them, which can create unintentional biases that could even be contrary to one's beliefs and intentions. These biases create barriers that should be recognized and mitigated proactively whenever possible in mixed-race mentoring relationships. Many of these challenges are based on unsubstantiated, yet common, stereotypes. For example, a white faculty member may worry without having evidence that minority trainees may not have enough commitment and resilience to enable them to complete their program. Some white faculty believe that overprotecting minority students will end up slowing down development of their independence and professional maturity. Others may worry about possible failure on their part in providing a minority trainee with a hospitable environment and successful experience that prepares them to advance their career. Such failure would likely be noticed due to the higher visibility and disproportionate scrutiny of mixed-race training arrangements. Negative experiences may discourage other minority trainees from joining the group in the future.

There are also concerns on the part of trainees from underrepresented populations about being trained by white faculty. Students of color are often unsure that a white mentor will identify with and understand their race-related challenges. There is also common implicit bias in evaluating the mentoring skills of a faculty member depending on their race. Students of color may fear that their white advisor would provide higher quality of training to white trainees as compared to those of color. The reverse is also true, as white male trainees generally believe that minority mentors may not be as effective as white men, particularly in advising whites.

Some trainees of color prefer integration of their professional and cultural identities. Including discussions of race and its challenges with their mentors therefore provides them with significant psychological and emotional support. However, there are often difficulties in accommodating these expectations. Many faculty members prefer color-blind mentoring relationships. They do this on purpose and with good intentions. Some worry that providing race-specific mentoring could make a minority student apprehensive or uncomfortable by feeling they are being singled out and treated differently. Moreover, discussing race often brings up difficult and uncomfortable conversations. A white mentor may worry about saying or doing something that could hurt the feelings of their trainees of color.

Providing a fair training experience to underrepresented minorities requires differentiating between the principles of equality and equity.

Equality has to do with providing everybody with the same tools and resources, based on the assumption or belief that everybody is starting the journey from the same point. Equity, by contrast, requires educated determination of the type and extent of resources to be provided to various trainees based on an individual's specific needs. It considers social detriments that have deprived certain populations of necessary elements of success. In applying equity, one should therefore consider the contribution of many factors that may hinder progress of minority trainees. Many students of color, for example, have background traumas that stem from racial discrimination and social oppression. Unfortunate recurring events related to this painful history during their education likely continue to revive and self-propel the feelings of pain. Others may be the first in their family to pursue postgraduate education, and some may come from a socioeconomically challenged environment. Together, these factors disadvantage trainees of color and place them at a different starting point compared to their white peers. They also result in distractions that do not afflict white students. Training plans should therefore be structured to compensate for this discrepancy and close the racial gap.

There are important pillars for building an effective mentoring relationship between a white faculty member and a trainee from an underrepresented minority group. The most important are trust, empathy, encouragement, and open communication. The same principles also apply to white students being trained by faculty of color. I recommend that you meet in person to impart warmth. Carving out time to attend to the trainee's needs conveys your dedication to care for them. Celebrate their successes. Help instill self-confidence. All mentors should invite trainees to share their challenges. Listen and probe deeper. Be sincere and candid in what you say and do, especially when it comes to making promises. Avoid equating the challenges a minority trainee faces with those that are common for whites at the same stage of training. Even though the nature and magnitude of the challenges may be the same, their negative sequelae may be exaggerated by background trauma and self-doubt in the case of a trainee of color. These hindrances would certainly be magnified even further if the mentee is suffering from racism during their current training. Stop when you feel discomfort in pursuing the conversation further. Resume the discussion when you meet again, preferably in small and intermittent doses.

You must act immediately and forcefully if a trainee shares present or recent experiences with racism. Do not just offer lip service. Find and confront the culprit if he or she is a member of your group. Train your minority mentee to navigate problematic situations related to racism. Explain the steps for filing a complaint or a grievance. Provide information on the college and institutional administrative structure and resources that deal with various issues of discrimination and encourage your trainees to use these resources whenever needed instead of continuing to suffer in silence.

Be an advocate for fighting racism, at least in your department and college. Serve on committees that handle matters of diversity and inclusion. Read literature on social justice, systemic racism and white privilege. Such experiences will position you to be more helpful, not only to your own trainees but also to the general cause of creating a just society that offers equal opportunities to all. It will mean so much to your trainees of color to realize that you are dedicated to understanding the nature and foundation of their challenges and are actively engaged in finding effective solutions.

One of the major difficulties I have personally faced in trying to pursue this approach is the resistance I met with from some trainees of color. One shared with me that while my attempts were appreciated, outsiders like me could not help much because they did not understand the roots of the problems and their widespread ramifications. I responded to indicate agreement regarding my lack of deep understanding but firmly stated that I needed help from this student and others to start understanding little by little, with the hope of fully understanding at one point. I truly believe it is detrimental to the cause of ultimately resolving racially based societal problems if each party continues to turn down attempts by the other to understand and to help. This approach would propel a vicious cycle of negativity and would halt progress toward finding a resolution.

Mentoring Across Genders and Sexual Orientations

To succeed in a mixed-gender relationship, a mentor must adapt their training style and content to address gender-related issues and meet the needs of mentees of all genders. It is therefore recommended that you seek to understand the gender-related barriers your mentees may be facing. Be a good listener. Empathize rather than jumping to diagnosis and deciding on approaches to treatment.

Female mentees often report more relational comfort with female mentors than with male mentors. Women mentored by women usually receive more psychosocial support than women mentored by men. Male mentors generally focus more on career-specific support rather than giving advice on matters outside the workplace—especially challenges related to having a family and an ideal work-life balance. This situation makes it difficult for female mentees to see their male mentors as suitable role models, mainly because of the imbalance in the roles of women and men outside the workplace, especially in serving the needs of their families.

Interestingly, relationships between male mentees and female mentors face far fewer challenges. In some cases, however, a male trainee may exhibit sexist behaviors and show disrespect for their female mentor. In these cases, the mentor must confront the mentee to discuss the basis of a specific behavior and work together to design an intervention plan to put a stop to it. The mentor must be clear about the harmful consequences of this behavior to individuals or groups. She should also discuss the expected negative effects on the career of the person who commits these negative actions. In many cases, these behaviors may simply be the result of oversight or ignorance rather than being intentional. Regardless, ending these negative behaviors is a necessary intervention to save the person who commits them from irreparably damaging their future career. It also helps maintain a positive environment for the entire group.

Male mentors face challenges in mixed-gender training relationships as well. They may hesitate to take on female graduate students or postdoctoral trainees for fear of having a close professional relationship be misinterpreted as romantic or sexual. While women have proven beyond any doubt that they are the equals of men as scholars and educators, some male faculty members still have their doubts regarding the ability of women to become successful and independent. These misgivings are the result of negative stereotypes that are dominant in society. Sadly, there are still a few academics who subscribe to these outdated beliefs. Be open with your trainees about your awareness of enduring stereotypes about men or women academics and those with other gender or sexual orientations. Share where you stand with regard to these stereotypes and inquire about how they have created roadblocks for your trainees. Benefit from learning about differences in perspective. Learn about the career and personal goals of your mentee and how they see their gender shaping their path. Acknowledge your privileges and your desire to help all trainees attain equal rights and opportunities.

Advising and Mentoring Across Generations

It is important to acknowledge and mitigate challenges imposed by generational differences between advisors and their trainees or staff. These differences even play a pivotal role in how you interact with and understand your colleagues. They include work habits, communication skills and preferences, and optimal life-work balance. Those from Generation X (born 1965–1981), for example, do not prefer the traditional instructive learning offered by most senior advisors. They enjoy learning by solving problems on their own and do not appreciate prescriptive approaches to how things should be done. Use a collaborative (rather than top-down) approach in designing collaborative projects and schedules for this group. Generation X individuals are known to react negatively to delayed gratification. Divide projects into clear segments with specific milestones that you celebrate together as they are met. Generation X members also prefer a healthier work-life balance. Allow them flexibility in their work schedule, as long as they accomplish their set goals.

Millennials (born 1982–1994) want work to be fun. They are generally independent, self-confident and optimistic. Millennials need to be heard and respected for their opinions. Provide them with a friendly work environment, listen to what they have to say, and avoid micromanaging them. Be cognizant of the negative impact of a rigid bureaucratic approach to management—for instance, asking everybody to show up on time every morning despite their preference for different work hours. Millennials may revolt and may become less productive as a way to express their dismay at your inflexible management pattern. Millennials are also known as "digital natives." They prefer any life activity to be mediated via the screen of an electronic device. You may want to take this preference into consideration by communicating with them digitally whenever a face-to-face meeting is not necessary.

Generation Y individuals (1995–2010) are totally technology dependent, sometimes at the expense of sacrificing personal relationships. They excel at multitasking but have a short attention span and expect immediate rewards. You should pay attention to these traits and carefully work with Generation Y trainees to get them to realize that some of these traits will likely hamper the progress of their professional career. Close connections with people are necessary for one to succeed in the real world. Also advise them to be patient while conducting their research projects. Achieving significant results usually takes a long time. Furthermore, the road is often full of obstacles and unanticipated failures. Train individuals in your group to be more realistic and resilient.

Mentoring Trainees with Diverse Career Preferences

I was trained at a time when the expectation and hope of almost every mentor was to have their trainees secure tenure-track academic positions, preferably in a research-intensive university. Only a few trainees at that time actively pursued industry or other non-academic jobs. (The majority of those did not make this choice voluntarily; rather, they were not successful in the academic job market.) As a result, advisors designed training for their graduate students and postdoctoral fellows with a focus on academic skills. They did not have the expertise to guide those who preferred a non-academic career and planned to explore employment outside large research-oriented academic institutions.

Things are quite different nowadays due to the availability of many career options that are equally attractive and satisfying to some trainees. Moreover, academic positions are scarce and quite competitive. Today's trainees are more aware of the cost-benefit analysis of life in an academic setting. They have a firsthand chance to observe junior assistant professors who must put in many extra hours to build up their team of staff and trainees and get their research projects off the ground. Junior faculty must go through many painful cycles of grant applications and rejections, and they must constantly juggle research, teaching and service. There is very little time left for family life, friendships or hobbies.

As a result, many trainees favor academic positions in small universities or colleges where their main responsibility is to teach undergraduate students. Others prefer non-academic careers.

A good mentor should make their trainees aware of various employment options within and outside academia, guiding them to explore their personal preferences and acquire necessary skills. Setting up informational interviews with people in different lines of work is an excellent way to learn about career choices and make informed decisions. These interviews provide credible information from those with real-life experience in a specific position. Past graduates or other individuals in the advisor's network are usually helpful in this regard. There are many core questions to ask during an informational interview: What are the main job responsibilities? What personal skills should one have to be successful in this line of work? Who does an employee interact with on a daily basis? Which necessary skills will one learn on the job? Which skills should a trainee acquire before they start job hunting by enrolling in targeted courses, workshops or internships? What else makes one competitive in this field? Finding answers to these and similar questions is helpful in more than one way. First, it will guide trainees to decide whether a given career is actually a good fit for them. Second, this information will give them an early opportunity to prepare for attaining necessary skills they may be lacking.

It has been quite valuable to me to know of my trainees' career preferences. This knowledge enables me to tailor their training and provide them with specific skill sets required for different types of academic and non-academic jobs. Back in the early 1980s, a doctoral student chose me as her thesis advisor simply because other faculty in the department turned her down once they knew of her firm intent to pursue a career in the pharmaceutical industry! I accepted her in my laboratory with the promise to design her dissertation project to be translational in nature and supplemented her training by sending her to workshops on project management and communication skills. Because she identified her career goals early, she had ample time to build up necessary skills. Upon finishing her training, she received multiple lucrative offers from big pharmaceutical firms.

Customized Training for Undergraduate and Professional Students

You will likely receive many requests from undergraduate or professional students to do short stints of research training in your laboratory, especially during summer break. To be upfront, this training does not usually result in much growth for a junior faculty member's research program. It takes personnel time and effort to teach these students the basics of handling instruments, reagents and biological material and to help them become competent at gathering and analyzing research data. Often, by the time they are close to mastering these skills, they are ready to depart. However, I still choose to train undergraduate and professional students, in spite of the expected negative benefit-cost analysis. I consider introducing them to research a moral responsibility. Many of my colleagues have done the same since volunteering to join a research group during their undergraduate years was their point of entry to doing research. Fortunately, there are success stories in which some of these trainees came back for additional training at a later time or enrolled in graduate education upon completing their degrees. A few have actually become superstars in their research fields. I consider this more than enough payback.

I usually assign these temporary undergraduate or professional student trainees to postdoctoral fellows in my group who have expressed interest in developing their supervisory and training skills. I mandate that undergraduate or professional student trainees get adequate exposure to the scientific way of thinking (for example, how to analyze literature to identify an important gap in knowledge, how to formulate a good research question or a hypothesis, and how to properly design well-controlled scientific experiments). I encourage including these trainees in meetings to discuss data interpretation and plan the next experimental step. I make it very clear that these junior students are not there to assume mundane chores such as washing research utensils or cleaning animal cages.

I recommend that you try hosting a couple of these students and determine for yourself whether doing so is worthwhile. However, do not feel obligated to take on undergraduate or professional students if you are not ready. Wait until you have enough of a critical mass of research personnel who would contribute to their training.

Summary

Advising and mentoring trainees is both an art and a science. Mentors must learn from their own experience, apply what they enjoyed and avoid what they did not appreciate when they were on the receiving end. They should also realize that giving advice to trainees specifically related to their scholarly projects must be supplemented with career guidance and enhancement of trainees' soft skills. There are common elements to successful mentoring and advising—namely, clear and aligned expectations and cultivating independence. Another important aspect of exemplary advising is meeting the needs of a diverse population of trainees.

Self-Reflection Exercises

- Contemplate what you found helpful in the way you were advised as a graduate student or a postdoctoral trainee.
- List the aspects of your training that you did not particularly enjoy or find conducive to building your career.
- In which aspects is your advising and mentoring style similar to or different from that of your doctoral and postdoctoral advisors? Do any of these practices resemble or differ from the ones you listed under the first two bullets?
- List the various ways you promote the career development of your mentees. What other methods have you learned from this chapter?
- What are the differences in the type and style of technical guidance you provide to junior and senior graduate students?
- How do you plan to challenge your students and postdoctoral fellows with new responsibilities to help promote their independence?
- Take an implicit bias inventory test: *https://implicit.harvard.edu/implicit/takeatest.html*

6

Team Management and Leadership

While it is important to be skillful at advising and mentoring individual trainees and staff, competence in this area by itself does not guarantee getting the best out of the entire group. Good team management and leadership ensure cooperation, harmony and high productivity for all. It elevates the whole group to a new height.

Management versus Leadership

It is vital that you understand and appreciate the difference between management and leadership. Management is essentially running the show at its current performance level. Leadership, by contrast, involves imparting transformation to guide a team to new levels of quality and productivity. Leadership therefore requires a higher set of intellectual and personal skills than management. A good leader must be inspiring, visionary and creative. She or he must excel at communication, decision making and delegation. In addition, an effective leader must have emotional intelligence, be it innate or developed through customized training. Emotional intelligence includes self-awareness of strengths, shortcomings, values and drives. An emotionally intelligent leader also has the social skills necessary for building rapport, trust and credibility.

It is rather obvious that it is easier and more common for academics to become good managers than to be effective leaders. Faculty are busy people who get entrenched in managing the daily operations of their team and responding to calls about the crisis of the day raised by peers or superiors. Junior faculty have not been trained in many of the necessary leadership skills. They focus their creativity and vision on developing new research directions and seeking funding. Most do not realize how to lead a team from good to great. Some are even terrible managers who do not know how to create a happy and inclusive work environment for their trainees. Creating such an environment involves providing constructive feedback, dealing with difficult people, rewarding those who are highly productive and motivating the underperformers. These practices pave the way to help team members grow, both professionally and personally. Given the lack of adequate training in management and leadership competencies during graduate school or postdoctoral fellowships, junior faculty end up running the business according to what they learned and observed while working with their advisors, regardless of whether they enjoyed this experience. They simply do not know any better!

Having said that, it is imperative for academic faculty to develop and sharpen their management and leadership skills. Doing so will pay off by increasing productivity and enhancing the quality of the group's work. Most offices of human resources in academic institutions offer management and leadership workshops. There are also many outstanding national leadership training programs. Moreover, a junior faculty member may benefit from books or podcasts on specific elements of leadership. I have made a habit of stopping at an airport bookstore whenever I fly to look for books on leadership skills. I usually find them in the business or the self-help section. Over the years, I have built an extensive library that I refer to quite often. This collection includes books on mentoring, motivation and rewarding, dealing with various challenges in the work environment, and so forth. Most important, junior faculty should seek advice from their mentors and senior colleagues on how to learn from their experience and enhance their own leadership abilities.

Your Responsibilities as a Group Leader

As you establish your research group, you will find that there is a myriad of responsibilities you must tackle. These duties will multiply as the size of your group expands over time. To begin with, you will be intimately involved in hiring employees or trainees. Work with human resources staff in your department or college to draft job advertisements and identify the most appropriate venues for posting a position to ensure getting utmost attention from your targeted audience. Get their advice on how to conduct effective interviews and make hiring decisions.

As you hire new members of your group, you will need to help them become acclimated when they start their job. Be welcoming and clear about expectations, responsibilities and evaluation criteria. Your responsibilities also include assessing the performance of employees and trainees and having a plan to motivate and reward them. Your team will depend on you to establish general research directions, obtain funding and provide technical advice. You are the boss; you set the tone and expectations.

Creating a Healthy Work Environment

A good work environment is essential for productivity and retention. It is usually based on major elements—namely, clear goals; division of labor; accountability; team participation in making decisions; opportunities for advancement, promotion and growth; transparent, consistent and fair guidelines for performance evaluation; appreciation and rewarding of good personal performance; and assistance to others.

You have a major role in setting the foundation of this environment. You are also responsible for maintaining and troubleshooting it. You must lead by being a good role model. People behave as they see you do, rather than according to what they hear you say or command. Be fair in dividing your attention among individuals. Be friendly, but avoid establishing close relationships with certain individuals in the group. Being too close makes it difficult to be objective or make tough decisions. Build trust by being genuinely concerned about the overall welfare and success of your trainees and wanting all the best for them.

Deciding on the Right Mix in Staffing Your Group

You have major decisions to make about personnel as you start your first faculty position. What is the ideal mix of technicians, graduate students and postdoctoral trainees? How do you get the highest output using the limited startup funds available to you? What type of past training and expertise should you look for? Should you aim for a junior or a senior research assistant? What is the most effective way to advertise positions? How do you attract a diverse population of applicants? What can you tell about a person beyond the content of their résumé or curriculum vitae? What type of interview questions should you ask to probe deeper into a person's character and ability to think on their feet? It is essential for you to hire individuals who demonstrate dedication, personal maturity and good problem solving. What are the human resources policies about how many people to interview for a given open position? How do you make a job offer? You may find answers to these and similar questions by discussing your specific needs with your department head, human resources staff and senior peers. Your mentors should be particularly helpful in this regard.

Most junior faculty start by hiring a research staff or an assistant to help them set up the research operation and carry out projects. Hiring a person with seniority to fill this position is a plus to save the time invested in training a novice. If you have sufficient funds, you may hire another research staff member, perhaps junior to economize spending your funds. At this early stage, you will probably spend significant time doing research yourself by being at the bench conducting experiments, collecting data or samples in the field or interviewing study subjects. A team of three would make a nice starting working unit. Your participation in the work will give you an opportunity to train the research assistants in sophisticated research methodologies and instrumentation and approaches to data analysis. It will also give you a chance to watch how your new staff operates and to intervene with advice when needed to correct noticeable errors. As time goes on, you will find yourself gradually gravitating toward staying in your office. You will conclude that you are more useful in doing higher-level work such as writing grants and manuscripts. This was my personal experience. As I became more senior, I craved doing experiments every once in a while. Unfortunately, my team members consistently sent me back to my office since I wasted their time and disrupted their attention by asking too many questions about where laboratory reagents or other items were located.

Technicians and other research staff are usually thought of as worker bees who receive orders to serve the queen bee (i.e., the principal investigator). Some directors of research groups treat them as such. It will behoove you, though, to engage your research staff intellectually in the project. Provide them with literature related to background knowledge that serves as the basis for their work. Discuss the project's anticipated impact. Get them gradually involved in writing drafts of various sections of manuscripts and grant applications. This approach will make them feel a sense of ownership of their projects. They will feel invested in their work. It will also provide them with self-confidence and transparency of the process in relation to the bigger picture.

Hiring postdoctoral fellows has significant advantages. Postdoctorals are at an advanced stage of training. They could hit the ground running and start contributing to the research projects right away. With time, they will be able to contribute to proposing and implementing new research directions. Of course, a junior faculty member must recognize the challenges of being able to attract the best postdoctoral fellows out there. Such stars usually seek apprenticeship by very senior researchers whose letters of recommendation will carry significant weight when they are ready to apply for future jobs. One may be fortunate, however, in finding an outstanding recent doctoral graduate in their own institution who is looking for a postdoctoral training opportunity. There are some graduates who have geographical limitations associated with family needs regarding where to do their postdoctoral training.

Choose postdoctoral trainees who possess both scientific and personal maturity. Favor ones with a good record of publications over those who have published little or none of their thesis work. Beware of those who enumerate a long list of manuscripts as being "in preparation" in their vitae. This status may suggest possible deficiency in their ability to bring projects to completion. However, give them some benefit of the doubt. Their doctoral advisor may be the one at fault for not providing necessary guidance in putting research findings out in a published format in a timely fashion. Hiring a postdoctoral scholar with different, yet complementary, experience could enable you to ask deeper research questions and to apply multiple approaches to test a hypothesis. In my experience, however, I found that there is a threshold of diversity of experience and interests, beyond which there is loss of common language and shared lines of thought.

Do not make the mistake of treating your postdoctoral trainees as technicians. Both you and a postdoctoral fellow should enjoy and benefit from their training and intellectual contributions. Do not completely let go, either. It helps to set up weekly meetings with a starting postdoctoral to discuss general aspects of their project, data interpretation and next steps. Train them to develop their independence in preparation for future stages of their career.

A serious issue often comes up when a postdoctoral fellow is ready to fly the coop. Sometimes there is tension that comes with defining which parts of their postdoctoral project they may take with them to pursue further. Early and clear communication about issues of research ownership and expectations regarding intellectual property is key to avoiding these uncomfortable (and sometimes relationship-damaging) conflicts later on. Failing to resolve these conflicts in a mutually satisfactory fashion may needlessly create professional enemies. It could also tarnish the good reputation of an advisor as a benevolent scholar and make it difficult for them to attract skilled postdoctoral scholars in the future.

Finding a good solution to the problem of research ownership becomes easier when a postdoctoral trainee is the main driver in framing and developing their project or when they have obtained independent funding to support their training. Be unselfish in these cases. Let them take their project and run with it. Most likely, however, you and any postdoctoral fellow will have jointly developed the concept of the research project and plans to execute it. Under these circumstances, it becomes tricky to parse out who owns which part. Open mindedness is essential for reaching a mutually satisfactory resolution. Consider your and the trainee's common goal of advancing knowledge in your field of scholarship. Work together toward achieving this goal. Avoid planning long-term collaborations with your postdoctoral trainees after they leave your research group. Continuing their association with you will hinder their efforts in demonstrating their independence.

Training graduate students is an important way for faculty to cultivate the next generation of scholars. However, you may not want to take on graduate students until your research group and setting are well established. Productively advising and mentoring graduate students requires your full attention and dedication. Training students in the nuts and bolts of research methods also requires contributions from other research personnel. This process could become taxing. Furthermore, graduate students usually spend most of the first two years in their program taking courses and preparing for their preliminary exams. Graduate students also come with a financial burden. Namely, the rate of their fringe benefits is markedly higher than that of technicians and postdoctoral fellows because of the ever-escalating cost of tuition. Carefully consider when the right time is to recruit graduate students to your group. Take into account their didactic background and research experience, if any. Insist they do a rotation in your laboratory for a couple of months. This experience will usually give you a more comprehensive picture and firsthand assessment of their intellectual abilities and personal character. It will also show how they interact with others. Remember, group harmony is necessary for your success! Never recruit a talented but obnoxious person.

Maintaining Effective Communication

Effective communication is the best preemptive approach to avoiding conflicts. From the start, discuss with every new member of your team policies on vacation, work hours, sick leave, and benefits. Clarify authorship guidelines. Have a conversation about their roles and responsibilities, as well as your expectations. In the same vein, tell them what to expect from you. Adjust what they should expect from you depending on their individual needs. Clearly inform new employees of parameters you use in assessing performance. Explain how you value both individual productivity and contribution to the team spirit. Develop a memorandum of understanding to be signed by both you and every new employee or trainee. Keep this document on file and provide them with a copy. Be cognizant of the differences in your and the trainee/employee's experience and developmental stage when you deliver instructions. Avoid jargon or acronyms that may not be familiar to them, especially the new hires. Assess understanding by paraphrasing, summarizing or asking open-ended questions.

Set up regular weekly meetings for the group, and allow time for everyone to discuss their research findings, interpretation of data and plans for the next steps. Invite feedback from the group. This type of knowledge exchange leads to wider understanding among the research team members by getting to know what others in the group are doing. It may also create opportunities for new collaborations between team members. Schedule additional one-on-one meetings with individuals to provide them with timely guidance and get into deep discussion of their specific projects. Block time slots every day for urgent matters.

You may want to delegate some chores to others as your group grows in size, seniority and maturity. For instance, you may assign fielding questions about the maintenance and calibration of instruments to an experienced technician. Delegate keeping track of compliance with regulatory matters to another. Consider involving postdoctoral fellows in advising summer undergraduate students, as doing so will help them develop mentoring skills.

Setting Work Plans the SMART Way

People who work without a clear plan will likely be busy but not necessarily productive. They may lack a sense of accomplishment in relation to the big picture. Involve each employee and trainee in putting together an individualized work plan. Help them connect short-term goals to the targeted outcome of the overall project. Share how you envision the plan contributing to both the individual's career development and the mission of the entire research group. SMART (*S*pecific, *M*easurable, *A*ction-oriented, *R*esults-focused and *T*ime-bound) is a popular approach in the business world for setting work plans. Instill this important concept into daily and long-term planning routines.

Be aware, however, that the nature of research necessitates flexibility in timelines and directions. Challenges arise. For example, many research operations had to be halted during the COVID-19 pandemic. Tribal wars may develop in the region of the world where you were planning to excavate for ancient ruins. Unexpected results or newly available resources may require redirecting the overall path of the project. Along the same lines, anomalies in research findings should be welcomed rather than be ignored or considered an annoying distraction. Unexpected (and perhaps counterintuitive) research findings have led to many paradigm shifts in humanity's overall body of knowledge.

Managing while Encouraging Professional Growth

Avoid micromanagement. Being a micromanager kills initiative, thoughtfulness and development of independence. Give your staff a chance to breathe and grow on their own. Do not fill everybody's daily schedule with experiments or other operational chores. Allow them time to reflect and plan. Stimulate them to dedicate time to reading background and recent literature and attending departmental and other relevant seminars. Keep in mind that their professional growth contributes to yours.

Whenever possible, seek input from individuals or the entire team in making major decisions. Of course, some emergent challenges require quick actions and therefore do not allow time for extensive consultation. You are the ultimate decision maker. Keep in mind, however, that explaining the rationale behind your decisions in such urgent cases is an invaluable learning opportunity for your staff and trainees. Teach them how to think about approaching solutions to problems. Discuss general work plans and approaches to problem solving with members of your team, but do not tell them how to do their job. If you always supply your trainees with solutions right away, they will never develop independence of thought in approaching sage problem solving. Instead, they will get used to coming to you for an answer. Allow them the opportunity to make mistakes when thinking on their own. Do not shame them if their chosen approach does not work. The majority of mistakes novices make are not harmful or too costly (for example, not including proper control groups in an experimental protocol). Other types of errors or oversights must be taken seriously (for example, ordering the wrong reagent used by everybody in the laboratory, forgetting to post an announcement for recruiting subjects for a study or failing to get written consent from individuals before enrolling them in a clinical trial). Educate your team members to recognize the difference in the gravity of various types of errors. Teach them how to decide when they must consult with others (especially you) when in doubt.

Have faith in your employees. Set high, but realistic standards and expectations, and guide them to meet these standards. Challenge your employees to perform more complex tasks. Spell out the benefits of this approach to the team to gauge their interest in developing professional independence. Allow them to assume a more active role in designing their experiments, interpreting data, and contributing to writing manuscripts for publication. Do not charge them with more than they are able to chew. Consider their educational background, career stage and individual abilities when you assign such tasks. Furthermore, cater to their specific preferences and work styles. I once had a technician who consistently begged me to tell him exactly what to do without feeling the need to explain why.

He frankly told me that he considered discussions that went beyond a "culinary recipe" pattern a waste of both his and my time. I had no choice but to abide by his wishes and assign him projects that required utmost precision. This area was where he excelled. I advise you to use this example as a way to assign different chores to specific individuals according to their unique strengths and shortcomings.

Provide necessary training to a person who lacks adequate experience to perform a new task. Instill confidence in another who undervalues their talents and abilities. Some employees may resist taking on new responsibilities, even though these new challenges may contribute significantly to their career development. Delve into understanding the underlying cause of this hesitation. It is possible that this employee had a past negative experience that made them overly sensitive to accepting new assignments. Their previous boss might have asked them to contribute to a project as a part of a team, but other team members did not perform their share of the work, resulting in the employee being a lone wolf with a mountain of responsibilities. Worse yet, one of the group members in this example who bailed out midway may have undeservingly claimed credit for the project's success upon its completion. In other instances, the new project may have failed because the employee's former boss did not provide the promised support or authority for execution, eventually placing full blame on the employee for not meeting expectations.

Dig deeper into these concerns and offer solutions. Clarify that you will be there to provide advice and guidance and to contribute to mitigating roadblocks. At a certain juncture, you may feel that the employee's concerns are legitimate and cannot be adequately resolved. In this case, you should assign the project to someone else who is more qualified. In other instances, however, you may sense that the employee is simply trying to avoid assuming new responsibilities, perhaps due to fear of the unfamiliar, even though you firmly believe they are fully capable of taking on the task. Use your authority and assign the project to this person. We all have to assume job duties that do not particularly appeal to us. Anticipate that the obstinate employee may try to find a way to wiggle out during the planning or execution of individual or team projects. Think and plan preemptively. Work with the employee to put in place a system for oversight and communication of frequent updates to make sure things are on track.

Building Skills of the Members of Your Team

Continue to advance the skills of your trainees and employees. This will result in their professional growth, increased job satisfaction, and, consequently, retention. It will also allow them to contribute more effectively to the research operation. New technicians and other employees need to get oriented to their new environment. They need to learn research techniques and methodology they did not perform on their previous jobs. Others may not have any research experience. Newcomers are also required to fulfill training related to safe operations, compliance and research ethics. Even personnel who have been working with you for a long time may need additional training at some point, such as when you plan to drastically change research directions. Another example is when some aspects of research regulations change, which requires updating compliance training and certification. Connect your staff with other research groups or send them to workshops to familiarize them with new methods and technologies.

A wise research group director customizes the opportunities they provide for growth according to individual appointments, training background and future plans. However, there are common elements of skill training that are helpful to all. Examples include guiding team members to pertinent literature or announcing important seminars and workshops. Do not assume that a junior research technician just wants to perform the work assigned to them. Many care and would appreciate the opportunity to understand the background basis and rationale of their project and its potential impact on society. Knowing this background makes a big difference in a person's enthusiasm and commitment to excel in whatever they are doing. It also provides them with clues that help them in independent troubleshooting.

Evaluation of Performance

You will need to develop a structure for periodically evaluating the performance of all employees and trainees. A new employee would benefit from an early assessment of the quantity and quality of their work to guide them to the right path. Ad hoc hallway conversations about such matters have a different purpose as contrasted with structured and planned evaluation meetings. The former type of interaction is particularly damaging to morale if you use it to deliver negative comments, especially in the hallways, where others may eardrop on the conversation. Stopping anybody on their way to do something else is a major disruption for your team members. Putting employees off guard makes them feel ambushed, scared and resentful. Similar concerns apply to asking someone out of the blue to immediately report to your office for instructions. If you use this approach frequently, group members will become anxious whenever you ask them to come to your office. It is also advisable to discuss performance in person rather than by email. Face-to-face evaluation meetings imply that you are inviting a two-way conversation rather than delivering a verdict that is not open to self-defense or appeals. These gestures show you care enough about an individual to dedicate time to a meeting to discuss performance and work together toward making improvements.

Invite your employees to assess their own performance. This practice is often telling with regard to possible blind spots. Apply a holistic approach to assessment. Evaluate quantitative work output, quality, completeness and timeliness. Do not disregard attitude, cooperativity, integrity and honesty. These behaviors have an impact on the spirit of the entire team, either positively or negatively. Encourage and support small successes. Relate your evaluation to the big picture, the career goals of individual employees and the progress of the group at large.

Listen actively; do not focus on anticipating the employee's response and preparing what to say next. Do not interrupt or talk over the employee being evaluated. Establishing trust is key to calm, open and effective communication. Relate your evaluation to the specific career stage of each trainee. Share your challenges at the same career stage. Acknowledge mentees' strengths, talents and hard work. Encourage questions. Ask for feedback on the quality and style of your advising and mentoring. Recognize and address cultural barriers to having trainees speak up. Assure members of your team that they are welcome to give you constructive feedback on your management and leadership style. Make certain you live up to your assurance to avoid losing both trust and respect.

Many supervisors apply the common refrain during evaluation meetings: "you put in a lot of effort in planning this project, but …!" That "but" or "however" makes the praise you started with seem like insincere sugar-coating. If you plan to deliver a mixed evaluation, I suggest you start by discussing the specific problematic issues, and then give praise on positive aspects of the employee's performance. Doing it the other way around makes the employee apprehensive, knowing that a "but" or a "however" will be coming out of your mouth at any moment. Moreover, the listener will usually remember the part of the statement following the "but" rather than the complimentary words that preceded it.

The Art of Constructive Feedback

It is necessary to keep a positive outcome in mind when you evaluate an employee or a trainee. Clearly articulate this goal to your employees at the outset of each conversation. Focus the discussion on how to improve their performance while avoiding injuring their pride or degrading their self-confidence. Your tone of voice and body language should reflect this intention.

I must interject here to clarify a common misconception about the meaning of the term *constructive feedback*. Many interpret it as a mainly "positive" evaluation associated with minor recommendations to enhance job performance even further. Notably, the *Merriam-Webster Dictionary* defines constructive feedback as "promoting improvement or development." This definition leaves ample room for "negative" constructive feedback—that is, constructive criticism.

Constructive feedback is based on information and data, and it is issue specific. It is quite different from general praise or criticism that are usually vague and based on feelings or groundless personal judgment. Boilerplate praise statements such as "Good job! Attaboy!" are usually perceived as hollow and insincere, especially if your trainees realize that you tell everybody the same thing. Furthermore, these statements do not let people know exactly what they did right. Contrast this approach to saying, "You did a good job finishing this project. You were proactive in putting together an effective plan and timeline. You identified roles of teammates and established clear expectations and metrics." Conversely, you should not tell someone you are unhappy with their performance without informing them of specific points that would help them work on focused strategies for improvement.

360-Degree Evaluation

This assessment format (also known as multilayer feedback or multisource assessment) involves evaluating one's skills and contributions with input from different stakeholders. These include peers, superiors and subordinates. This process also requires self-assessment and reflection. It targets assessment of an employee's skills in management or leadership, teamwork, interpersonal interactions, independence, work habits, dependability and accountability. This approach provides a more comprehensive picture of one's performance from different vantage points.

It is best to use an anonymous survey to seek 360-degree assessment. Formulate questions under each category of evaluation and use a Likert scale to enable gathering quantitative data. You should also solicit open-ended comments. Most important, ask responders to indicate their work relationship with the employee being reviewed. This step will enable stratifying evaluations by peers and superiors. Of course, there is a challenge in maintaining the anonymity of responders in a small group, where it will be easy to guess who said what. You may construct different questions for each group of responders depending on the work portfolio of the evaluated employee. However, include questions on work aspects that affect all stakeholders, such as communication skills, integrity and dependability. Conflicting responses to this type of question are often quite revealing. One may receive accolades from their supervisor for being respectful, for instance, while their subordinates consider him or her utterly rude. This is the real value of 360-degree evaluations. They reveal weaknesses (and strengths) that do not become obvious when you limit employees' performance solely to the judgment of their advisors.

Some group leaders voluntarily ask for 360-degree evaluation of their own performance. They will therefore seek feedback from their boss, peers, employees and trainees, in addition to self-evaluation. This approach is, of course, optimal in making one a better manager, advisor, mentor and leader. Consequently, it will help build a more effective and happier workplace. It you opt for this type of evaluation, be aware that you will be placed in a very vulnerable position. Of course you would like to know what people like about your work style. But do you really want to hear negative comments about your aptitude as a team leader or research advisor? One must be extremely humble and self-secure to volunteer for this type of exercise.

Many years ago, I attended a leadership workshop in which requesting 360-degree evaluation from people I interacted with was one of the assignments. This was an amazing eye-opening experience. Some of my work habits were admired by my peers but loathed by my employees. My peers, on the one hand, appreciated my willingness to seek extensive counseling from various constituents to explore alternate approaches prior to making decisions on important issues. Some of my employees, on the other hand, resented being consulted about matters that were "above their pay grade." Similarly, I received high marks from my peers for being open to reasoning and showing flexibility by changing my mind as a result of hearing convincing arguments. My employees, by contrast, labeled this practice waffling and indecisive. I applied this feedback constructively to improve communication with my staff by starting conversations with explaining the reasons why I needed input from specific members of the group. I also became more selective when seeking feedback and choosing who to involve in these conversations. It paid off.

Most faculty I know are not open to being evaluated by their employees, graduate students or postdoctoral trainees. This is quite unfortunate since academics often have blind spots that make them continue on their straight path believing they are doing their best. They cannot take the time to self-reflect or seek comprehensive multilayer feedback on how to improve their work relationships and habits. Some may overhear complaints about the way they treat their laboratory personnel but prefer to live in denial or deem this an irrelevant issue as long as their employees are being as productive as they want them to be. Faculty often do not bother to participate in collegiate or institutional workshops on improving various managerial or leadership skills. They commonly believe these remedial events are aimed at the "other" problematic folks—sad, but true! In fact, I have consistently noticed that attendees of such workshops are mostly those who excel at the targeted skill to be taught but would like to become even better at it.

How to Motivate and Reward High-Performing Members of Your Team

Motivation and rewarding are necessary for enhancing productivity. They demonstrate your appreciation for good work, in both quality and quantity. Employees who are acknowledged and rewarded for their exemplary performance develop loyalty. They will not be tempted by job offers, regardless of how lucrative they may be. They will tend to work even harder and strive to further improve their skills. Pay increases naturally make it to the top of the list of desirable rewards. Unfortunately, there are bureaucratic challenges that may limit the extent of salary augmentation for an excellent employee. These obstacles are usually more evident in the case of technical staff. Maximum annual raises may be capped by the institution. Certain classes of employment are governed by policies and guidelines of unions or bargaining units in which everybody receives the same annual raise regardless of the quality of their performance. Furthermore, an employee may be at the highest level of pay for their employment class, in which case their supervisor will need to submit paperwork to reclassify their position to a higher-paying rank. This is usually a time-consuming process that involves multiple steps.

There are many ways for you to provide rewards in addition to pay raises and promotions. For example, you may offer a research staff member a chance to lead projects, assign them more challenging duties, involve the employee in higher-level planning meetings, recommend and pay for developmental workshops and courses, suggest and support specific educational opportunities, offer extra time off to compensate for working overtime, or allow a flexible work schedule that better fits the employee's life circumstances. You may also choose to market your employees and increase their visibility or nominate them for awards. Tailor the reward according to the career plan and specific needs of a given employee. Be creative in finding alternative approaches to rewarding your team. Let the employees tell you what they would find most rewarding at the specific stage of their career.

Coaching Underperforming or Disruptive Employees

There are problematic traits associated with underperforming employees that are more prevalent and serious than others. These include frequent absences with or without "creative" excuses, tardiness, inaccuracy or lack of thoroughness, low output, missed deadlines, and irresponsible or unsafe research practices. Some employees may exhibit social behaviors that negatively influence other members of the group (for example, lying, backstabbing, sabotage, off-color humor, profanity or vulgarity, negative stereotype remarks, ridiculing or insulting others, threatening, manipulating and misleading).

Do not allow these destructive behaviors to fester by not dealing with them instantly. Do not wait for the employee's annual evaluation to intervene. It is best to provide feedback when a certain negative action is fresh in the mind of the offender. Consider these guiding questions in assessing the nature of the individual's behavior: Does the behavior affect the productivity, quality of work or morale of the team? Is it unethical? You may tolerate a messy desk in someone's office but not clutter on a laboratory bench that may lead to spilling hazardous chemicals. Similarly, you should not expend energy in trying to change the social nature of an introvert but must put a stop to an extreme extrovert who consistently interrupts others' work with endless social conversations. Along the same lines, you should never tolerate someone who makes sexist or racially inappropriate remarks or another who plays loud music that interferes with others' ability to concentrate. Most seriously, you should immediately stop and reprimand employees or trainees for unethical research practices. These include falsification or fabrication of data, as well as plagiarism. It is your neck that will be on the line if such behaviors are allowed to continue.

Confronting the Culprit

Be as specific as possible in identifying issues of concern. Set up a private meeting. Give the employee a heads-up about the nature of a negative issue you plan to discuss; this is not a surprise intervention. Give them a chance to reflect and think of ways to improve. When you meet, be direct and get to the point. Do not start with delivering judgments or commands. State the behaviors you noticed, not how you interpret them (i.e., report the precise action you observed instead of characterizing it). Avoid saying, "Don't take this personally." This statement is meaningless and misleading since you are about to discuss issues related to the specific individual to whom you are talking!

* * *

Be an active listener. Do not interrupt or talk over the employee. Allow for moments of silence so that he or she can collect their thoughts and probe their feelings. As you sense a transition in the conversation, paraphrase what you just heard to ensure correct understanding. Be both objective and polite in commenting on the proposed approaches for improving performance. Find out the rationale behind the employee's thinking and do your best to steer the conversation toward a positive and productive outcome. Invite the employee to participate in the discussion. You may sometimes face silence or answers such as "I really don't know" or "I never thought about it." In this case, I recommend that you give the employee a few days to ponder, and then invite them back to continue the conversation.

You need to not only get to the cause of the problem but also plan a path for moving forward. Do this by asking open-ended questions. Start with "what" or "how" queries, as questions that start with "why" sound accusatory. You may also trigger deeper discussion by using statements that begin with "tell me," "explain," "elaborate" or "describe." Here are examples of questions/statements you might use to explore why an employee failed to finish a project by a designated deadline:

- Tell me your understanding of your responsibilities related to this project.
- What do you think you accomplished?
- What fell through?
- Elaborate on your perception of how what you left unaccomplished affects the plans of the team.
- Tell me why you did not perform your duties in a timely fashion as planned.
- Were there special circumstances that interfered with your plans?
- What do you think you would do differently to prevent similar lapses in future projects?
- In which areas do you need more guidance or training?
- How may I be of assistance in helping you succeed to make necessary changes?

Common barriers to a constructive conversation include preaching, long-winded interruptions and blocking communication by failing to really listen. Watch your tone of voice when asking questions. An angry tone causes anxiety and invites defensiveness. Do not introduce sarcasm as a way to lighten up the conversation; it will likely backfire. Do not dominate the conversation. Remember the rules of active listening (detailed in chapter 3), and avoid distractions or signs of boredom, such as scrolling on your cell phone, looking out the window, or shuffling paper. Be mindful of disrespectful body language such as rolling eyes, head shaking in disagreement, crossed arms, pounding on a table, pacing around the room or pointing fingers. It is never a good idea to compare someone's substandard productivity or lousy attitude to the high output and exemplary behavior of a specific person in the group. This comparison will likely create ill feelings among team members.

Here are some examples of helpful and unhealthy styles of confrontation.

EXAMPLE 1: A CHRONICALLY TARDY EMPLOYEE

Effective confrontation style: I noticed you often arrive late. I realize you stay longer than others in the evenings and you even work over weekends to make up for that. Sometimes, however, your being late interferes with the work of other team members who collaborate with you on projects and must synchronize their work with yours. Please share with me the reason why you are unable to come to work on time. Is there anything I might do to help circumvent these challenges?

* * *

Poor confrontation style: You are quite irresponsible when it comes to sticking to regular work hours. You'd better come to work on time from now on, or else there will be grave consequences.

EXAMPLE 2: A CLUTTERED LAB BENCH

Effective confrontation style: I noticed your laboratory bench is usually very crowded. As you know, having a cluttered laboratory space may lead to many hazards. Do you agree? Please tell me how you plan to change this habit to ensure your safety and the safety of everyone in the workplace.

* * *

Poor confrontation style: You are very sloppy. You must immediately eliminate the clutter on your lab bench. This is a research laboratory, not the kitchen at your home!

EXAMPLE 3: NOT DEDICATING ENOUGH TIME TO READING LITERATURE RELATED TO AN ASSIGNED PROJECT

Effective confrontation style: When you present your work in group meetings, I have observed your unfamiliarity with pertinent literature related to your project. As you know, good research is based on a foundation of knowledge published in various formats. Do you agree or see things differently? Are there reasons why you do not give more attention to reading literature? I would really like to see you dedicate time to this important activity that one needs to develop their scholarly independence. I will be glad to help you develop time management skills and will also recommend pertinent literature to help you achieve this goal.

* * *

Poor confrontation style: You will get nowhere without keeping up with the literature. I expect you will be a total failure when you lead your own group of researchers.

Example 4: An Irresponsible Research Assistant

Effective confrontation style: It is unfortunate that this project failed. Your specific role was to supervise mice breeding to ensure that there were enough animals for both the control and the drug-treated groups. There weren't. Nobody was alerted to the problem until the day before the experiment. Please share with me why you did not deliver as promised and what you plan to do in the future to avoid a recurrence of this problem. I would like to help you avoid such a major oversight in the future. Learning from failures is an invaluable opportunity for personal growth.

* * *

Poor confrontation style: As far as I am concerned, your incompetence is the reason why this project has failed!

* * *

In adopting the healthy styles of confrontation discussed above, you are essentially applying the main principles of coaching. Your role is to guide the employee or trainee to discover the nature of obstacles that hinder their progress. The goal is to make it easier for them to dig down deeper in their soul to figure out the background of actions or behaviors that result in suboptimal performance. It will also help them explore how to apply their inner strengths to overcome weaknesses. People respond differently to coaching cues. They vary in the extent of their contribution to the dialogue. Base your approach to coaching on the resourcefulness of the employee or trainee in self-analysis and reflection.

Whichever style you decide on, approach your coaching in a holistic manner. Realize that the behavior and traits of any individual are based on the sum of all aspects of their life. Holistic coaching also connects the quality of an employee's performance with their role on the team and the nature of their relationships with other team members. This comprehensive approach to coaching obviously takes time to conduct and achieve results. It is totally worthwhile, though. Doing so will likely result in effecting real and long-lasting change in the performance and productivity of the employee and the way they go about accomplishing their work with dedication and pride. Having said that, avoid acting as a therapist, nutritionist, parent, friend or legal advisor. Do not provide advice on personal matters outside the work environment. Recommend professional resources instead. Your institution likely has an employee assistance program that provides help with personal problems free of charge.

To be fair to your employees, be forthcoming when you notice performance or behavioral issues that need realignment. As stated previously, be as specific as possible in providing this feedback based on your observations. In deciding on and communicating an action plan for improvement, create an account of what needs to change and by what time. Involve the problematic employee in crafting these plans. Hold follow-up meetings soon thereafter to track compliance with the agreement. If no significant change is made, you must issue a written warning to the employee. The warning should detail all aspects of the problem. It should also state action items necessary to correct performance deficiencies. Be clear about the consequences of not meeting these performance expectations by a certain time.

In evaluating the performance of employees and trainees, it is highly advisable to keep records of meeting dates and what was discussed and agreed upon. Documentation is essential in order to legitimately fire an employee. Human resources policies usually mandate three warnings to an employee before a supervisor can legitimately issue a termination notice. These are commonly known as steps 1, 2 and 3, with heightened degrees of escalation regarding the seriousness of the warning from one step to the next. Advancing from one stage of warning to another must happen within a defined period. Otherwise, the process restarts at step 1 the next time that same employee underperforms. Naturally, it is less complicated to fire someone during their probationary period, usually during the first three to six months of their employment. Take advantage of this opportunity if you have serious doubts about the abilities of a new employee as a result of observations you or other members of your research group have made in interacting with this person early in their employment. To be fair, however, you should provide them with early and frequent feedback to improve their performance. Decide to fire if the trajectory is predictive of continued unsatisfactory performance. It goes without saying that you must consult with your college or institutional human resources experts every step of the way to be fair and avoid legal consequences.

How and When to Let Go of an Employee or Trainee

Contemplating firing someone should not come as a surprise either to you or to the employee. An expert in human resources shared with me that many of the employees she was charged with delivering a layoff notice to surprisingly expressed relief. They were aware of their poor performance, but their lack of expertise or distaste for the job stood in the way of doing a better job. You should not suddenly face serious doubts about the performance of a given employee or trainee at or near the end game when you are about to ask them to leave. An astute manager bases such tough decisions on the overall track record of the employee rather than on a single incident (with the exception of proven criminal or ethical offenses, of course). While you should always strive to provide tools and opportunities to help an underperforming employee readjust their path, sometimes these efforts do not produce the desired results. One's patience often runs out at a certain juncture. There is usually a last straw that breaks the camel's back!

Most managers find it difficult to decide when and how to fire an employee. The experience brings many turbulent emotions to the surface (for example, guilt, pity, self-doubt and fear of the employee's negative reaction). Many questions come to mind that cloud one's ability to make a firm decision. Here are some examples:

- Have my expectations been commensurate with the particular stage of this employee's career?
- Have I been fair in assigning appropriate responsibilities to this employee based on their education, training and personal strengths?
- Have I provided necessary training for the particular tasks they have failed to perform?
- Have I fairly balanced evaluation of the good and poor aspects of this particular employee's performance?
- Does this person face special social or health challenges that hinder their ability to achieve their full potential? Could these challenges be mitigated?
- Is this employee amenable to further training?
- Are they aware of what it takes to succeed?
- What is the employee's expected reaction to being terminated and how should I respond?
- Do I need to provide an explanation of the termination to other employees and trainees in my group? When and what should I tell them?
- How do I handle rumors surrounding the basis of the termination while still maintaining confidentiality?

As you answer these questions, be aware of possible prejudice and assumptions, particularly those stemming from the employee's gender identity, sexual orientation, race or religion. Prejudice is usually the result of hidden unconscious or implicit bias.

Summary

In my opinion, managing people is one of the most difficult tasks a junior faculty member has to tackle. It involves so many intricate and interrelated aspects that are necessary for the group to operate smoothly. These responsibilities do not stop with making wise decisions on who to hire but continue into training, motivating and reprimanding employees and trainees. The group manager is also responsible for setting the tone for a harmonious team working together in a happy and safe environment. This process involves both management and leadership skills. The main challenge is the lack of adequate training given to most junior faculty in these important areas while they were graduate students or postdoctoral fellows. This shortage may easily be corrected through reading, attending relevant workshops and seminars, and learning from senior colleagues, especially designated mentors. It is not advisable for one to learn these skills by trial and error. This approach would likely lead to a long and painful journey to achieve sufficient knowledge in this regard.

Self-Reflection Exercises

- Consider a recent difficult conversation with an employee or trainee. Reflect on what worked, what did not and how you would better handle similar conversations in the future.
- List how you approach developing the careers of your staff. Consider different employment and training categories and stages of individuals' careers.
- Contemplate the pros and cons of requesting a 360-degree performance evaluation for yourself.
- List approaches to rewarding each member of your group based on their career ambitions and personal needs.
- Imagine a hypothetical situation in which you have lost one of your research grants and you must lay off one member of your research staff. Contemplate who among your team you would choose to let go and why. Imagine how you would convey and explain your decision to that employee.

7

Benefiting from Mentoring

Need for Mentoring

Mentoring of junior faculty members by their senior colleagues provides a wide range of benefits that are necessary for the progress of their careers. These include maximizing the use of their time without getting burned out and improving teaching and writing skills. Mentees also learn how to better manage their research teams and develop healthier relationships with superiors and peers. In addition, mentors guide junior faculty in setting goals and then structuring realistic plans to achieve these goals. Most important, they serve as role models and advocates for junior faculty.

The specific skill set to be targeted through mentoring depends on the background and knowledge base of a particular mentee. Junior faculty vary in their personal and professional experiences and skills. They worked with different graduate or postdoctoral mentors who used diverse approaches to prepare their trainees for the next move. A comprehensive self-inventory of a mentee's existing proficiencies and specific areas that require further development would provide a helpful roadmap. It will also help to choose mentors who have special expertise to fill the specific needs of a given junior faculty member.

Research competencies that may be augmented through mentoring include short- and long-term goal planning, setting priorities, writing skills, structuring research projects as publishable units, writing successful grant applications, and identifying proper funding agencies and types of grants. A junior faculty member may also learn many useful tricks pertaining to their ability to manage and lead their research teams, such as hiring, rewarding, motivating, dealing with problematic employees and trainees, giving constructive feedback and creating team spirit, maintaining accountability, guiding professional and personal growth of their trainees, advising and mentoring group members, and engaging in proper fiscal and project management. Mentors may be of great help in guiding a junior faculty member to become an effective teacher through introducing them to active learning, team teaching and problem-solving strategies. They may share their experience in creating effective presentations and ways to keep all students stimulated and engaged. This is of paramount importance due to the increased diversity of the student body, particularly in preferred modes of learning.

The most important category of knowledge to be gained from senior mentors is how to deal with people. This includes making connections in and outside the department and the university; conflict resolution; negotiation skills; learning when and how to say no; assimilating into the department, college and institution; and dealing with difficult people. Other keys to success to be learned from mentors include structuring a healthy work-life balance, managing time and energy effectively, delegating tasks, and learning about university structure and policies related to career advancement. The most important policies related to this final aspect are those pertaining to annual performance reviews, in addition to promotion and tenure. Knowledge of these policies and associated procedures and criteria will help a junior faculty member adjust their priorities to focus on what matters most in attaining their career goals.

What's in It for a Mentor?

Contributing to developing someone's career naturally has significant psychological and emotional rewards. It provides a sense of self-fulfillment. Preparing future scholars who will lead various academic fields ensures continuity of the academic lineage and profession. Thus, the most effective mentoring is often based on self-satisfaction and self-motivation on the part of the mentor rather than through obligation or coercion. When I was a teenager, my grandfather (and most influential mentor) once told me that teaching a person knowledge that they subsequently pass on to others makes one's soul eternal. What a great source of gratification that is!

However, not all mentors are willing to selflessly donate their time and pass on their experiences. Some may worry that good mentoring would consume much of their time, putting them behind in their own work. Others may believe that helping develop a superstar may well create a fierce competitor, particularly if the mentor and mentee work in the same or close fields of scholarship. A selfish and territorial person may fear that the new kid on the block will end up becoming more successful in securing research funding, attracting top trainees and being invited to give talks at top institutions and conferences. Sometimes assigned mentors may lack essential abilities such as clear communication skills and knowing how to distinctly align expectations or to provide stewardship toward independence. In rare cases, a mentor may be unreasonable, abrasive, abusive, disrespectful, or controlling. In the mentoring world, such individuals are often described as "de"mentors or "tor"mentors!

Structured versus Ad Hoc Mentoring Relationships

Mentoring in the academy is often an ad hoc and informal practice, which makes it vulnerable to inconsistencies, mostly reflected as lack of commitment and investment by all parties involved in the mentoring relationship. Both mentors and mentees are busy and distracted by many other pressing tasks on their plates. There is also evidence that informal mentoring does not suit some of the special needs of minority and women faculty. This misalignment usually takes place when the mentor is a white male who may not be aware of the many challenges faced by this population. Mentoring should therefore be an intentional and well-planned exercise. Many elements should be considered in designing a successful mentor-mentee relationship—most important, thoughtfully matching the mentor's abilities and mentoring track record with the specific needs of the mentee. Compatible personality traits are a plus.

Role of Department, College and Institution in the Success of a Mentoring Experience

Research has shown that having formal, functional mentoring programs organized by colleges or institutions is the second highest predictor of faculty advancement in research (the first being a faculty member's passion for the discovery of new knowledge and teaching). The success of structured mentoring programs depends on the quality of support and investment provided by the department, college and institution. Most institutions mandate that departments and colleges draft documents that detail faculty mentoring policies and guidelines. However, some do better than others in practicing and rewarding mentoring. There are also significant variances in institutional cultures that drive commitment to good mentoring. These include whether high-quality mentoring is acknowledged and whether adequate resources are provided (for example, administrative staff support). Some departments have established clear criteria for the successful outcome of a mentor-mentee relationship and benchmarks for attaining its goals. This practice facilitates objective evaluation of the caliber of mentoring. Unfortunately, some department chairs do not even include mentoring activities as a parameter of faculty activities during annual evaluations of senior faculty. Others include it but do not reward it appropriately. I find this style of leadership shortsighted, knowing the many benefits mentoring provides to the overall professional growth of faculty and, therefore, to departments, colleges and universities.

Departments also vary widely in the extent of required documentation and evaluation regarding the quality of faculty mentoring. Some expect a senior faculty member to submit detailed narratives that describe the time commitment, frequency of meetings with the mentee, and in what ways mentoring has helped advance the career of the junior faculty member. Others simply ask senior faculty to list the names of those whom they mentored in a given year. The latter approach is not informative enough. It does not enable the department head to gauge the caliber of mentoring, in terms of both quality and quantity. During my academic journey, I have noticed many cases in which a senior faculty member claimed a certain junior faculty member as their mentee, while the proclaimed mentee did not list that individual as a mentor. This contradiction represents a clear case of the mentor misunderstanding the required elements of effective mentoring. It also suggests that junior faculty are often more aware of these elements than their senior colleagues.

I believe generational gaps are the main contributor to such misaligned expectations. Most senior faculty started their careers as independent investigators at a time when resources were plentiful. Public institutions enjoyed more financial support from their states. It was not uncommon for a faculty member to have a grant application funded on the first or second submission. There was no page limit for grant applications—or even a limit to the number of proposal revisions and resubmissions. (I recall reviewing a proposal that was revised eight times before members of the review panel asked the committee administrator to call the applicant to beg them not to apply for a ninth time. Luckily, the applicant gave up and developed better research ideas and questions.) Funding lines were quite generous back then. This is obviously the antithesis of the current bleak funding situation.

During these earlier times, researchers also had more access to types of grants designed to give an investigator a chance to gather preliminary data to support bigger applications, such as the R03 and R21 funding mechanisms from the National Institutes of Health. These applications did not require inclusion of supporting preliminary data. While such funding mechanisms still exist, the way they are evaluated is quite different. Nowadays, reviewers of these seed grants favor applications that include a significant volume of preliminary data as proof of concept, which obviously defeats their main purpose. There are equivalent small grants for starting research programs in the social sciences and humanities (for example, from the Wellcome Trust). However, those are becoming rather competitive as well, in part because some senior faculty who are better at marketing their ideas apply for these grants to support changes in the direction of their research.

Thus, faculty who started their careers a couple of decades ago did not require mentoring in grantsmanship to the extent that current junior faculty need it. A junior faculty member usually needs about a year to set up their laboratory and hire staff before they embark on submitting grant applications. The process of reviewing applications by funding agencies is quite slow. Most funding agencies allow only one chance for revising and resubmitting applications. Meanwhile, the promotion and tenure clock continues to tick. Having a major research grant in hand is key for promotion to associate professor with tenure. There is little opportunity for learning by trial and error. All of these serious challenges make it absolutely necessary to provide frequent and well-planned guidance to junior faculty through mentoring.

Some institutions provide training to mentors in optimizing the practice of mentoring. As with parenting, senior faculty tend to mentor mainly in the way they were mentored, even though there were likely negative aspects to their training experience. Therefore, mentors need to be familiarized with different mentoring styles and formats, as well as how to maximize the process's rewards for the mentee. Effective training programs are designed to help establish evidence-based guidelines, tools, and mechanisms for regular assessment. They also emphasize the importance of aligning expectations and defining the roles and responsibilities of both the mentor and the mentee. Furthermore, this type of training provides helpful tools for mitigating different types of challenges that may arise in the mentoring relationship.

Common Models of Formal Faculty Mentoring

Mentoring by a Senior Faculty

This traditional style of mentoring is hierarchical in nature. It involves assigning a single senior faculty mentor to each junior faculty member. The assignment is often made by the department head. This type of mentoring is usually more oriented toward improving research or teaching skills. However, it is amenable to incorporating career planning and goal setting.

While such arrangements have historically worked well, they are subject to numerous possible roadblocks. The major obstacle is the usual high demand for good senior mentors, especially women and minority mentors. There is also the possibility of a mismatch in the relationship since assignments are usually made on the basis of individual mentors' availability and equal sharing of mentoring responsibilities by all senior faculty. For example, the junior faculty member may need training in areas at which the senior mentor may not excel. Different preferences in the mode and style of communication often result in serious clashes. Such a mismatch creates a serious problem for the mentee due to the existing power differential with the senior mentor. While selecting a mentor who works in a research area close to that of the junior faculty member can work well, this approach could easily result in a conflict of interest with serious negative consequences. For example, the mentor may claim some research questions as their own territory and force the mentee to take different, less interesting directions. The senior partner may also exploit the mentee by coercing them to include the mentor as an investigator on grants or as an author of research publications. These problems tend to arise more often when the junior faculty member was trained in the same institution where they were appointed as an assistant professor.

I must admit these examples are worst-case scenarios that happen infrequently. Having said that, the fact that they do happen warrants making junior faculty aware of the possibility. They should watch for early symptoms of trouble and treat the problem as early as possible. Better yet, issues related to such conflicts should be resolved preemptively during a discussion of mutual expectations at the outset of the mentoring relationship.

Organic mentoring relationships develop from actual experiences in dealing with a given senior faculty member. A junior faculty member may witness a senior colleague in action. They may notice their candor, wisdom, integrity and respect for others. The senior faculty member may provide sage advice as an informal mentor. Feelings of comfort and trust in the relationship may lead the junior faculty member to negotiate creating a formal mentoring connection. One may find this person in another department. Their area of scholarship may be far removed from that of the junior faculty member, but they may contribute much in helping the mentee understand institutional culture, develop networks and improve personal skills. This scenario is, of course, ideal. However, having a junior faculty member find such a person on their own and develop a productive relationship may take time. The fact is that a junior faculty member needs mentoring from day one on the job, perhaps even before their arrival on campus. My recommendation is to have the junior faculty member request input in the department's selection of mentors. They should ask around regarding the personal traits and mentoring styles of different senior faculty who are available to assume a mentoring role. More important, a mentee should interview junior faculty who have been mentored by the senior faculty of interest. They must politely talk their department head out of assigning a mentor they do not feel comfortable with, for whatever reason, and be ready to justify their request for a different mentor.

Mentoring Teams

It is difficult, if not impossible, to find a single mentor who can adequately cater to all the needs of a given mentee. It is also hard to predict whether a mentor assigned by their department is the best choice. A senior faculty member who is an expert in the junior faculty member's area of scholarship may not necessarily be a role model for managing their research team, or they may have poor teaching skills. This is why mentoring teams may be more advantageous than having a single mentor. Individual members of the team could help the junior faculty member build different skills related to their own professional experiences and personal strengths.

A junior faculty member may select a mentor to help them with scholarship and others in the areas of teaching or people skills. They may add one who has had experience in guiding other junior faculty to a successful career, or another with specific technical expertise. Junior faculty specializing in certain lines of research, for instance, may benefit from having a statistician mentor who would guide them to proper experimental design and data analysis. Furthermore, a mentee may be hesitant to candidly share their weaknesses with a mentor from the same department, one who will eventually vote on their promotion and tenure. It is therefore recommended that a mentoring team include at least one mentor from outside the mentee's department, even from outside their college.

Finding a sufficient number of qualified senior faculty represents a major challenge to team mentoring. Scheduling meetings that work for everybody's calendar is not an easy task, either. Furthermore, a junior faculty member may receive contrasting advice from different members of the team. This disagreement creates a potentially awkward situation in which the junior faculty member may have a hard time deciding which advice to take or leave. It is best to bring such problematic issues to the attention of the entire group for discussion of the pros and cons of each suggested approach. It will save the junior mentee from having to take sides on their own.

Group Mentoring

In this style of mentoring, one or a few senior mentors work with a small group of mentees. Such an approach could be useful to both early and mid-career faculty. The usual application of group mentoring is to help faculty gain competence in individual elements required for their professional advancement. Teaching and writing skills are common examples. Participating in group mentoring allows mentees to exchange success stories, best practices and challenges. I have had firsthand experience with applying this approach to critiquing grant applications by a group of junior faculty, in which both mentors and mentees in the group provide suggestions for improvement. Receiving feedback from peers with different backgrounds, scholarly interests and specializations ends up producing a document of greatest clarity to experts and nonexperts alike, a situation that closely mimics the makeup of a grant review panel. This approach works best at the very early stages of composing an application—for example, when one develops the main frame or the "specific aims" page of the proposal. At this time, the main thrust of the proposed project is still pliable. It is much easier to alter its path. Emphasizing the specific aims ensures their coherence and clarity. These qualities are fundamental in setting the tone of the entire application. Most important, they mentally direct a reviewer to be either an ally or a foe as they read the rest of the proposal. I liken this very early stage of grant writing to what is known as "curb appeal" in real estate, as it is commonly believed that home buyers make up about half of their mind on a certain property based on the way it looks from the outside. It is also similar to presenting an attractive lure while fishing. (I prefer the latter analogy since it also applies to maintaining the attention and interest of the reviewers until they read the last page of the application, similar to slowly dragging the lured fish toward the boat and bringing it onboard.)

Group mentoring may also be structured to address various soft skills. Examples include team building, rewarding and motivation, conflict resolution, networking, negotiation, time and energy management, and setting goals and priorities. The main challenges to group mentoring are the varied needs of individual mentees, the need to manage group dynamics, time commitment and turnover of members.

Peer Group Mentoring

Peers may meet one on one or in groups without mentors to discuss challenges and share approaches to finding solutions. The group will ideally be composed of faculty at different stages in the early part of their careers to allow for varied levels of experience. This structure is largely devoid of hierarchy, which makes it easier to be open and discuss issues freely. Group peer mentoring works best for a critical mass of junior faculty and when members honor their commitment to attend meetings and come prepared to offer candid and constructive feedback on others' work. Peer group mentoring requires skillful facilitation of discussions to give everybody an equal chance to speak and voice their opinions. Facilitators should also be adept in steering conversations in a constructive direction. Peer mentoring in general creates a warm sense of camaraderie and also enhances a junior faculty member's self-confidence in realizing they are not alone in facing a certain obstacle that is standing in the way of advancing their career.

This type of mentoring is commonly built around getting a collaborative project done or a specific type of professional activity. Writing is a common topic that benefits from peer mentoring. Members of the group collaborate to establish a timeline for sharing specific sections of papers or grant proposals with the group members. They meet regularly to critique and edit each other's manuscripts and grant proposals. In addition to improving the quality of an individual's drafts, group members learn by making suggestions for changes in others' writing. It also obliges participants to meet deadlines for drafts and therefore pushes the process forward. Peer mentoring may also be centered around challenges in the work and family environments, as well as work-life balance issues. The group may invite a guest senior colleague to benefit from their experience. Doing so provides participants with a role model to emulate.

Online Mentoring (E-Mentoring)

A junior faculty member may opt to include a mentor from another institution to complement their mentoring team. Communication tools include email, chats and virtual conferencing. This approach to mentoring expands the available mentoring network beyond one's institution, especially when there is a dearth of senior faculty mentors with expertise that fits the mentee's needs. In fact, the e-mentor may be in another country or continent (i.e., "mentors without borders"). This flexibility is most advantageous in the case of small academic institutions. Being mentored online by someone from another institution also allows the junior faculty member to candidly share their weaknesses with someone who will not play a role in their formal evaluation or promotion decisions.

Roles and Responsibilities of the Mentored Junior Faculty

A mentee has a very important role in making the mentoring relationship yield its expected return. Mentors, especially among senior faculty, are very busy people who have to simultaneously juggle numerous tasks. They often mentor a handful of junior faculty, in addition to their graduate students and postdoctoral trainees. Mentors may not be as proactive as a mentee may expect or hope in checking in periodically or in initiating meetings. It is therefore the responsibility of the mentee to organize regular meetings according to the agreed frequency. A junior faculty member should also be proactive in approaching their mentors with questions when challenging situations arise, and they should be candid about their needs and what they aim to get out of the mentoring relationship. In addition, they should not hesitate to ask probing questions to develop awareness of what services their mentor or mentoring team is willing to offer and of the boundaries of the relationship.

A junior faculty member benefits the most from mentoring when they are actively engaged in identifying specific career development goals they need help achieving. They should participate with the mentor in putting together a plan for accomplishing various goals and establishing a timeline for deliverables to which they must adhere. The mentee should strive to accept constructive criticism and take ownership of the changes they need to make. Some of the steps on the modified path may fall outside their comfort zone, which will require conviction and commitment on their part in order to succeed in making the necessary changes. The more engaged a junior faculty member is with their mentors, the stronger advocates the mentors will become at the time of promotion and tenure. Close engagement provides mentors with firsthand experience in evaluating their mentee's performance. This personal touch will add credence to their testimony of what an outstanding individual the mentee is.

Roles and Responsibilities of the Mentor

Mentors should be committed to making themselves available to meet with their mentees and to respond to their needs in a timely manner. They should be active listeners and adept in working across boundaries of race, ethnicity, gender, culture, religion and sexual orientation. Mentors should invest necessary time in carefully reviewing work plans and critiquing drafts of manuscripts and grant proposals. A good mentor is one who is both encouraging and candid in giving feedback. She or he simultaneously plays the roles of cheerleader and coach! Their focus should be on helping the mentee set realistic career goals and have an appropriate vision.

Ideal mentoring is comprehensive in nature. It should aim to help the mentee grow in both professional and personal skills. Mentors should also be sponsors who advocate on behalf of the junior faculty member by recommending them to serve on grant review committees and nominating them for internal and external junior awards. One of the mentor's most valued roles is making the junior faculty aware of resources that are not widely advertised for one reason or another. Senior faculty benefit from "institutional memory" that makes them aware of these resources. They have learned about them over time during their many years of service. These resources are not only technical (for example, specialized research core facilities or library archives) but also intellectual. Serving on different institutional committees allows senior faculty to get to know who is who outside the college and therefore makes them well positioned to orient others to unique opportunities for networking and collaboration. This knowledge saves junior faculty ample time and effort in unearthing these resources on their own.

A caring mentor feels comfortable with being vulnerable by sharing lessons learned since they started their academic life—what worked for them and what didn't. They are open to communicating about their failures and how they got back on track. They also reflect on what they would have done differently if they had the opportunity to restart their journey. This type of sharing imparts warmth to the mentoring relationship. In addition, it gives the junior faculty member insight in realizing that the senior faculty member also walked through a rocky road in the early stages of their career, but they eventually made it with flying colors.

A good mentor commits to maintaining confidentiality of conversations and shared information. They acknowledge their limits of expertise and recommend other resources to the mentee. Effective mentoring requires considering the big picture of the mentee's career goals. It involves not being hasty in offering solutions to challenges expressed by the mentee. Mentoring works best when it is based on coaching strategies. A skillful mentor will therefore ask a variety of open-ended, probing questions to guide the junior faculty member to the roots of a problem, as well as proper solutions. This process includes having the mentee contemplate and contrast a variety of approaches and specific actions they laid out.

Sharing Expectations About Mutual Roles and Responsibilities

A mentee and a mentor should collaborate on deciding their specific roles in the relationship, as well as what to expect from each other. Both sides should also share their expectations regarding boundaries to the relationship. For instance, they should work together to agree on the frequency and length of meetings; preferred mode of communication, especially on sensitive or confidential matters (phone or in person versus email); the mentor's availability to attend classes to evaluate the mentee's teaching; and both parties' willingness to critique drafts of manuscripts and grant applications. If a junior faculty member is being mentored by a team, this conversation must be had with each of the mentors.

Some recommend that each mentor-mentee pair work together to draft a document that spells out expectations and boundaries—namely, a mentoring compact agreement. While this approach is favored by some, others deem it too rigid and excessively formal, almost like a legal contract. I recommend that the mentor-mentee pair settle on some version of formal or informal documentation of mutual expectations to use as a guide as they proceed to work together, but documentation is key here.

One of the empirical aspects of a good mentoring relationship is upfront planning for its closure. The mentor and mentee should agree on when and how to taper off or terminate the relationship. Some mentoring arrangements go sour to the point of being beyond repair. There are usually early signals that reflect different aspects of such a dysfunctional relationship. Misdirection for selfish reasons, lack of commitment or accountability, or breaching confidence are common red flags that should set off alerts. Alternatively, the mentee may develop far enough in their career that they no longer require as much feedback from their mentor or mentoring team. It is also possible that the needs of the mentee will change in a direction beyond the expertise of the assigned or self-selected mentor. In this case, the mentee should seek other, more appropriate mentors.

I highly recommend keeping in touch with past mentors and continuing to benefit from their special talents and wisdom. An academic never ceases to need advice from others related to furthering their career, no matter how senior they become. Maintaining a relationship with past mentors is also a good indicator that the mentee did not have to work with them only during a time of need. I still consult with my doctoral thesis advisor and professors from my graduate program and have often received very sage advice on how to proceed in sensitive and complicated situations (especially when I first experienced serious academic politics in which I was coerced to take sides in a matter I had no stake in). I also recommend that mentees acknowledge the assistance they received from their mentors and how mentoring has helped shape their careers. A mentee should give mentors credit for contributing to their success, both during and following the termination of the mentoring arrangement. One way to repay this debt is to nominate mentors for internal and national mentoring or achievement awards.

Summary

Mentoring is essential for a junior faculty member to build up a complete profile of technical and soft skills. More important, one could learn valuable skills that are essential for proper time and energy management, achieving a fair work-life balance, and dealing with difficult people and challenging situations. Mentoring may be achieved through a single person or a team of senior faculty or through peer junior faculty. Due to the importance of effective mentoring in guiding faculty during their early employment period to advance their career, some departments, colleges or universities provide structured mentoring programs and offer training to mentors to maximize their positive input. Furthermore, healthy mentoring relationships are based on a foundation of mutual trust and clear expectations regarding roles and responsibilities.

Self-Reflection Exercises

- Compare and contrast the pros and cons of the various mentoring models according to your personal preferences and needs.
- Identify your top mentoring needs in scholarship and teaching.
- List the soft skills you need to strengthen through mentoring in these areas: writing, speaking, team management, conflict resolution, time and energy management, work-life balance.
- Draft an inventory of what you are currently getting out of mentoring and what you are missing.

8

The Path to Promotion and Tenure

Being promoted to the rank of associate professor with indefinite tenure is one of the most coveted accomplishments in one's academic career. It represents the stamp of approval that a junior faculty member has successfully gone through the initiation period of probation and proven they are worthy of joining the cadre of the elite. Naturally, this distinct honor comes with a hefty price tag. It requires full dedication by a junior faculty member to their work. More important, careful planning and prioritizing are also needed.

The Probationary Period

It is natural to harbor marked angst during the six years of probation for tenure-track faculty. There are so many different tasks to attend to but a limited amount of time in which to do them well. Things take longer than expected and are never as easy as they seem or as advertised by others, especially those with deeper experience in the matter. This rule applies to getting a paper published or a grant funded. Longer work hours and less downtime are needed to keep up with the crazy pace of the academic environment. This sacrifice usually comes at the expense of time dedicated to family and self.

There is vast new territory to explore and become familiar with as a junior academic. When dealing with research group members, staff and colleagues, a new faculty member may begin to regret not having had formal training in management and leadership, mentoring and advising, or general people skills that prove to be a big part of the game. There is also the tangled web of academic politics, a concept that one did not realize existed when they were graduate students or during their postdoctoral training. A junior faculty member must be very tactful in expressing their point of view, especially when it diverges from the stance of senior colleagues. They constantly sense the potential danger of the power differential, personal turf and the role of senior colleagues in influencing votes on promotion and tenure. This situation makes a junior faculty member feel vulnerable and intimidated; he or she may feel like they are constantly walking over eggshells. Families and friends try to be empathetic and supportive, but it is not easy for them to comprehend and identify with the complexity of the situation and why anybody in their right mind would choose to stick with this unreasonably demanding environment rather than get a 9–5 job with higher pay and better benefits.

When you interviewed for your first academic position and during the first few months on the job, you likely heard numerous promises that all your needs would be taken care of. The dean of the college may have said, "Don't hesitate to walk in whenever you feel my intervention in any problem is needed." Your department head may have promised to offer total protection to your time to allow you to set up your research program and obtain funding. This honeymoon effect lasts longer in some cases than others. The truth is that people are busy with their own agendas and challenges; they have their own priorities. The dean and department head likely have jam-packed calendars, every day, and may go home to continue working until the wee hours. While your challenge may be quite urgent or time sensitive as far as you are concerned, the first available appointment to meet with either person may be in a few weeks. Moreover, promises of protecting your research time may start to evaporate sooner than expected. As an example, your chair may approach you to jump in to cover some or all of the teaching of a colleague who unexpectedly left the college in search of greener pastures. Or perhaps a new task force has been established to explore adding more advanced classes in genetics or healthcare journalism, and you happen to be the local expert on the subject matter. Your research time thus appears to be shrinking, adding to your anxiety.

Dealing with the Imposter Syndrome

Junior faculty can be classed in three categories when it comes to evaluating their abilities. Some are extremely confident, while others are realistic about the mix of their strengths and shortcomings, and a few lack significant self-confidence. Obviously, it is healthy for someone to be confident while being aware of their need for improvement in specific areas. Overconfident, perhaps arrogant faculty become devastated by failures, even minor ones. Their exaggerated confidence may lead them to refuse to admit ownership of their role in having research staff leave soon after they are hired or in having a grant or a manuscript be rejected. This behavior leads to their lack of awareness regarding the need to better themselves. However, it is equally dangerous and self-defeating for one not to believe in their ability to do a good job and to be on a par with others who have successfully navigated a similar journey. These negative feelings and predictions of doom hold them back from trying and may fester further to become paralyzing to their growth. Fear of ultimate failure may stop junior faculty from enjoying and celebrating small successes along the road. At some point, such self-doubting faculty may start feeling like imposters or frauds. What an unfortunate and uncomfortable position to be in! Seeking help and support from mentors and professional career coaches is advisable in such cases.

The Process of Promotion and Tenure

Your performance will be evaluated annually during the probationary period. Each year your department head will assess your productivity and potential for promotion and tenure. They will recommend whether to approve continuation of your probationary period for another year or terminate your employment. While the latter situation happens quite rarely, the tone of the department head's comments on your performance may vary and will undoubtedly be taken into consideration when you are considered for promotion. In approving continuation of your probationary position, it also makes a huge difference if your chair comments that you have "met" or "exceeded" expectations. Your performance evaluation at the end of the third year carries the most weight. At this juncture the department head and senior faculty will decide via a formal vote whether you have the potential to be promoted and tenured by the end of your sixth year. Passing with a high proportion of negative votes should be taken quite seriously as a most alarming signal. It means that the probationary faculty member must do much more to reverse this shaky impression of their performance and to meet the criteria for promotion and tenure when they apply.

At the end of your fourth year of employment, you will inform your department head of your plan to come up for promotion and tenure. You should then start to put together your promotion dossier to be reviewed and voted on by your department promotion and tenure committee. Votes will be documented in the dossier along with comments as to why some of your senior colleagues voted not to support your promotion to the rank of associate professor with indefinite tenure. Following a majority positive vote, you will work with your chair to come up with a list of external reviewers. The department chair will send your dossier to reviewers accompanied by the department vote and the department/college criteria for promotion and tenure. The chair will frequently ask reviewers to comment on whether you have the potential to be promoted and tenured at their institutions. It is noteworthy, however, that the main scale to be used in judging your productivity and qualification for promotion is the documented criteria in your college and institution. Once the external letters are received, they will be added to your dossier, which will then be forwarded to the college promotion and tenure committee for review and voting. The committee will provide the voting tally to the dean accompanied by a letter that summarizes your accomplishments and the basis of the committee's vote. Some universities allow submission of a report from committee members whose evaluation of your performance conflicts with the votes of the majority. The dean is the final decider at the college level, and the tone of their letter and recommendations to the provost or chancellor bears significant weight. Note that you will have a chance to comment on or rebut in writing decisions made at all levels of the departmental or college reviews of your promotion and tenure dossier. The rebuttal documents you provide will be appended to your dossier. Furthermore, you are allowed to add new material to your dossier at any stage of the process (for example, listing a newly funded grant or a paper that was recently accepted for publication) until a specified date.

If there is strong support for your promotion at the college level, it is almost always the case that the university will concur with the college recommendations. You cannot be that confident, however, if you were recommended for promotion with a split vote by your department and college peers. Split college evaluations force university-wide promotion committees to be consistent across the board in assessing cases of faculty from different departments and colleges. Decisions at that higher level are made based not only on the faculty past accomplishments but also on the trajectory and promise of their continued productivity after getting tenure, since some faculty tend to slow down at this juncture. One common predictor of the possibility of "tenure crash" is having a sudden flurry of research activity a year or so before coming up for promotion, as opposed to a steady stream of publications and grants equally spread throughout the probationary period. If this pattern is associated with a weak majority vote in supporting promotion at the college level, the main question becomes why anyone should offer a person a lifetime commitment for employment if the writing on the wall clearly says that making it to this stage of the marathon may well be their last hurrah.

Preparing Your Promotion and Tenure Dossier

A typical promotion and tenure dossier includes a complete and up-to-date curriculum vitae. Most institutions mandate a prescribed

8. The Path to Promotion and Tenure

format for content and sequence of items in a vitae, and some require using specific software to generate it so as to maintain consistency. This approach makes it easy to compare vitae of faculty from different colleges at the institutional level. Annual performance evaluations of the probationary faculty by their department head and departmental promotion committee are appended, in addition to supplementary materials such as student evaluations of teaching and reprints of representative publications. At later stages of the process, letters from external reviewers and votes by various administrative bodies that evaluate the promotion and tenure quest will be added to the dossier.

Carefully study promotion guidelines from your first day on the job to know what is eventually required to reach your goal. There may be separate guideline documents for each department or a single shared one for the entire college. Consult with your department head and mentors on the meaning of vague statements and criteria such as "must have obtained one or more large research grants from highly competitive sources," "must have published a significant number of original research papers in premier journals in the field," or "must have established national prominence in the research specialty." What do these requirements really mean in quantitative terms? Get to know what documentation and data you need to include in your promotion dossier and save them in a folder as you acquire them. Doing so will save you ample time in digging for this information under stress later on. Regularly take notes on individual accomplishments or contributions in research, teaching and service. This information will become handy when you formulate your statements in these areas. Start building various components of your dossier about a year from the date when you have to submit it. Ensure that your vitae includes all your past and present teaching and service activities. Highlight service on editorial boards and grant review committees. List every presentation at local, national or international conferences, and highlight the ones at which you were invited to speak since they carry more weight in judging your reputation in your field of study. Do the same with invitations to deliver research talks at other institutions. Help reviewers of your dossier learn about your specific role in publications.

Work on developing your personal statements on research, teaching and service. These statements should not be a simple regurgitation of what is included in your vitae. Information presented in this section does not even have to be in chronological order. Write in a way that reflects your unique professional identity. Tell a story and, if possible, use common themes in the statements on research, teaching and service—for example, your passion for discovering and teaching knowledge and for serving the community as a shared driver of all of your academic activities. Do your best to provide succinct summaries/take-home messages about the novelty and wider impact of your efforts under each of the three academic domains. In a way, you are helping reviewers by providing summaries they may use as sound bites in composing their reviews.

Interestingly, it is rather difficult for some to boast about themselves and adequately convey the real value of their research achievements. Most stop at listing journal impact factors, citation count and the number of invitations to give talks. I strongly advise you to blow your own horn as loud as you can. Talk about the uniqueness of your research questions, how your findings have contributed to society by bettering lives, and how your work possibly challenged dogmas in your field. Mention whether your research has led others to realign the direction of their own investigations or to make important discoveries based on yours. Talk about your personal philosophy, values and career goals. Clarify how they are reflected in the way you approach your academic duties. Talk about your future plans and goals. Provide assurance that being promoted to associate professor with tenure is not going to be your end game.

Accomplishments matter the most, but style and presentation also play a role, especially if the substance of the promotion dossier is not of highest quality or if the person expected to review the dossier is not an expert in your field of scholarship, which will likely apply to your dean and the provost or chancellor. Ideally, aim to impart a positive impression in both substance and presentation. Read recent promotion and tenure dossiers from your department and others. Select and adopt the style that appeals to you the most, one that speaks to your personality.

Cultivating External Reviewers

Network forward to cultivate reviewers. Become visible by getting involved in national organizations. Most institutions ask the promotion candidate for a list of suggested reviewers as a starting point, with indications of why they qualify as appropriate judges on the matter and their relationship (if any) with the faculty member coming up for promotion. Some institutions stipulate that reviewers be chosen from peer institutions with similar missions and stature. Reviewers cannot be collaborators or past advisors. The list should include those who are familiar with your work and know you personally, along with others who work in a similar or/related field but do not know you directly. This task is difficult in very specialized areas of research in which the cohort of scholars is rather small. The department will likely select some reviewers from your proposed list and add others.

One way to network early with potential reviewers is to invite them to give seminars in your college. Rub shoulders with key figures in your field at research conferences. Provide sincere and honest remarks on their recent publications and ask questions to seek elaboration on key points. When I was a junior faculty member, I made it an annual habit to send reprints of my publications to a select group of researchers in my field who I thought would qualify as reviewers when I submitted my promotion dossier in a couple of years. A few of these individuals were actually independently identified by the department as reviewers. Familiarity with my work enabled them to comment on the magnitude and timeline of progress I had made and the trajectory of professional growth I had achieved from one year to the next. Their intimate knowledge of my research added a personal touch to their assessment of my productivity.

In recommending reviewers, aim for those with high stature in the field and those who come from world-class institutions. This high caliber will impress internal reviewers of your dossier. However, be cognizant of the likelihood that reviewers may be asked whether you would be promoted and tenured in their own universities. Standards vary. While your institution may require having at least one major federal grant, elite universities may ask for several. In addition, differences in promotion standards may apply to the required number of publications and ranking of journals in which you publish. Thus, you should also include on the list of recommended reviewers some from peer institutions that have similar criteria for promotion and tenure.

At many institutions, junior faculty are allowed to specify who they do not wish to serve as external dossier reviewers. This list may include research competitors who are wedded to their own theories and are therefore unwilling to accept your challenges to their dogmas, or perhaps a disgruntled candidate for chairmanship of your department or deanship of the college who was not selected for the position by the search committee you served on. Limit your "do-not-contact" list to the smallest number possible. You do not want to give the impression that you have a high number of professional enemies. Avoid appearing paranoid by claiming that there are many scholars who you think plan to steal your ideas or sabotage your progress.

Keys to Promotion and Tenure

The quantity and quality of your teaching play an important role in the promotion and indefinite tenure decision. Students will judge your style of teaching and the content of your presentations and, even more so, evaluate you as a person who cares about their future. There are many ways for you to let students know that you do care. Being an extrovert, I enjoy chatting with students. At the end of my lectures, I hang around outside the classroom for a few minutes in case some students have questions about lecture content or need my help in addressing challenges they are facing in their education. I ask how they are doing both academically and in life in general. I use this opportunity to share common interests in hobbies and encourage them to keep a good life-school balance. Students know of my keen culinary interests, so they often exchange recipes with me. I share challenges I experienced when I was a student and how I managed to turn failures into success stories. I connect with them through LinkedIn and continue to offer my assistance to further their careers in the following years, even after they graduate. It thrills me to no end to read comments by students about my character, describing me as a person who has made a difference in their lives. These comments mean much more to me than those about the quality of my teaching.

Your professional success is mainly dependent on the caliber of your work and accomplishments—most important, the novelty of your research questions or results and their impact on society. This much you have control over. You just have to submit more high-quality manuscripts or grant applications. Unfortunately, this is not all. Your fate is partially decided by reviewers of grants and referees of manuscripts, so that many other factors contribute to the outcome, be it good or bad. Decisions may vary significantly depending on who from the review committee or editorial board is assigned your proposal or manuscript and whether the most qualified reviewer is available to referee the paper or participate in the review cycle of your grant application. As bad luck may have it, your worst and most unfair competitor may get invited as an ad hoc reviewer for your grant application due to the unavailability of a regular member of the review committee who would have normally been assigned to assess your proposal. Your best preemptive defense is to craft the most convincing documents you can come up with, ones that even your worst enemies would have a hard time finding major faults with.

Benefit from permitted extensions of the tenure clock. Many institutions grant additional years of the probationary period when a faculty member of either gender has or adopts a child. Take advantage of these leaves to allow you more time to demonstrate higher productivity through submitting papers and applying for research funding. Better yet, protect your research time by applying for a career development award. These awards mandate protecting 50–75 percent of a junior faculty member's effort toward research. They also provide funds to pursue professional development endeavors to fill in gaps in research expertise or soft skills (for instance, by attending courses and workshops). Your department head and dean must formally attest that this level of time protection is adhered to. For example, the Wellcome Trust offers research development awards in humanities, social sciences and bioethics. This program supports scholars who aim to develop leadership in creating sustainable research agendas that take risks and push academic boundaries, building a diverse and collaborative research community and developing the careers of its members. The National Science Foundation also offers prestigious career development grants to early-career faculty in the fields of mathematics, engineering and physics who have the potential to serve as academic role models in research and education and to lead advances in the mission of their department or organization. Activities pursued by early-career faculty awardees should build a firm foundation for a lifetime of leadership in integrating education and research.

For those in biomedical sciences, there are many examples of career development awards from the National Institutes of Health (NIH), as described on their website.

K01—Mentored Research Scientist Career Development Award

The purpose of this program is to provide support and protected time for an intensive, supervised career development experience in the biomedical, behavioral, or clinical sciences leading to research independence. Some institutes use the K01 to enhance workforce diversity, for individuals who propose to train in a new field, or for individuals who have had a hiatus in their research career.

K02—Independent Research Scientist Development Award

This program aims to foster the development of newly independent, outstanding scientists who can demonstrate the need for a period of intensive research to enable them to expand their potential to make significant contributions to their field of research.

K08—Mentored Clinical Scientist Research Career Development Award

The purpose of this program is to prepare clinically trained individuals for careers that have a significant impact on national health-related research needs. This program provides support and protected time for an intensive, supervised career development experience in the fields of biomedical, behavioral, or clinical research, including translational research.

K12—Clinical Scientist Institutional Career Development Program Award

The purpose of this program is to support institutional career development awards designed to prepare newly trained clinicians who have made a commitment to independent research careers and to facilitate their transition to more advanced support mechanisms (e.g., K08 and K23).

K22—Career Transition Award

The goal of this program is to facilitate the transition of investigators to independent, productive research careers. It is a one- or two-phase award—an initial period of mentored research, followed by a period of independent research at an extramural institution.

K23—Mentored Patient-Oriented Research Career Development Award

The purpose of this program is to support the career development of individuals with clinical doctoral degrees who have the potential to develop into productive clinical investigators and who have made a commitment to focus their research endeavors on patient-oriented research.

K99/R00—Pathway to Independence Award

The purpose of this program is to increase and maintain a strong cohort of new and talented, NIH-supported, independent investigators. This program is designed to facilitate a timely transition of outstanding postdoctoral researchers or clinician-scientists from mentored research positions to independent, tenure-track or equivalent faculty positions, and to provide independent NIH research support during the transition that will help these individuals launch competitive, independent research careers.

Maintaining a Focus While Allowing Space for Good Opportunities

You should consider three main elements when you decide on a research focus: first, what you are trained to do; second, what you are

8. The Path to Promotion and Tenure

passionate about; and third, which research questions have highest impact. It takes skill and experience to optimally balance diversification of research interests and questions and claiming expertise in specific subfields. I should also emphasize that a defined research focus does not conflict with diverse research questions or multidisciplinary collaborations to delve deeper in answering questions of common interest. By contrast, too much diversification would make one a research generalist who cannot claim fame or stature in specific areas of scholarship (i.e., a jack of all trades but a master of none).

The time of research generalists is over. There were days when scholars explored many different areas of research and contributed to various inventions that cannot be placed in a common bucket. Take Ben Franklin, for example. His inventions include the lightning rod, bifocal eyeglasses, swimming fins, the Franklin stove, the odometer and urinary catheter. There were no funding agencies in the Franklin's time; he financially supported his work with his extensive wealth and did the work himself. Additionally, research used to be more descriptive in nature. For example, the scientists who discovered the anesthetic properties of chloroform used themselves as experimental subjects who, for the sake of having fun, tried sniffing a variety of substances. They therefore did not need any research funding. I always find it quite amusing to read excerpts published in recent issues of the journal *Nature* from papers published in the same journal one hundred years ago. Here is an example from a paper published in 1917:

> In the summer of 1850 a small party of engineers arrived at Dover in order to lay a cable across the Channel.... At that period it was considered absolutely unnecessary to test copper wire.... The project excited much good-natured ridicule amongst the town folk. A man was found cutting the cable with his knife to show his friends that there was a wire inside.... On an ideal calm day the pioneers laid the cable from Dover to Grisnez, but they were destined to bitter disappointment ... the anchor or the trawl of a fishing-smack cut the cable in two not many hours after it was laid. They were thus prevented from carrying out experiments which would probably have enlightened them considerably on the laws governing the transmission of submarine signals. As it was, they had no conception that their failure was mainly due to ignorance of the laws of electrical capacity and induction.

The current research scenario is vastly different. Modern research requires very sophisticated equipment and expensive reagents. Very few scientists are able to financially support their own research. Therefore, the freedom of switching research directions often and asking questions that extend in multiple directions has been lost since it is usually not appreciated by funding agencies. One has to focus on their claim to fame and style their research track record in a way that appeals to those who are paying the bills. Reviewers readily see through attempts by some individuals to go after new sources of money regardless of the research questions they are genuinely interested in. Examples include those who suddenly change their research emphasis to benefit from increased funding for certain diseases, such as AIDS or COVID-19. I have coined the term "prostitution of science" to describe this insincere approach to supporting research.

Having said that, there are currently exceptional scientists who contribute to studies that vary widely in the type of questions being asked. Take, for example, an expert in magnetic resonance imaging. This person may have a specific focus on a given health condition or disease, but he or she could also contribute their expertise to studies of other diseases led by different investigators. However, such technical experts sometimes spread themselves too thin and may be thought of as investigators who are awaiting *any* question to be addressed by their favorite instruments. Someone described a scientist who has published imaging studies on topics ranging from Alzheimer's disease to toenail discoloration as "willing to image anything that moves"! This is not a good reputation to have. Other examples include statisticians who offer their services in study design and data analysis to researchers in a variety of disciplines. Most do not generate their own data or have a defined research interest. They just provide services as needed. Clever statisticians, however, also develop their own focused projects that rely on mining the extensive body of available databases.

Narrowing your research focus too much is not a good idea, either. I know scientists who have devoted their research careers to rare diseases that afflict only a very small number of people. These researchers had a hard time convincing grant reviewers of the wide impact of their investigations. At times when research dollars are scarce, it is natural for funding agencies to favor projects that have wide applicability and impact. It is also quite risky to stick with the same technique or methodological approach to answer research questions without keeping up with technological advancements that would allow for many more degrees of freedom. There were, for instance, days when biological research was based on making gross qualitative or quantitative observations of changes in animal behavior due to a disease or the administration of different pharmacological agents. Scientists working in these areas who refused to move on and supplement their research arsenal with modern molecular methodologies to explain the cellular basis of these behaviors were left behind. The old-fashioned questions they proposed were eventually dubbed "log cabin research."

Another type of harmful narrow focus is for one to be wedded to a specific hypothesis to the point of becoming blind to newly developed evidence against it. All scientists have their own pet hypotheses that are near and dear to their hearts. While we pursue testing these hypotheses with fervor and passion, our eyes should be wide open to evidence to the contrary. I have seen blind love and unhealthy attachment to favorite theories cause researchers to reject manuscripts or grant proposals by others that attempt to legitimately disprove their pet hypothesis, either in part or in total. This is not good practice of scholarly investigation. It actually leads to stalling scientific advancement. It is reminiscent of the dark days four centuries ago when the idea of a heliocentric solar system was so controversial that the Catholic Church classified it as a heresy and warned the Italian astronomer Galileo Galilei to abandon it.

It is important to convey the main focus of your research to both experts and non-experts in your field. Your promotion and tenure dossier will be reviewed and evaluated by different individuals and committees, starting with your department faculty and ending with the university provost. The more the process progresses, the less familiar your area of research will appear to those who read your dossier. You need to help those folks figure out what you are an expert in; they certainly will not invest the time to actually read your publications word for word to gain this knowledge. One simple trick is for you to define a few terms to include in the headings of most or all of your published articles (e.g., Alzheimer's disease, tablet dissolution, Greek history, bereavement, centrifugal force, animal husbandry). Non-expert dossier reviewers will therefore readily know what your research focus is and what you are known for.

Keeping a Healthy Balance

Your journey toward promotion and tenure does not have to feel like a prison sentence. There are healthy ways to travel this road while maintaining balance in various aspects of your life. Seek relief by doing pleasurable things with your family and friends and on your own. A relaxed mind is a more efficient mind. Many of my European friends who are also in academia wonder why their American counterparts seem to be addicted to work. One of them made a clever observation that a collaborator from the United States finally committed to take time off work, but he spent it making repairs to his home. One may argue that his activity could bring him joy and a chance to get his mind off professional work. A valid counterargument, however, is that going on an extensive hike in the mountains or sunbathing by the ocean is certainly further removed from being categorized as work than fixing shingles on a house. Getting away from the norm is both physically and spiritually important for cleansing and rejuvenating the soul.

Celebrate small and big successes. Establishing prominence in one's field usually takes a couple of decades to come to fruition. It involves the culmination of many types of activities and accomplishments, including publishing papers, giving research presentations, teaching various classes and obtaining grants from a variety of sources. It also encompasses gradually building a network of collaborators and mentors. One would be mistaken to wait until they receive a glamorous award that reflects their high status in the scientific community before they start acknowledging and celebrating their success. Promise yourself rewards that bring you pleasure for accomplishing individual milestones in long-term projects (including the promotion and tenure journey itself). I always treat myself to dinner with my wife at one of our favorite restaurants whenever I "submit" a large grant proposal. My justification is that writing and submitting the best proposal I could produce are the only steps over which I have control. I have no say in what transpires after that. Of course, this ritual has never stopped me from celebrating again once a grant application gets funded, this time with my entire research team and collaborators.

It is also wise to know when to stop and change tracks. A few years back, I was at a critical juncture in the professional aspect of my life. I was quite unhappy with the trajectory of my career but was scared to pursue a different path. I thought things might change for the better if I maintained my resilience and continued on the familiar road I had followed for many years. I was fortunate that a good friend of mine taught me a very valuable and timely lesson over a delicious lunch at a Chinese restaurant on campus. She said, "Only the wise realize when to stop trying and make a timely decision to get out of a bad situation. Others keep going, hoping for miracles to happen and circumstances to change." One may apply this wisdom in deciding whether to terminate a research project that has proven to be intellectually and financially consuming without having produced results for a long time. What usually makes one hesitate to pull the plug is that so much effort has been invested and will be wasted if such a project is abandoned at this late stage. If you are ever faced with a dilemma of this kind, use your skills as a scholar to rely on trajectories and projections in making your decisions. Cutting your losses and running away may be the wisest option in certain circumstances. Remember, only the wise know when to stop and change tracks.

Which of Your Accomplishments Matter the Most?

I have read hundreds of external reviews in support of promoting faculty at different ranks. In the majority of these letters, there is detailed evaluation of the candidate's publication track record in terms of numbers, venues and citation numbers. The letters also include a narrative on the impact of the promotion candidate's work and their stature in their scholarly area of specialization. The same level of emphasis applies to research funding in terms of dollars, consistency and prestige of funding sources. In sharp contrast, referee letters usually include cursory coverage of the candidate's teaching, usually with brief comments on teaching quality as judged by students and peers. Comments on service are usually the briefest. Reviewers often place more emphasis on editorial services and membership on national or international committees of professional societies or federal agencies, especially those involved in grant funding. Obviously, one does not get asked to serve in this capacity unless they have demonstrated special achievements and recognition. Less is typically said about service on college or university committees, since outside reviewers are often unaware of the impact of these committees and the time commitment dedicated to serving on them. These arguments further support the notion that adding extra components to your vitae in the research section means much more than serving on another committee or teaching another course. It is extremely rare (perhaps even unheard of) for a junior faculty member in a research-intensive university to get tenure on the basis of excellence in teaching and service while showing few results in the research arena. Recognition of these facts should guide you in deciding whether to accept or decline requests for added responsibilities that do not contribute to your research accomplishments, as they will undoubtedly take away from your research time. Do not buy into the belief that making everybody happy by agreeing to new assignments will get you tenured. Keep your eyes on the prize—that is, promotion and tenure. Pay attention to what counts the most (i.e., research productivity).

In his book *Tenure Hacks*, Russell James spells it out quite clearly: "Do you want to win the [tenure] game? Win the curriculum vitae. Winning the vitae isn't about sitting down at the end of a year and trying to remember the stuff you have been doing. Winning the vitae means thinking about it every day, every day. It means filtering every work decision through the lens of the vitae. Before spending time on anything work related, ask yourself, 'how will this look on my vitae?' First consider 'can I put this on my vitae?' Next ask 'if I put it on my vitae, will it make it stronger or just longer?'" James even suggests that it is better for you to spend time with your family, go to a movie or even take a nap than to do something that does not conform to these criteria! However, this opinion may represent an extreme in self-protection. Taken literally, James' advice may make you look like a selfish citizen and could lead to losing important supportive relationships. It is best to assess every request for additional service or teaching on its own merit through careful and holistic cost-benefit analysis. (There is more information on when and how to say no in chapter 4, "Time and Energy Management.")

On Publishing

Both the number and the quality of publications count in the tenure game. Pay special attention to annotation of each publication listed in your vitae. State your specific role in conceiving the research question, designing experiments, analyzing data, and writing the manuscript. Being first or last on the list of authors means different things in different fields of scholarship. You therefore need to highlight articles on which you served as senior corresponding author. This information is quite important, especially if your research is based on collaboration with other scientists, in which case your name will usually be among many others on the authors list. More elaborate delineation of your role is needed if the published work was the result of collaboration with senior researchers who are well established in their field to indicate that you played a major role in the generation of such publications.

Some institutions also require including the number of citations of an article by others and impact factor of journals. Reviewers of dossiers for promotion from assistant to associate professor with tenure typically do not expect a high number of citations since this requires significant time to build up from the date when a publication comes out in print. However, I have seen citations of more than a hundred for seminal papers published by very junior faculty. I recall meeting a junior faculty member in my university during his first year on the job. He shared with me his dream of developing a research method that would enable him to turn specific genes on and off at will to study their role in various cellular processes. A year later, I was impressed to see a paper on establishing this technique in his laboratory published in the prestigious journal *Nature*. This paper was cited very frequently as soon as it was published. In little more than a decade, this junior faculty member has become a distinguished full professor, one who receives frequent invitations to give talks at premier institutions around the world.

At the early stages of my career, I used to look up to such successful junior scientists to give me inspiration for making it to that level of accomplishment if I put my heart and soul into my work. I recommend that you do the same, but do not feel discouraged if you do not make it to the same high mountain peak as quickly as others. Earthshaking discoveries that lead one to a distinguished status in the research community do not happen that often, as they usually are the culmination of a variety of factors (for example, the type of research, training and experience, academic environment and creativity). Serendipity also plays a crucial role in seminal discoveries. Being at the right place at the right time matters. Memorable examples of the role of serendipity include a scientist's observation during a seminar of the sequence of the analgesic peptides—the enkephalins—within the sequence of very large pituitary hormone. Another is the unearthing of the underground catacombs of Kom El Shoqafa in Alexandria, Egypt, when a donkey fell through a hole in the ground. These catacombs have special historical significance since their features and content merge Pharaonic, Roman and Greek cultural aspects. A lucky professor of archeology happened to be on hand to witness the poor donkey falling through the cracks.

Be aware that some journals in a very narrow area of research may not have a high overall impact factor, but they may be in the top quartile in their respective fields. Make sure you highlight these facts in annotating your publications. It is not a good idea to only publish a few articles in premier journals, nor is it advisable to have a high number of papers published in mediocre journals that are known to have an acceptance rate close to 100 percent. A good mix works best. Be wise and realistic in assessing the novelty and impact of your work when selecting a journal. If you and your mentors truly believe a given piece of work meets the high standards of a top journal in your field, then go for it. It is worth a try, especially since the turnaround time for having the editorial office triage your manuscript to be sent out for reviews or reject it flat out is usually pretty quick. If you receive a rejection, go for a second-tier journal.

Deciding to try the highest-impact journals also depends on where you are on the tenure clock. If you are far along in the game but still need more publications, I do not recommend that you risk submitting manuscripts to the most prestigious journals in your area of scholarship. Even if your work is deemed good enough to send out for reviews, you will likely be asked to perform significant additional work that will take a long time to complete. It is also not unusual for papers submitted to such elite journals to undergo several rounds of revision and resubmission. In addition, journal selection depends on whether postdoctoral fellows or graduate students who are about to finish their training and move on to the next stage of their careers are involved in the work. It is harmful to their career trajectory to aim at perfecting every piece of work to qualify it for prime time. Like you, they need to have a good number and mix of trophy and medium-size fish on their string at the end of the day. Also realize that once they leave your group, they will become busy with their new job and may not have the time or the initiative necessary to complete writing their unpublished work.

I have also heard it said that four figures and two tables constitute a paper to be published somewhere! While numbers matter when it comes to evaluating publication productivity, do not be tempted to divide your research findings into minimally publishable units just to be able to claim more publications on your curriculum vitae. Sometimes this practice (especially if it becomes habitual) will deprive you of the opportunity to finish the research and publish wholesome and highly impactful pieces of work in top journals. As a friend of mine elegantly put it, there is eventually a home for any piece of work. However, there is a bottom line below which you should not drop. It is a bad idea to publish work in one of the numerous unranked journals that sprout on almost a daily basis. These are the journals that send you invitations to serve on their editorial boards if you submit papers and accept paying exuberant page charges. Do not be fooled by noticing names of highly respected scientists among the membership of the editorial boards of such journals. Some of these fly-by-night unscrupulous publishers concoct such impressive—but fake—membership lists without the knowledge or consent of those whose names are listed.

Do not waste any valuable but incomplete pieces of research. Find creative ways to add to the unfinished work to make it worthy of publication in a decent journal. In my own experience, assigning such tasks to graduate students doing rotations in my laboratory or to summer undergraduates works best. In fact, some ended up being coauthors on publications resulting from their work.

What about writing review articles and book chapters? How valuable are those in building an impressive vitae? The bottom line is that they are not valued as much as peer-reviewed original-research publications. They also require significant time and effort to write. Therefore, I advise you to focus your efforts on publishing your research findings. There are exceptions, of course. Becoming engaged in writing a review article or a chapter in a book would be a good idea if your research is at a lull for any reason—for example, if you are waiting for animals to breed or are unable to carry out archeological excavation in a country that is affected by war or natural catastrophes. (A case in point is the closure of research operations across the country during the recent COVID-19 pandemic.) Another creative approach to writing review articles and book chapters is to collaborate with one of your senior graduate students or postdoctoral trainees in composing these articles. Listing this type of publication on their curriculum vitae is impressive at their early career stage. Finally, do not turn down requests to write review articles for top journals in your field or to contribute a chapter to a new edition of a highly respected textbook that is commonly chosen by instructors for their classes (for example, *Gray's Anatomy*, *Goodman and Gilman's The Pharmacological Basis of Therapeutics*, *A*

History of Archaeological Thought, The People's History in the United States). These books are considered the holy grail of knowledge in their respective fields.

On Research Funding

Research grants are associated with overhead (administrative or indirect costs). The amount varies depending on funding sources, type of research and agreements between individual institutions and funding agencies. This money is supposed to pay for research and office space, utilities, animal husbandry, and so forth. In reality, however, it is not enough to cover all of these expenses. In fact, universities end up losing significant amounts of money in covering the extra costs. Why, then, are research grants so highly coveted? The answer is simple. Research-intensive universities recognize their unique role and responsibility in being a haven for the discovery of new knowledge through research, thereby contributing to improving various facets of life. Additionally, the total amount of funding to a research-intensive institution determines its prestige, reputation and ranking among peers. This stature entices students and outstanding faculty. It also motivates private donors to give more money, as they feel confident that their contributions will be put to good use. Finally, research grants support faculty salaries and graduate students' stipends and tuition.

The time will eventually come when you will not be able to renew one or more of your research grants. It is therefore advisable to diversify sources of financial support for your research in order to add security to the stream of funding. Running out of money is not a pretty picture. You will have to fire highly skilled people in whom you invested significant training time. Your graduate students who are about to finish their dissertation work will be in limbo; it will be too late in the game for them to change research advisors. If you are in the biomedical sciences, life sciences or engineering fields, seek funding from more than one federal agency (the National Institutes of Health, the National Science Foundation, the Department of Defense). Analogous resources for the humanities and social sciences include the National Endowment for the Humanities, the American Educational Research Association, and the American Political Science Association. Complement federal funding with financial support from state offices and national foundations. Examples include the Alfred P. Sloan Foundation, the American Association of University Women, and the American Council of Learned Societies.

There are also private funding sources for your research. Work with the development officers in your college or institution to help you seek funding from private donors who may have a stake in your research project—for example, having a family member who is afflicted by the disease that is the focus of your research. However, do not spontaneously make connections with such private parties on your own. Raising funds is a science and art in its own right. Institutions usually have lists of wealthy individuals to approach for large sums of money at opportune times. Having a researcher directly contact these individuals to ask for tens (or even hundreds of thousands) of dollars messes up the big game.

Withdrawing Your Application for Promotion and Tenure

While denial of tenure is not very common, it is still a reality with which some junior faculty may have to contend. Being denied tenure could be associated with significant psychological trauma and possibly a permeant stain on the official record that would negatively affect one's chances of getting a job at other institutions. Denial of tenure is less damaging if one works for a top-tier research institution that has excessively high standards.

There are usually overt and covert warning signs that a junior faculty member may not be on a trajectory to achieve indefinite tenure. These are usually communicated in annual performance reviews or through feedback from mentors. However, such negative signs may not become clear until the early stages of promotion dossier evaluation—for instance, receiving shaky enthusiasm for promotion from the department or college committees or receiving lukewarm support from external referees.

One option in these situations is to take a chance and move forward knowing that the odds are not favorable. Another is to withdraw the bid for promotion and tenure. If one chooses to proceed with the process, I highly recommend that they start applying for jobs at other institutions as soon as possible, while preparing to withdraw the application for promotion before a final negative verdict is pronounced at the institutional level. He or she should identify allies in their current department (preferably senior faculty) to write letters of reference in support of job applications.

I have colleagues who used projections for not making tenure as a wakeup call to reconsider their career and life priorities. Some decided that the demanding journey of a tenure-track or tenured faculty member was not for them. They did not want to continue such a highly stressful and competitive journey in getting grants funded and papers published. They discovered more passion for teaching or service than research and were glad to change their career paths to benefit from their strengths at the same institution or others.

8. The Path to Promotion and Tenure

What If You Did Not Get Tenure?

If your quest for promotion and tenure is denied, allow yourself time to mourn and vent. When you calm down, start objectively assessing the situation and what really led to the negative outcome. Involve your mentors in helping you perform a fair and educated analysis and weigh different options for moving forward. An assistant professor may choose to appeal being denied tenure at the level of the institution and even in courts, if such becomes necessary. The odds of success are better if there is compelling evidence that the negative decision was based on some type of discrimination or retaliation. I do not recommend taking this route if you have a tenuous case to make. Becoming labeled by peers as a litigative troublemaker will make others hesitant to hire you.

Another option is applying for a job in other universities. One should be aware, however, that it may be difficult to make a lateral move to a peer institution of equal stature. It would be wise to seek employment at a lower-tier institution for a few years to allow time to build a strong case for moving back up. While it may be difficult to get a tenured position right away, one may be able to successfully negotiate a shorter period for coming up for promotion and tenure at the new academic home. This option would actually be advantageous not only to the applicant but also to their new institution. Their ability to make it to the finish line will be assessed in a short time period, thereby avoiding the cost of investing the regular six years only to meet with another disappointing decision.

If a faculty member who is denied tenure chooses to pursue this route, they should structure their cover letters for job applications in a positive way in detailing both past accomplishments and future plans. They should acknowledge (but not dwell on) failing to make tenure at their current institution and should not share conspiracy theories regarding why their petition was denied. The applicant must be realistic and describe what they would have done differently if given a second chance (for instance, developing better projects or using better time management skills), in which case they should provide specific plans for mitigating these deficiencies. They should structure their vitae to reflect what projects are close to being finished, including publications and grant applications. He or she should describe how they see themselves fitting in the department they are applying to, perhaps even better than they do in their present department. Some faculty who are outstanding and passionate teachers may have been denied tenure by an institution that values research dollars and publications more than teaching. Their special strengths would be a great fit for a smaller institution where teaching excellence is the highest priority.

Should you be denied tenure, an analysis of your own strengths, career goals and preferred life-work balance may lead you to consider employment outside academia. Do not think less of yourself if you reach this conclusion; the days when non-academic PhDs were considered and treated as second-class citizens are over. One can clearly see this change in the fact that the brightest doctoral graduates and postdoctoral trainees often prefer non-academic positions, even though they could easily become assistant professors at one of the best universities in the country or around the globe. The options beyond academia are endless. You might consider working for a federal agency (for example, the Food and Drug Administration or the National Aeronautics and Space Administration). You may also choose to work as a market research analyst or a technical writer, a political advisor, an economics analyst, or a writer for a newspaper or a television station. A colleague of mine who is passionate about design and writing left academia to work for a biotechnology company, where he is responsible for designing graphics and instructions for molecular biology reagent kits. Another left a position in a prestigious institution to become a grant review officer at the National Institutes of Health. Neither regretted making this bold transition.

The transferrable skills one builds while getting a doctorate afford great versatility in career choices. The most important of these are analytical skills. In doing research, one learns how to critically evaluate and distill information, identify gaps in knowledge, determine the importance of specific data points, design pertinent questions, analyze data and disseminate the results as publications or presentations. These skills apply to a wide variety of careers. You should answer the following questions in order to determine the degree of matching a given career to your aptitude and personal preferences: What is your real career passion? Are you oriented to the overall picture or to details? Do you prefer dealing with data or people? What do other people say you are good at or most often ask you for help with? You should also prioritize the elements of an ideal job in terms of money, time flexibility, freedom in exchange of information, and geographical location.

Summary

Reaching the rank of associate professor with indefinite tenure is both a sprint and a marathon. There is so much to be accomplished in a limited time span, but one also needs to expend their time and energy judiciously to get to the finish line without crashing halfway. In your first few weeks on the job, you should start keeping track of your accomplishments and document them in your vitae. Identify key figures in your field, and network with them in anticipation of having them serve as external reviewers of your promotion dossier. Most important, understand both published and word-of-mouth criteria for promotion with indefinite tenure. Bear these criteria in mind as you prioritize your activities.

Self-Reflection Exercises

- What have you done so far to cultivate external reviewers of your promotion dossier? What else do you need to do toward accomplishing this important goal?
- Take notes on all your activities in a given week, and then rank them according to their importance in contributing to achieving promotion with tenure.
- At the end of each semester, tally the responsibilities you took on that have minimal bearing on your path to promotion. Design a strategy to get rid of these tasks and avoid similar ones in the future.
- Establish a timeline for the milestones for each item on your list of targeted short-term and long-term accomplishments based on its current state of completion.
- Take note of unfinished pieces of scholarly work and design a plan to complete them and make them ready for submission to a journal.

9

Maintaining the Vitality of Mid-Career and Senior Faculty

Mid-career and senior faculty are essential to maintaining an institution's vitality. They are valued for their experience, their stature and their service as role models for junior colleagues. Senior faculty, particularly full professors, currently represent the majority of faculty in well-established institutions due to the elimination of obligatory retirement by a certain age.

Being tenured offers many perks, but it also imposes obligations to continue to be productive. I know some faculty who have remained quite productive past their eighties. However, I also know others in their fifties who have lost interest in pursuing a competitive research career. It is sad to see this happening since these individuals, who have given up for one reason or another, have to remain in a coasting mode for another couple of decades or more. This situation will likely result in loss of self-worth and is therefore psychologically degrading. Loss of faculty productivity at this young age also has a tremendous negative impact on their institutions. Faculty stagnation imparts a bad image that may harm recruitment of outstanding faculty, graduate students and postdoctoral trainees. Moreover, such inertia and disengagement are usually infectious and may therefore cause others to slow down. Most important, the high salary of a disengaged full professor may easily be sufficient to hire two highly productive assistant professors who are looking for employment to start running a vigorous, state-of-the-art research program. There are so many exceptionally talented junior scholars out there waiting for an academic position to open up.

Merits of Achieving Associate Professorship with Tenure

Getting indefinite tenure provides job security and a feeling of safety. At this juncture, you have learned the ropes and know how to navigate the institution. You will enjoy more academic freedom and confidence, allowing you to engage in academic debate without fear of negative repercussions. In essence, you will establish your right to think and act freely according to your beliefs and become the true you in research, teaching and service. To be clear, however, academic freedom does not entitle a faculty member to harass, intimidate, abuse or impose their views on colleagues, staff, trainees or students. Nor can a tenured faculty member act in any way that violates university, state and federal regulations. The most important guidelines to adhere to are those regarding responsible research conduct. Academic freedom does not allow a scholar to plagiarize or falsify data. Furthermore, being tenured does not offer protection against sanctions due to poor performance. A tenured faculty member who repeatedly receives poor teaching evaluations from students and peers may be denied salary raises or career development opportunities (for example, sabbatical leaves).

When you get to this stage of your academic career, you will have the luxury of picking and choosing among research directions and projects. You have protection if you decide to embark on more challenging research questions, the ones that are both risky and highly impactful, or to move from publishing many small papers to producing only a few that have much higher quality and impact. You will be able to decide on the upper limit of engagement in new projects to allow time for self and family, while avoiding the stress caused by carrying an excessive load of responsibilities.

You also have more freedom to do things in a way that suits you and avoids academic bureaucracy. When I served as associate dean for graduate education in my college, I wanted to develop a series of workshops for graduate students on soft skills. I proposed this idea to the faculty, who in turn asked whether I had strong evidence that students were missing such skills. To my utter surprise, they even questioned the value added by acquiring these skills, even if students express an interest in gaining them. As is usual in an academic setting, a couple of task forces were formed to explore these questions and were asked to report on their findings in six months. If you ask me to name one thing I despise about academia, it would be such bureaucracy, hands down. To me, the goal was quite important. In fact, I was asked directly by student representatives from different graduate programs in the college about the possibility of organizing workshops of this nature. Furthermore, bookshelves and the internet are full of indisputable evidence that mastering soft skills is necessary for success in any career direction graduate students opt to pursue upon obtaining their degrees. They undoubtedly need to master writing, presenting, and conflict resolution, and they must develop skills in interviewing for jobs, grantsmanship and networking. I had to look for other solutions to get the job done. Being a tenured professor gave me the freedom to do that.

I ended up striking a deal with various student organizations in the university at large to offer these workshops as part of their programs and initiatives. This approach did not require the blessings of my college administration or the faculty. I started on a small scale to test the waters by offering a workshop on job interviewing skills and another on resolving conflicts between students and their advisors. I was pleasantly surprised to find that the large auditorium where I presented was full to its capacity, with standing room only. Many of the attendees were actually graduate students from my own college. Student evaluations of the events were outstanding, with many requests for more workshops on developing other soft skills. Of course, I did not run to my colleagues to show them what they had missed getting credit for. I trusted that word of mouth would eventually reach them. This initial success motivated me to build up these workshops into a year-long series that covers many topics relevant to helping graduate students succeed in their career endeavors.

Does Tenure Guarantee You a Job for Life?

While by definition indefinite tenure provides a permanent faculty appointment, there are circumstances in which tenure may be revoked. One example is having a mandate to downsize the faculty upon declaration of financial stringency by an institution. Such situations, however, usually jeopardize the jobs of tenure-track and contract faculty before they affect tenured faculty. It is also important to realize that tenure is associated with a tenure home, usually a department in a college or a college that has a single department divided into several multidisciplinary units. Sometimes universities decide to eliminate departments or colleges, perhaps for financial reasons or to increase operational efficiency. This change would allow institutions to fire faculty employed in the eliminated units, tenured and non-tenured alike.

Preparing for Promotion to Full Professor

It is best to start preparing for promotion to full professor in a few years as soon as you achieve the rank of associate professor with tenure. The process is still fresh in your mind. Consult the guidelines for promotion to find out what it takes to get promoted to the next level. Determine the required number and caliber of publications and research grants, and create a plan to meet these requirements. Identify roadblocks and devise approaches to circumvent them. It should be noted that criteria for

9. Maintaining the Vitality of Mid-Career and Senior Faculty 165

promotion to full professorship in many institutions are less clear than those for promotion to associate professorship. However, there is consensus regarding the need to demonstrate significant national and international reputation in the field of scholarly inquiry. Of course, this requirement is intimately related to your research productivity and dissemination of your findings in the form of publications in highly ranked journals. There is usually more emphasis on the quality and impact of publications than numbers when one is being evaluated for promotion to full professor. You also need to seek opportunities to serve on national and international committees and task forces. Target key international conferences where you may connect with known figures in your area of scholarship who could provide testimonials to your stature and the impact of your research findings on the field. These connections will also help you initiate productive research collaborations.

As discussed later in this chapter, you must continue to guard your research time from being invaded by additional teaching and service. You have essentially lost the protection you enjoyed during your junior years. More important, designate specific times for writing, as this particular activity often falls through the cracks while being bombarded with so many other responsibilities.

Evaluating the Performance of Tenured Faculty

Senior faculty, like their junior colleagues, are asked to submit an annual report of their scholarly, teaching and service activities. This report is used as the basis for a performance assessment by the department head or a department review committee. The results of such reviews influence merit salary raises and renewal of contracts for clinical, teaching or research faculty who are not tenured. Department heads and deans should apply different measures of productivity at various faculty career stages. While junior faculty should have a high number of publications, focus their research emphasis and avoid risky projects, senior faculty should be encouraged to pursue long-term, sometimes high-risk but high-impact projects that may result in fewer but more influential publications and contribution to new knowledge. Senior faculty participation in service is unique and highly valued because of their experience. Unfortunately, service is usually assessed by the number of committees and hours of meetings regardless of impact or roles played by the individual. Mentoring is often not appropriately recognized or rewarded. In a recent conversation with a department chair, I inquired why he does not include mentoring as one of the categories in reviewing faculty productivity. His response was that "there is no need.

Everybody does it. It is expected." I truly believe that this approach is absolutely discouraging and demoralizing to those who dedicate significant time to mentoring junior faculty and trainees.

Astute department leaders use the review process as an opportunity to discuss with mid-career and senior faculty their trajectory and goals for the coming years. It is best to formulate an individual development plan as a collaborative endeavor between the faculty and the department head. The plan should contain short- and long-term goals, along with strategies to achieve them with specific actions and a timeline of deliverables. This plan should serve as the foundation of subsequent annual reviews. Well-thought-out annual reviews therefore represent a stitch in time that provides timely guidance to continued high performance while avoiding tenure burnout. Unfortunately, while recommendations by department heads geared toward avoiding stagnation of senior faculty may be taken seriously by some, others may let these proposals fall by the wayside.

Post-Tenure Review

Many universities have instituted extensive reviews of tenured faculty at the ranks of associate and full professor, usually every four years. In some institutions, this process is triggered any time a faculty member receives two consecutive "unsatisfactory" annual performance evaluations. The review is designed to seriously evaluate productivity in relation to expectations for a senior faculty member at a given rank. The post-tenure review system was created to enable institutions to get rid of deadwood faculty who have stopped being productive in research, teaching and service—that is, those who have become professionally incompetent. In practice, however, it is almost unheard of for a tenured faculty member to be fired as a result of the post-tenure review process. Thus, many consider this laborious scheme inconsequential and a waste of time. However, post-tenure review still serves the important function of working with tenured faculty to establish development plans and strategies to maintain their vitality.

An ideal post-tenure review includes all contributions a faculty member makes to their academic environment. In evaluating teaching, for example, there should be consideration of the individual's ability to meet the needs of a diverse population of students and to develop student-centered learning strategies. Students and trainees should be polled to determine the impact of the faculty member being evaluated on their knowledge, abilities, and progress of their career. In regard to scholarship, special consideration should be given to projects that involve collaborations with or high impact on the community. This type of community engagement is important in letting the public become aware of what goes on inside the "ivory tower." Senior faculty should also be valued for their impact on their field of scholarly pursuit. They should be rewarded for their role in training graduate students and postdoctoral fellows, as well as mentoring junior faculty. They should also be valued for serving as thought leaders who effect paradigm shifts in the academic mission, both in their institution and at the national level through serving on key committees in federal and professional organizations.

Changing Responsibilities After Tenure

Junior faculty in most research-intensive universities are protected to allow them ample time to establish their research programs. They are usually assigned a low teaching and service load. It is rare that a tenure-track assistant professor would be asked to direct a course or chair a committee. However, the kid gloves are off once tenure is achieved (sometimes even once the promotion dossier is submitted for evaluation). Senior faculty tend to enthusiastically nominate the newly promoted associate professor for additional teaching and service duties. The honeymoon is over, kiddo! It's time to pay back and carry your weight! Associate professors will likely be assigned service on higher college and university committees and task forces now that they have the experience and credibility. They may also be asked to play a leading role in revising the curriculum. Some are even appointed as department heads. Together, these significant changes in roles and responsibilities mandate readjusting one's priorities and effort distribution.

The Tenure Malaise

Mid-career professorship is generally associated with a lack of clear expectations combined with diminished support. Some faculty burn out following the stressful journey to tenure and do not bother to pursue the path to full professorship. This goal no longer seems to fit into their ambitions or priorities. A recent survey of faculty in my college indicated that about a quarter of them are disengaged but would like to find a way to reengage. Sadly, another quarter expressed comfort in being disengaged without having the desire to reconnect with their academic environment. In watching eternally disengaged colleagues, I could sense some becoming antagonists to progress of the academic mission in the college. They diverted their energies and plentiful spare time to oppose "any" proposal posed by "anybody." Sometimes they would even strongly criticize proposals they had initiated a couple of years back, having forgotten their previous involvement. (I took pleasure in reminding them of this history!) Similar negative behaviors must be controlled before they become toxic to the work environment.

While obtaining tenure provides many opportunities to enhance faculty productivity, there are forces that work against maintaining vitality, both overt and covert. Becoming stagnant is essentially the result of job security due to granting indefinite tenure combined with a lack of significant carrots and sticks regarding further career advancement. Let me start by discussing the lack of attractive rewards for maintaining hard work. Merit raises are often minimal, with minute differences between performance stars and those who barely meet expectations. Even worse, a senior full professor who serves on a search committee to recruit an assistant professor may discover that their department is willing to offer candidates for this position a salary that equals (or sometimes exceeds) that of most full professors in the college. Institutions must compete for outstanding junior faculty candidates, which leads to continuous escalation in their market value.

A highly productive tenured faculty member may end up doubting their wisdom as they watch unproductive colleagues lead a happy and relaxed life. These poor performers do not have to deal much with the stresses of meeting deadlines and confronting rejection of papers and grant applications. They have ample time to enjoy their families, friends and hobbies. What compounds these feelings even more is when family members stop understanding why a tenured faculty member has to give up spending time with them and continue to put in longer hours of work, even when they are home. They were under a false pretense that their sacrifices were limited to the probationary period of the faculty appointment. This situation naturally leads to a gradual loss of family support and empathy. In addition, repeated rejections (particularly of grant proposals) may create an inferiority complex that stops mid-career and senior faculty from trying again. This sad scenario is often the result of failing to keep up with modern research technology and methodology, due to lack of good mentoring and having to attend to the myriad of responsibilities added to a tenured faculty member's portfolio.

Women faculty face special challenges. They often postpone having children until they successfully jump through the tenure hoop. Children require attention and nurturing, which naturally takes away from the focus on work matters. Furthermore, maternity leave may disrupt a faculty member's momentum and disconnect them from recent advances in the field.

Challenges and Solutions to Maintaining the Vitality of Mid-Career and Senior Faculty

Maintaining the vigor of mid-career and senior faculty is supported by both intrinsic and extrinsic factors. Intrinsic elements include subject knowledge, keeping up with recent technological advancements, work habits, diversity of projects and funding sources, commitment, passion, socialization and networking. Extrinsic factors include institutional support for career development, rewarding, positive climate and resources. Ideally, institutions will provide a critical mass of investigators with similar or related research interests. Strategic institutions keep this fact in mind when they recruit new faculty. They also cluster researchers from different departments and colleges to be physically close to those who do research on similar topics to stimulate collaborations. The local academic community of the department and college is also a great source of professional and psychological support. To remain vital, however, a faculty member should reach out to communities within and outside their institution. He or she should establish a strong network with national and international scholars in their field. This network plays an important role in providing validation, mentoring and collaborations that ensure continued renewal.

Many senior faculty started their academic careers when research funding was abundant. Advancement of research technology and methodology was rather slow. It was common for a researcher to keep asking different questions using the same techniques and methods throughout their entire career. This practice was quite acceptable as long as the questions were novel. In fact, staying the course using the same experimental setup used to provide credence and confidence in the researcher's expertise. In the past few decades, however, new methodologies have been developed to make it possible to ask questions that are more mechanistic or deeper in their nature and scope. Examples include DNA cloning and mutagenesis, transfection of cells with foreign genes, gene suppression, genetic analysis, cell and organ culture, immunohistochemistry, proteomics, metabolomics, informatics, simulation, artificial intelligence, and use of laser technology in archeological excavations. Lately, the pace of developing these tools has markedly accelerated. Such advancements have led grant and journal reviewers to expect more mechanistic rather than phenomenological research questions. In essence, the main direction of many lines of research has changed from asking "what happens?" to wondering "how does it happen?" This change has required senior faculty who have not kept up with the pace of technological advances to alter their methods. Fortunately, there are several approaches to acquire this knowledge (for example, by attending workshops on specific technologies and methods or taking a sabbatical to learn them from an expert group).

The best way to maintain vitality after you get promoted to associate professor with tenure is to keep up your momentum. Immediately start writing down your short- and long-term goals and plans. Assess your strengths, developmental needs, strategies and milestones. Documenting these thoughts will create a very useful roadmap that will guide you to remain rejuvenated. Contemplate what really matters to you, with special consideration of whether your top priority is to achieve fame, wealth, or simply the satisfaction of making significant scholarly discoveries. Assess the competitiveness of your research program in terms of the questions you ask and the methodology you use. Some research directions become stale and therefore unattractive to funding agencies and publishers. Think of how you could elevate your teaching skills a couple of notches and what modern teaching tools you would like to experiment with. Consider whether pursuing academic administration may be a possibility in the near or distant future.

Those who work hard during their junior years mainly for the sake of attaining tenure as a final endpoint will likely fizzle out upon reaching this short-term goal. A junior faculty member should work hard for the reasons they chose to be in academia in the first place—namely, to teach the next generation of professionals and scholars and to unearth new knowledge. I believe there is no joy comparable to designing a new medication for a common disease, inventing a better heat-resistant material to be used to construct outer shields of spacecraft or discovering fossils of an extinct animal. Similar self-fulfillment becomes evident when a faculty member learns of the success of one of their students or trainees. When faculty slow down or stop because of weak drive, their job satisfaction goes down the drain and gets replaced with boredom, stagnation and self-doubt.

Maintain a competitive spirit—honest and fair competition, that is. In general, the main driver for scientists is the joy of discovering things first. This way they maintain the child inside them who wants to brag "I found it first!"—the same child who asks "why" almost every minute of the day. Nourish this drive by keeping the scientist kid inside you healthy and happy. Joy is more powerful than guilt or obligation; use your assets to create an enjoyable and satisfying experience. Continue to build new initiatives, whether updated research directions, fresh scholarly or teaching collaborations, revised curricula, or establishing a new teaching or research interdisciplinary institute in your college. Learn modern techniques in teaching such as team teaching, active learning, and problem-based learning. Use teaching consultants in your college or university to guide you. Apprentice with others who successfully apply these modern approaches.

Until recently, it was common to have a single researcher design and execute their research studies. In fact, departure from this prevailing model was sometimes frowned upon. Reviewers of a faculty member's annual progress or their promotion dossier, for instance, were less impressed by colleagues whose name appeared among many authors on publications or grant proposals. In fact, faculty who often published with other investigators were criticized for lacking independence. However, the model of a single principal investigator has gradually become a relic from the past. Research questions have morphed to be more complicated and require contributions from teams of researchers from the same or different disciplines to give them due depth and justice. There are numerous examples of how collaborative research has enabled researchers to pose very unique research questions that are more appreciated by grant reviewers than mainstream inquiries related to a single discipline.

There are different categories of collaborations that people often get confused. Intradisciplinary teams are composed of investigators from a single discipline who have complementary expertise, while multidisciplinary work involves researchers from different disciplines. Historically, both approaches have resulted in significant paradigm shifts in knowledge. Multidisciplinary research that involves physiologists, engineers and physicians, for instance, has been the main foundation of inventing many medical devices that are used for diagnosing and treating various diseases. Such successful endeavors have resulted in new educational and research disciplines, such as biomedical engineering.

Senior faculty should be encouraged to work with others to keep their research programs on the cutting edge. This includes initiating partnerships with other faculty in their department, college, institution and other universities. Advances in communication technology have made it possible to build highly functional working relationships with researchers anywhere on the planet in real time. Collaborations between senior faculty and their junior colleagues in particular offers many mutual advantages. Such cooperative efforts often result in productive interdisciplinary and multidisciplinary research programs that are based on investigating unique and highly impactful research problems. A senior faculty member would benefit from revitalizing their research methodologies through the expertise of the junior partner. For example, a scientist who uses behavioral methods in animals to study the phenomenon of drug addiction would benefit from adding questions at the cellular or molecular level to explain the biological basis of the observed drug-seeking behaviors. This approach would enhance their competitiveness in obtaining research funding by making their grant applications "sexy." Furthermore, trainees in the senior investigator's group would benefit from learning and applying new research technologies. The junior faculty member, in turn, would gain the ability to move their test tube findings in a translational direction by finding out how the measured but unseen changes in the makeup of a given brain region relate to visible changes in behavior. Collaboration with senior faculty also gives junior assistant professors a valuable apprenticeship opportunity to learn how to express their clever research ideas in words that are more convincing to grant reviewers. The long history that most senior faculty have in submitting grant applications (and, more important, serving on grant review panels) makes them an invaluable resource in this regard. Multi-generational research collaborations also have the potential to develop into a mentoring relationship in which the junior faculty member would learn many people skills that are mandatory for advancing in an academic community.

Mid-career and senior faculty must remain hungry for knowledge. They should strive to attend as many seminars and professional conferences as they can. There is always something to learn to rekindle their excitement about research. These gatherings also provide a good way to discover new collaborators. When I go to conferences, I make it a habit to walk through poster aisles dedicated to topics far removed from my specific research interests. I find this approach more profitable than limiting poster viewing to my immediate area of expertise. This practice has created fertile ground for serendipity that inspired ideas for more exciting research questions. I find visiting posters in my field more important for connecting with my colleagues in other institutions than for learning significant new information. Let's face it: the content of most posters presented at scholarly conferences has already been published in full since scientific organizations usually have deadlines for abstract submission many months ahead of the conference date. A colleague of mine goes a step further, as he purposefully attends conferences dedicated to topics outside his immediate research interests to learn something new. Stepping out of his comfort zone has stimulated ideas for new research directions. It has also enabled him to connect with researchers in different fields to construct truly interdisciplinary research endeavors.

In essence, successful mid-career and senior faculty do not and should not settle for comfort. They always challenge themselves to learn new technologies and methodologies, refusing to stay in their comfort zone. They renew their vigor by following directions in scholarly exploration that excite them the most, instead of sticking to the same project for life. They are more aware than others that any project based on a well-defined set of questions is apt to approach a dead end, in which continuing research would lead merely to small steps of incremental new knowledge.

9. Maintaining the Vitality of Mid-Career and Senior Faculty   173

While scholars who maintain their vitality are fearless about learning and applying new technologies, they recognize the limits of their knowledge and consult with experts as needed. Most likely, introducing new methodologies involves sending graduate students, postdoctorals or senior technicians somewhere else for training (for example, to another laboratory or a technical workshop). It is therefore imperative to consider a potential employee's aptitude for learning new things when hiring trainees or staff. My advice to all my trainees and mentees is never to let the technology they are familiar with dictate the research questions they pursue. Instead, they should ask bold, novel and impactful questions, and then seek whatever new technologies and methodologies may be needed to answer these questions in a comprehensive manner. I also advise them to let the results of their research lead them to the next logical step. Highly productive senior faculty take advantage of their increased liberty to pursue high-risk, high-impact research questions by applying such modern technologies since their jobs are protected by indefinite tenure. They therefore have the time and the leverage. They do not have to meet deadlines for applying for promotion from one rank to a higher one. (For those at the associate professor rank, for instance, there is no prescribed number of years after which they must be considered for promotion to full professorship.) The love for scholarship is a main element required for resilience and longevity. This love leads researchers to be amenable to renewing themselves and adapting their approaches.

Professor Richard Weinshilboum, a revered long-time mentor and colleague at the Mayo Clinic, recently shared these thoughts with me:

> Dr. El-Fakahany asked me to address the question of how/why I have continued to remain engaged in and have maintained scientific productivity. Most of us would never get to that point without having benefited from strong, supportive mentorship early in our careers. I was terribly fortunate to have been accepted in the laboratory of Dr. Julius (Julie) Axelrod at the National Institutes of Health—where I learned what biomedical research was and how to do it. Julie gave me what were then the cutting-edge technical tools of biomedical science, tools such as exquisitely sensitive radiochemical assays to measure enzyme activities. He was unique, having received his PhD at night school at George Washington as he approached 50 years of age after having already published approximately 100 papers while he was a technician at the NIH. Julie was exciting to be around, always generating new ideas and suggestions—most of which were totally crazy—but one out of ten of which was brilliant. I was lucky enough to be in his lab—and was sent out to purchase champagne the day that he received the Nobel Prize in 1970 for his discovery of a novel mechanism for termination of the action of a class of neurotransmitters. The tools provided at Julie's laboratory made it possible for me to assay enzymes that play a role in brain function in large numbers of subjects to discover wide variations in the activities of those enzymes, variation that was under genetic control. Please

remember that this was a time before any genes had been "cloned." Once it became possible to clone genes, my laboratory spent a decade cloning and characterizing sequence variation in genes encoding those same brain enzymes, followed by a decade of doing something that would have seemed impossible to Julie—scanning the entire genome for genetic variation that contributed to risk for and response to drugs used to treat both cancer and neuropsychiatric disease and now—today—taking blood samples from patients suffering from those diseases and generating brain cells and "brain organoids" to use for drug testing. It must be clear that it is not just necessary but essential that a biomedical scientist needs to embrace change and use every new technique and apply it to the science that he/she is pursuing. I also go through this list to remind us of the scientific journey that we have all taken in just a few decades. It is this stunning science that attracts the students and fellows, and it is the union of exciting science and the youthful enthusiasm of those students that propels scientific productivity.

Professor Weinshilboum also believes that key elements for maintaining senior faculty's vitality include receiving effective mentoring early on and then giving back by mentoring others, in addition to family and institutional support:

> Before I get to the rewards of being a mentor, there is one major influence who needs to be acknowledged, my original department Chair, John Blinks. John was a cardiovascular pharmacologist who knew little about my scientific interests in genetics but he was a stunning mentor. As I walked through the door at Mayo, he said "You need to write an R01 grant." I said "Great. Could I see one?" I had never seen a grant—ever! When I wrote that grant, I thought that it was truly a thing of beauty, but I was wise enough to tell John that it was a "rough draft" when I gave it to him for suggestions. It came back covered with rude comments in red ink (there were no "tracked changes" then) and he commented "Rewrite it and this time make it presentable." I did. Over the ensuing years, I have served as a mentor for generations of students, fellows and junior faculty members. Those experiences have occasionally been frustrating, but they have also been the most rewarding aspect of a career in biomedicine. To have the opportunity to be of some help to these young people has been and remains the aspect of a biomedical career that I find most rewarding and exciting.

Moving into completely different areas of research within one's discipline is another effective way to maintain vigor. One of my favorite professors in graduate school, Stephen Brimijoin, started his career in the mid–1970s investigating how biological substances such as enzymes diffuse through neurons. Interestingly, he currently works on pharmacological strategies to control addiction to cocaine, which is far removed from where he started. His keen observation of exciting research findings led him to drastically alter the main path of his research program. I have to mention here that this malleability in pursuing intriguing observations

9. Maintaining the Vitality of Mid-Career and Senior Faculty   175

perfectly fits his general personality traits, particularly when it comes to hunger for learning new things. In his senior years, for example, he challenged himself to learn to play the piano and became quite good at it. He also became proficient in several foreign languages. At social gatherings, it is difficult to realize that he is somebody who pursues research in a specific discipline (namely, pharmacology) as one listens to him talk with confidence about a very wide spectrum of topics, ranging from the role of mysterious black holes to why polar bears hibernate! He is well read and well rounded. I have always wondered whether his free spirit is a combination of his unique personality and his training with Professor Julius Axelrod, a Nobel laureate in physiology and medicine who encouraged his trainees to unleash their hunger for discovery and let research findings become their guiding beacon. (I hope you recognize that Dr. Axelrod trained two of the most highly resilient, motivated and productive senior faculty members I have ever met in my long academic career, Professors Weinshilboum and Brimijoin. This fact speaks volumes regarding the importance of placing a junior science student on the right path from the very beginning. Somehow this initial dose of genius sets their path forward and makes them a magnet for attracting additional tools for success as they go on.)

In drastically changing research directions, one must make the transition gradually. Develop credibility by publishing papers on the new line of research in peer-reviewed journals. Grant reviewers are usually not risk takers. They would not recommend giving significant amounts of funds to a researcher without full trust in their expertise on the subject matter. One idea for supporting new research directions is to establish collaborations or submit joint proposals with researchers with high credibility in the new topic of inquiry. Another is to generate a convincing body of preliminary data that support the new research direction, but this option requires money. Fortunately, most institutions provide seed funds to facilitate transitions into new scholarly paths. One may also use external research funds the university presently has available to produce the required supportive data. However, an institution's willingness to allow faculty to veer away from the specified goals of funds at hand varies according to the type, source, and diversity of research funds. For example, research contracts are associated with specific deliverables that must be met. Research grants, by contrast, allow more flexibility, but one must ensure that expending resources in pursuit of a new direction does not hurt progress toward achieving the major goals of a funded grant. Research gifts provide the highest degree of flexibility since they come with no strings attached. Gifts are mostly donated by individual philanthropists or by companies for which a faculty member provides technical consultation. Diversifying one's sources of funding expands the degree of freedom available in pursuing new and more exciting research directions. It is also an insurance policy that protects researchers against the possibility of being totally unfunded. It is a matter when (rather than if) one will lose one or more grants that have been going on for a long time.

Tenured faculty should not neglect modernizing their soft competencies portfolio. There are always new things to learn, especially when it comes to communication technology and networking through social media. LinkedIn, for instance, is an amazing platform for professional networking. Twitter is another venue for fast and efficient exchange of information and knowledge. Younger generations are certainly more adept in using and enjoying the tremendous benefits of these tools. They are usually able and willing to mentor senior faculty in this regard.

Discussions with many highly productive senior colleagues have revealed a consensus about the importance of family support and taking good care of one's own needs. Many of these scholars exercise regularly, eat a healthy diet and maintain enjoyable hobbies. The majority take their full vacation days to get away to fun and exciting places with their families or friends. While they do their best to disengage their minds from work while on vacation, I have heard from more than one that very exciting new directions were conceived as a result of serendipitous observations while they were enjoying their time away from the routine and bureaucratic work environment. I identify with this phenomenon; I often generate my cleverest research ideas while I am watering my flower garden.

One of the best examples of such relaxation-induced serendipity is the invention of the polymerase chain reaction. Kary Mullis, a chemist who worked for an industrial firm, had been dreaming for a long time of finding a way to replicate DNA in a test tube. He knew that DNA has to be heated in order to separate the two strands of the double helix, each of which would then serve as a template to synthesize a partner molecule using replication enzymes. His dilemma was the fact that DNA-replicating enzymes would be destroyed at the high temperatures used to separate the two strands. For some odd reason, the image of bacteria that inhabit hot geysers in the bottom of oceans came to Dr. Mullis' mind while he was away at his cabin in the California woods back in 1985. These thoughts made him wonder how these bacteria replicate their DNA under such hostile conditions. Could they have a thermostable type of DNA-replicating enzymes? *Eureka*—they do indeed! This realization led him to a monumental discovery that enabled amplification of a single molecule of DNA many times over, dubbed the polymerase chain reaction, which has endless applications, most significantly genome sequencing and producing large amounts of DNA from tiny specimens (hair, dandruff) for application in forensic criminology. Dr.

Mullis was awarded the Nobel Prize in Chemistry in 1993. He also licensed his patent for the handsome sum of $3 million.

Senior faculty should think deeply of what kind of legacy they would like to leave behind at the end of their academic career. Training and mentoring graduate students often gives a sense of continuation and legacy, even though they have become rather expensive due to the escalating cost of tuition. Mentoring graduate students, postdoctoral fellows and junior faculty is an excellent way for a senior faculty member to pay back for all the mentoring they received during their early academic years. It is important, however, that mentors strive to sharpen their mentoring and advising abilities through attending workshops or reading related books and online articles. Senior faculty's experience enables them to contribute to advancing the research of others, even in areas that are vastly different from their own. Their expertise as grant reviewers makes them skilled in providing educated critiques of presentation clarity, coherence of aims and general important elements of the study design. Most often, junior faculty write grant applications anticipating that they will be read by a reviewer who is an expert in their narrow field. This may be true in the case of primary reviewers. However, some do not realize that secondary reviewers likely do not specialize in the same areas, but rather in related ones, and that tertiary reviewers may well come from very different fields. A successful grant application must be written in a style that appeals to and excites all three reviewers, since their scores of applications' merit have equal weight in determining the funding outcome. Moreover, the institutional memory of senior faculty enables them to recommend collaborators or other resources the junior faculty may not be aware of, especially in very large institutions that have many colleges and departments.

Professor Dorothy Hatsukami, a world-renowned scholar in the area of drug addiction, shared with me these words of wisdom regarding how she has maintained her vitality over the years:

> The primary reason for my continued academic success is finding an area of research that continues to fascinate me and the attitude of wanting to learn about new areas of investigation and research methods within this research domain. The research area I have chosen, nicotine addiction and its consequences, has led me to explore many of its facets, from the biology and genetics of nicotine addiction, its characteristics and ways to treat it and more recently tobacco regulatory policies to minimize addiction. In choosing research topics within this area, I have always envisioned where I think science is going, the research gaps that exist and the types of research that might have the biggest impact on public health. In this journey, I have found my collaborations with junior and senior faculty from various disciplines to be most meaningful and valuable. In each evolving phase of my research, I have had wonderful

collaborators who have been my teachers and who have contributed to my thinking, research directions and experimental designs. These collaborations have been bi-directional, where I contributed to their research as well. Many of these collaborations have resulted from proactive networking with other scientists and even funding agencies, which exemplifies the importance of communicating with other scholars about your own research and reaching out to scientists representing different disciplines as well as from different academic institutions. These collaborations, my tendency to develop frameworks that integrate various areas of science, and wanting to be bold and not intimidated by challenges have led to establishing a team of scientists who are interested in addressing a particular research topic from different angles. Our research team has successfully sought generous research funding from the National Institutes of Health through the program projects and research center's funding mechanisms. Just as important as the research collaborators, having a strong and trusted research staff is also crucial. I have been fortunate enough to have staff who can implement, problem solve and run the studies without much direction from me. The research staff are also active contributors to the research design and ideas. Finally, being involved in leadership roles or on certain committees for scientific organizations and being selected to serve on a number of governmental and academic advisory boards have provided me with a broad perspective on scientific priorities and policies that nourish my thinking on directions that I believe are worth pursuing.

Professor Stephanie Huang also shared tips on how to strategically design one's successful academic career to remain highly productive. She believes that her love for solving problems and the pride she takes in generating useful knowledge to truly impact human health in a positive way are major drives that have kept her motivated and resilient. She also enjoys seeing her trainees thrive, especially when one of them lands a dream job, publishes a seminal paper, wins an award or receives a grant. She considers everybody on her research team a member of her family. Professor Huang's approach to maintaining high productivity after she was granted indefinite tenure involved surrounding herself with great collaborators and allowing team spirit to lead the way. She believes that having an individual scholar work very hard in isolation will never produce the same result as having a harmonious team work together. She has been intentional about recruiting collaborative team players to join her group and to nourish a positive collaborative culture.

Role of the Administration

Senior faculty are often perceived by academic administrators as untouchable or uncontrollable. This common misconception often leads the administration to ignore senior faculty's need to be mentored. Department heads have their hands full with managing hiring, budgeting, curricular issues, and so forth. They dedicate the little time they have left to paying attention to the needs of tenure-track faculty. As a result, many senior faculty suffer from benign neglect. In reality, department and college administrators could and should have a positive impact on maintaining the vigor of mid-career and senior faculty. First and foremost, they should ensure continued engagement of tenured faculty in department and college functions and operations. Feeling marginalized often leads to the loss of one's enthusiasm.

Senior faculty have so much to offer due to their experience and wisdom. Administrators should nominate them to serve on higher institutional committees. They may also be asked to serve as leaders of focus groups responsible for revising curricula and department missions or for documenting and enacting college values. Department heads or deans should keep their eyes open for opportunities to express appreciation of senior faculty's contributions to the college mission, perhaps by nominating them for prestigious awards, particularly at the national and international level. Department and college administrators could also play an important role in recommending various types of career development workshops, conferences or publications that help senior faculty update their skills and maintain their vigor. Keeping senior faculty connected with the research and teaching activities around them is a great way to ensure their continued engagement and motivation. This result may be achieved through establishing research or teaching focus groups to facilitate exchange of expertise or creating local symposia that highlight contributions of senior faculty to a given field and make them aware of others' work.

I will always have fond memories of an initiative started by one of the departments in my institution, coined the "Friday Night Fight." At the end of the workday on every Friday, faculty, trainees and staff gathered around food and drinks to hear and critique the general outlines of a future research project presented by one of the faculty. The general format was designed to permit the audience to do their best in ripping the proposal apart by highlighting holes in the underlying hypothesis or experimental design. All was done with good intentions and in a friendly spirit. "Fights" ended with no bad feelings or resentment against those who were more vocal in criticizing the proposed project. This was an amazing learning experience, both for the presenter and for the audience. Graduate students and postdoctoral trainees benefited the most by learning how to be critical of their own research proposals.

During my service as associate dean for research in my college, I initiated research retreats that included faculty in my college and those in other colleges of the university. The goal was for faculty in each college to share not only the types of research projects being carried out in individual laboratories but also knowledge of available technologies and equipment in their college at large. The outcome of such retreats was astounding. This program led to many new research collaborations and joint grant applications, some of which revived the research programs of senior faculty who had lost their competitive edge in obtaining funding on their own. However, I met with significant resistance when I proposed applying the same model to research gatherings that would include faculty from different departments within my college. Opposition was based on the assumption that "everybody" already knew "all" of what others were doing. In testing this prevailing dogma, it became clear that this proclaimed knowledge was quite limited in nature. As an example, while one of the faculty knew that Professor X did research on nanoparticles, he failed to provide any details beyond this general taxonomy. This limited knowledge is certainly insufficient for two or more faculty members to initiate discussion of potential collaborations. I therefore gathered my courage (relying on the fact that I am a fearless tenured professor!) and held an interdepartmental research retreat. Ahead of the meeting, I preassigned specific roles to as many faculty as I could to ensure good attendance. The retreat was an absolute success and resulted in many new collaborations between faculty in different departments. More surprising, new collaborations between faculty from the same department also sprouted as a result of gaining deeper knowledge of what individual faculty members actually did in their own ivory tower. The dogma was put to rest.

Role of Mentoring of Mid-Career and Senior Faculty

There is usually focus in academic institutions on mentoring junior faculty at the assistant professor level. They are new to the game and require significant guidance to enable them to launch their careers. This type of mentoring is often offered by senior faculty in the same or other departments. Interestingly, and perhaps surprisingly, this mentoring is rarely reciprocal, even though junior faculty have much to share in terms of new technology and cutting-edge research questions. There is also a prevailing thought that senior faculty do not need, or want, to be mentored. They have already made it through the promotion and tenure hoop and have demonstrated independence and competence in building their own career. What more do they need?! This is far from being true. Faculty need mentoring at all stages of their career. They need guidance in maintaining a well-funded research program and modernizing their style of teaching and advising. They also need guidance when they decide to move to administrative positions. The most effective type of mentoring is provided by peers who have found ways to maintain joy in what they are doing.

The Concept of Resilience

Resilience empowers a person to face and circumvent challenging life events while maintaining self-determination, positivity, hope and well-being. While individuals differ in their innate resilience, there are ways for this essential trait to be learned and gained. There are also external factors—mainly related to the individual's social and professional network—that play an important role in building resilience. Innate resilience is associated with one's psychological makeup, especially in how their neural networks handle stressful situations. It is also supported by their level of competence in what they do and their social skills. Resilient people generally look at challenges as opportunities. They are hopeful, optimistic and self-confident. They derive resilience from experiencing general joy in life and recognizing the difference between what they can change and what they have to live with. In my opinion, their stockpile of internal satisfaction and happiness offers a formidable and effective protective wall against stress or feelings of defeat. They bank "spare happiness currency" that they expend wisely during challenging times! A good part of their feeling of joy is related to their contribution to the success and happiness of others. This experience is to be contrasted with the low resilience linked to negative traits such as rumination, angst, hypervigilance and being overly self-critical.

Humans are social animals who derive support from others. Being surrounded by caring family, friends and colleagues is a great asset for gaining resilience. Such connections provide resources and psychological support. The work environment also has a significant effect on fostering resilience in individuals. Positive resilience-inducing work communities are based on respect, renewal, collaboration, justice and equality. In an academic environment where these values are practiced, a faculty member feels strong emotional and professional support from their colleagues and superiors at times when a grant is not funded or a manuscript is rejected. The opposite is true in settings where colleagues enjoy watching others fail. The latter scenario compounds the negative consequences of failure. It makes one quite anxious while waiting to hear the outcome of any of their initiatives, fearing being disgraced in others' eyes if they hear of a negative outcome.

There are many approaches for strengthening your own resilience. As a starting point, you must dig deep into your soul to identify the sources of stress in your life, their relative roles in causing anxiety, and the patterns of your stress and relaxation cycles. Do not hesitate to seek professional counseling if you think you need it. Interview colleagues, particularly mentors, to understand their secrets to handling stress in order to develop coping skills in dealing with failures, overcommitment or other challenging situations. Offices of human resources in academic institutions often offer workshops or provide individual counseling on resilience. Be aware that resilience training may be embedded in general programs geared at wholesome well-being. There are also resilience applications for smartphones; these apps provide resilience inventories, goal setting outlines, action plans and training videos.

Changing Path to Maintain Career Fulfillment

Being tenured gives a faculty member the freedom to expand or drastically alter the focus of their academic endeavors. As one deeply contemplates future goals and what gives them job satisfaction, they may consider paying more attention to teaching or service instead of having research continue to be at center stage. Some who favor teaching over other academic activities may divert their scholarly work toward the pedagogy of learning. Others may decide to contribute more to mentoring graduate students and postdoctoral fellows. Having served for so many years in academia provides senior faculty with invaluable intellectual wealth that could benefit the next generation of scholars. These include competence in writing convincing grant proposals, time management, conflict resolution and networking. Some senior faculty may opt to develop structured programs to share strategies for effective mentorship with their colleagues. They may also develop interest in contributing to the scholarship of mentoring and advising. Guidelines for promotion to full professorship usually have clauses that permit counting such activities toward promotion credits. What matters the most is that an individual plan for a productive academic career in a way that meets their career and life goals and makes them proud of the legacy they intend to leave behind.

Some, like me, opt to prepare for pursuing leadership roles. I made this conscious decision to effect change in the academic environment, particularly in providing high-quality mentorship to scholars at all stages of their careers. I will always be thankful for having made this pivotal decision. In fact, having this experience has been the most rewarding and fulfilling practice in my entire career. Senior faculty often become more involved in serving their professional societies and make stronger connections with outside communities surrounding their institutions. This approach frequently leads them to gear their research toward placing more emphasis on questions that have strong societal impact. I also have known senior scholars who have entrepreneurship tendencies. They followed this passion by starting small companies.

Should One Remain in the Same Institution After Attaining Tenure?

Associate and full professor faculty who remain productive represent an attractive target to other institutions. The attraction is based on the possibility of gaining faculty who have already established their career and stature in their respective fields. These individuals have demonstrated ongoing enthusiasm and vigor after getting tenure, thus proving they are in it for the long haul. In addition, productive faculty at this stage of their career are usually well endowed with sizeable research grants that they could take with them when they move to a new university. While research equipment is theoretically the property of the institution to which the grant was originally given, most universities allow faculty to take this equipment when they move, especially if the equipment is highly specialized and would not be of use to others. Another valuable gain for institutions when they recruit high-caliber senior faculty is that their stature creates a magnet for recruiting top faculty and students to colleges and institutions.

After spending several years in one institution as an assistant professor, a faculty member gets to know the real picture of its academic environment. They become aware of available resources, both technical and intellectual. They experience how supportive department and college administrators are and whether they walk their talk when it comes to their declared mission, vision and values. They are able to accurately judge the level of intellectual stimulation and mentoring they receive from interacting with their colleagues. This experience plays an important role in their decision to either stay in the same institution or move to another.

One should not make the decision to switch institutions lightly. They should take a wholesome approach, realizing that the criteria for an ideal academic setting differ from one person to another. More important, one should realize that there is no utopia. Every environment has its good and bad points. Sometimes negative aspects of a new academic environment are not readily apparent when one interviews for a job, or even during the first few months on the job. A faculty member who is considering joining another university must do careful investigative homework to find out the real story about the climate of the new workplace. There are also factors to be taken into serious consideration that lie outside the academic circle. One example is the happiness of one's family in the community where they live regarding safety, cultural resources, caliber of education for children and job satisfaction of a spouse or significant other. In Minnesota, we have lost a few faculty whose families could not tolerate the cold weather! Of course, the relative contribution of the various factors to be weighed depends on marital and parental status, age of children, and proximity to relatives and others who play a significant role in supporting the family. Another element to be taken into consideration is the psychological cost of uprooting one's family and moving to an unfamiliar place to start building new friendships and discover all types of resources all over again.

Most faculty remain at the same institution upon being granted tenure and promotion to associate professor if they are happy with the environment of the institution and outside community and receive sufficient support from their colleagues, leaders and friends. However, some decide to move to higher-ranked research-intensive institutions upon attaining tenure, even though some elite universities may not honor the tenure status granted at the original institution due to differences in standards for receiving tenure. In this case, the faculty member will likely be appointed as a tenure-track assistant professor or associate professor without tenure and then come up for a tenure decision in a couple of years. Other newly promoted associate professors may decide to move to a lower-caliber university that places more emphasis on good relationships between employees and providing career development tools over the level of research conducted by an individual faculty member. One may make the latter type of a move as a result of being lured with significant financial perks or leadership positions. The move may also be based on being close to extended family or supportive communities. If you take this route, understand that you are expected to help others grow their research programs without harming yours. Selecting one or the other type of institution is never an easy or straightforward matter. As a wise colleague of mine put it, it is always a tough choice between wanting to become the head of a snake or the tail of a dragon. In other words, one could opt to be either the brightest star at a medium-level institution or at the bottom of the hierarchy in one of the elite institutions.

Moving to other institutions may be associated with significant perks. Examples include higher salaries and exuberant startup packages. Other lures include being given an endowed chair or being asked to build a new research institute. Some individuals may even decide to move to an institution that contributes in part or in full to college tuition of faculty members' children if they decide to enroll in one of the colleges of this university. There are groups of institutions that have agreements for reciprocity of waiving tuition for children of faculty.

Generally speaking, one has to be wise in considering the totality of a financial offer instead of limiting their judgment to the salary amount. First, the purchasing power of a dollar differs across the country, especially in relation to buying a home. Second, universities vary significantly in the nature of fringe benefits provided to their faculty (some are more generous than others in contributing to healthcare and retirement plans). Finally, some institutions or colleges guarantee only a portion of the salary. The rest is derived from research, teaching or clinical revenue. Thus, a faculty member's salary may go down if they lose their research funding.

Should One Remain in Academia Until Retirement?

Successful mid-career and senior faculty also become desired by major industries. A creative and prolific faculty member who specializes in aerodynamics, for example, may be pursued by Boeing to contribute to its program in improving plane navigation in severe storms. The pharmaceutical industry would be very interested in recruiting a medicinal chemist with expertise in synthesizing and screening large libraries of new compounds as drug candidates for the treatment of various diseases. Of course, moving to industry usually comes with significant financial perks in the form of higher salaries, annual bonuses and stock options. Furthermore, a faculty member who transitions to the corporate world no longer has to go through the pain and stress of writing grant proposals to submit to funding agencies. High-priority industry projects receive unlimited funds and personnel support. Equipment is often top of the line since speed and efficiency are of utmost concern to win the race with other firms that work on developing similar products. There are no futile "academic" meetings that do not lead to firm decisions or action strategies. The entire operation is goal oriented based on analysis, strategies, role assignment, accountability and measurable milestones. Employees of large corporations are often flown to conferences around the world in the company's private jet. It is a completely different world that offers so much glamour.

However, these advantages also come with a significant cost. Job security is at the top of the list. A couple of decades ago, I was recruited by a large pharmaceutical firm to head one of its divisions. I was impressed, and so were they during the job interview. While I was contemplating whether to pursue this opportunity further, I received word that the company high management had decided to close the division I was recruited to lead. I considered myself fortunate that this sudden change happened before I actually uprooted my family and moved them across the country. Here is another example of job insecurity in the corporate world: One of my graduate students who was employed by Big Pharma went to work one day to find that her entry card and computer account had been deactivated. What a shock that was! Such decisions are not uncommon in this industry. They are usually made unilaterally by the management based on the odds of profits versus losses of certain research projects. In other cases, closing divisions is the consequence of being acquired by another company that has different research and development priorities and emphases. If a faculty member decides to move to industry, they have to live with this reality and be willing to move frequently, sometimes even to other countries or continents. Another graduate student of mine who chose the pharmaceutical industry as a career made an educated choice to accept employment at a firm located in a region of the country endowed with a high density of similar industries. She wisely purchased a home that is right in the center of the area where these companies are located. Amazingly, she never had to relocate her residence, even though she changed jobs many times, either being forced to or voluntarily moving to more attractive positions.

A scientist in industry does not have a free hand in choosing their group's research direction. These decisions are made by the management, based on projected financial returns on investment. She or he may not have the luxury of exploring "academic" research questions that lie outside the company's interest in making money. They may even be discouraged from pursuing research questions that have the potential to reveal negative properties of the targeted product. Essentially, the remarkable perks that industry provides are associated with loss of academic freedom in pursuing self-selected research projects.

One also has to be careful in analyzing the pros and cons of moving to a certain company versus another, since firms differ greatly in their intellectual environment. In serving as a consultant to large pharmaceutical firms, I found some more loyal to their employees than others. One firm offered retraining to employees in research divisions that were about to be eliminated in skills that would qualify them to join another division in the company. I have also noticed marked differences in how companies apply academic scholarship principles in terms of basing projects on solid, hypothesis-driven backgrounds. When I visited certain companies, I really felt as if I were in a highly dynamic academic institution. There were many postings of seminars by outside speakers. Scientists were encouraged to publish their findings in top-tier journals and to consider adjunct faculty positions at neighboring institutions to enable them to teach and advise graduate students. Of course, scientists working for industry cannot and should not submit publications or give public presentations that jeopardize the company's intellectual property rights.

The group I worked with applied an amazing interdisciplinary approach to conducting research. They functioned as a team composed of chemists, pharmacologists and statisticians who conversed and jointly made decisions about the next steps. This approach made them aware of what was happening and who was doing what at each stage of the project and gave them a chance to offer input and timely feedback to adjust the path. The group even included someone from marketing, who made helpful comments based on requirements for success in marketability once the product was released. I have seen other companies, however, approach drug discovery in a hodgepodge manner. Chemists randomly synthesize thousands of compounds on a weekly basis and then pass them on to pharmacologists for screening without any communication between the two groups of employees. They even blindly purchase chemical libraries from academic institutions and other smaller companies, hoping for a miraculous uneducated hit. One must take these stark differences seriously in deciding whether to leave academia and move to a given company. Either of the two above scenarios may be heaven to some but hell to others.

The soft transferrable skills, especially analytical approaches to problem solving, make academic scholars successful in a variety of careers. A faculty member who is not happy in academia, for example, may decide to work for a federal or state agency. I know a couple of colleagues who became involved in the grant review process in funding agencies. Others with passion for writing became editors for newspapers or consultants for television stations in their respective fields of expertise, be it economics, social justice or politics. One with expertise in forensic toxicology actually got a lucrative offer from a movie company. Her role was to authenticate the physical appearance of homicide victims and provide advice on symptoms of poisoning and how fast various poisons commonly used for murder would act. After all, no self-respecting film company wants to be laughed at for having a victim poisoned by valium (a sedative) shown in a movie as suffering from hyperactivity or convulsions since these are signs of excitation rather than suppression of the activity of the central nervous system. A mathematician or a statistician could easily work as an analyst in a financial investment corporation. Some other careers may necessitate additional training to gain important skills (for example, working in the areas of intellectual property or regulatory affairs).

Summary

Being promoted to the rank of associate professor with indefinite tenure is only one stop on a long journey. It represents validation of one's ability to continue producing new knowledge, teaching students and training the next generation of scholars to prepare them for carrying the torch. It should not be taken as an opportunity for slowing down past this critical stage because of the job security granted by the tenure status. A tenured associate professor or full professor should enjoy what tenure offers regarding the freedom to explore controversial topics or take on risky research projects that have the potential for significant impact. Senior faculty should continually sharpen their research tools to be able to address cutting-edge questions. However, department and college administration also play a paramount role in appreciating and encouraging continued vitality of mid-career and senior faculty.

Self-Reflection Exercises

If you are a tenure-track assistant professor:

- Who in your department or college are role models for productive mid-career and senior faculty?
- What do you think would change in how you approach your work and life in general once you become tenured?
- What are the pros and cons of staying at the same institution versus moving to another when you become a tenured associate professor?
- How do you think your department and college could do better in maintaining the long-term vitality of faculty?

If you are a tenured associate or full professor:

- What has changed in your attitude about work and life since you were granted tenure?
- What personal factors have contributed to your continued academic success? What would you improve?
- How has your department and college administration helped in keeping you motivated and productive? How would they do better?
- What are the factors that contributed to you or your colleagues slowing down over time after attaining tenure? How do you plan to get back in the saddle?

10

Preparing to Become a Future Academic Leader

Most faculty in the early stages of their career do not see assuming a leadership position in the department, college or institution in the cards for them. Some, like me, even vow that they will never become one of those bureaucratic and useless administrators. I was wrong, as so many others have been. There may come a time in a person's life when they realize they could do a better job leading than being led. They may aspire to be a conduit to effect significant changes that require being in a place of power and authority in a way that would allow them to leave more remarkable fingerprints on the academic environment than if they continue to do what they have been doing for a long time. In my particular case, for example, I am confident that I have made more significant contributions to advancing scholarship by having created or improved initiatives for mentoring graduate students, postdoctoral fellows and junior faculty than by doing my own research. I therefore advise you never to say never!

Planning for Transition to Leadership

Deciding to pursue an administrative position should not be taken lightly. Much homework needs to be done to ensure a good fit. The goal here is not only to figure out whether one would enjoy this career path but also to determine whether they have the necessary abilities that enable them to deliver the best leadership possible and make the highest impact. A person who is contemplating transitioning to leadership must have a purpose that will provide fulfillment and self-satisfaction, in addition to service to others. I highly discourage going after an administrative job for the sake of prestige or monetary gain in the form of administrative augmentation; it really is not worthwhile.

If you are considering leadership as a career direction, I recommend that you start by discerning your motivation for making the move through asking these questions: Are you seeking new challenges or personal growth? Do your career goals include giving something back and creating chances for success for others? As a second step, I suggest digging deeper using this set of ancillary questions: What are the specific changes you would like to make? How do you plan to make them? How realistic are you in your vision in light of your skills and the institutional culture with regard to being open to change? How will you know whether you have succeeded in your mission? How will your past experience help you? How strong are your people skills in communication, aligning expectations, motivation, and conflict resolution? Be as specific as possible. More important, be honest with yourself. This exercise must represent your candid and realistic internal calibration of your leadership aptitude. There are many other questions to ask to figure out whether administration is a good fit for you and vice versa. How do your personal values conform to what the position needs and the organization's values? How much leverage and authority will you be permitted? Will you be expected to maintain the status quo or develop new initiatives?

I also advise you to consider your personal vulnerabilities and how you plan to mitigate them to prevent them from becoming roadblocks on your journey to create positive change. What triggers your negative emotions and reactions? How open and capable are you toward owning up to your mistakes? How resilient are you when you face failure and see people pointing the fingers at you? How do you react to being blamed? Recall actions or spoken words that you wish you could take back. Think of their triggers. What would you do differently if given a second chance? What is the cost of self-restraint for your energy level, stress and ability to sleep soundly? What types of difficult people do you loathe and how do you plan to transform them from hecklers to allies? Thinking of interactions in your personal life may guide you in answering these questions. My own pet peeve, for instance, is dealing with a person who is incapable of or unwilling to ever admit that they are wrong or that they do not know something. Another is one who claims credit that is not fairly theirs.

You may consider testing the waters by easing gradually into the administrative region. Consider becoming director of graduate studies or associate department head. Some institutional administrative positions are part time (for example, assistant vice president jobs). Try them out if you get a chance. Be aware of the time commitment, however. While many department heads, for example, have up to 50 percent administrative appointments, the two halves of their job usually add up to much more than 100 percent in a practical sense. This imbalance may end up harming the progress of their academic careers, especially in terms of having sufficient time to manage their research teams, publish papers and apply for research grants. Department head appointments are annually renewable at the pleasure of the college dean, and some institutions limit the number of years in which an individual may serve in this position. A department head, therefore, would be wise to maintain their professional productivity to avoid having a gap in their vitae as a result of their administrative services. Another disadvantage of part-time administrative positions is having to answer to and satisfy multiple bosses, each of whom will expect 100 percent dedication from you regardless of the formal structure and effort distribution of the position.

Benefit from the wisdom of your mentors to help you probe your motivation and qualifications in seeking administrative positions. They will help you understand the roles and required competencies for a given leadership position and will guide you to acquire important skills you are missing. They will also work with you to determine whether this move is wise at a particular juncture of your career. Better yet, you should arrange for informational interviews with colleagues who currently hold or have held similar positions. Ask questions to learn details of what the job entails and the culture of the administrative unit you are considering joining. An aspiring leader will not be able to create or facilitate changes and improvements if they have to report to one or more micromanagers who subscribe to the status quo.

Desired Skills of Academic Leaders

An academic leader serves as a role model for ethics and integrity. He or she motivates and inspires, collaborating with all stakeholders to put together shared values that guide plans and actions. He or she should build a sense of community based on mutual respect for all. A successful leader is consultative and inclusive. They rely on shared governance and charge various governance bodies with clear responsibilities and authority in crafting policies. They also listen to consultative bodies that ensure adherence to the established policies. They should be willing to consult with others but still be decisive when they weigh in on plans and actions. A confident leader does not hesitate to delegate some responsibilities as appropriate and should establish approaches for succession by grooming others to replace her or him when the time comes for them to step down.

Good leadership is based on motivation and appreciation. A department head, for instance, should reward faculty and staff through promotion and annual salary raises based on documented performance criteria that are clear, fair and equitable. For instance, they may construct detailed rubrics that allow them to be consistent in assessing performance and determining commensurate rewards. It is demoralizing when a faculty member works hard and then finds out they received more or less the same evaluation and salary raise as others who have not contributed as much. It is not really about the money; rather, it is about feeling valued and appreciated. It hurts morale and motivation to take on more responsibilities when a department head allows floundering faculty to enjoy the same benefits as top performers, including research space and services. This behavior tempts others to slow down and enjoy life instead of stressing themselves out by working hard all the time.

A good leader aims to fulfill the needs of people around them, whether individuals or groups. They sacrifice their own needs and personal goals for the good of those they serve. They provide their constituents with guidance and empowerment. Good leaders are also transformational, charismatic and highly skilled in creating and nourishing relationships. They motivate and inspire people to do better for their own sake and for the progress of the entire institution. Reliability is an important trait of effective academic leaders. This quality lets stakeholders rest assured that their leaders will be looking for their best interests when the going gets tough. Reliability combined with transparency are the basis for establishing trust. Strategic leaders recognize and value ethical behavior and act accordingly. Integrity is their guiding beacon. These values gain them forgiveness by others when they make mistakes. In these cases, people trust that their leaders have done their best, but their best was not good enough. Good leadership means responding to concerns, both in words and in actions. Effective leaders realize that asking for feedback to help solve arising problems and then totally dismissing it is very disheartening and disengaging. This harmful behavior discourages people from responding to different types of surveys, which they perceive as a meaningless and time-wasting exercise.

Good leaders value everybody's contributions. A department head, for example, should express appreciation for the work of all faculty, staff and students. They should also establish rapport with and express appreciation for managers and staff of units that serve departmental needs (for instance, facilities management, graduate school, human resources and janitorial staff). These relationships will ensure that the department receives timely and high-quality service. A good department chair or dean leads by example by showing respect for others and not talking about them behind their back. They should keep conversations positive and professional.

An academic leader may learn valuable lessons from the business world, but they must recognize essential differences in the drivers and motivators in leading a department, college or university versus managing a business entity. Corporate leaders emphasize financial gains to satisfy their investors. While finances are important in the academic arena as well, they usually are not (and should not) be the main driving force in planning. Achieving high-quality education, research and services must come first. Having said that, financial challenges facing academia have slowly transformed priorities to emphasize financial gains to make ends meet, leading to a scary trend of valuing the amount of generated dollars as an indicator of the performance of faculty and academic leaders at all hierarchical levels. A university president or provost, for example, may express more appreciation for deans of colleges who accrue the greatest amount of research funding or tuition-generated dollars as compared to those whose faculty produce more publications in prestigious journals or stand out for their teaching skills. Likewise, enhancing the institution's financial health may please the board of regents or trustees more than anything else. After all, members of boards of regents or trustees in many academic institutions mostly come from the corporate world. These trends trickle down to influence how deans evaluate department heads, as well as how heads evaluate faculty. Another factor that drives using financial gains as the main indicator of an academic leader's success is that money is an entity that can easily be counted. It is therefore more objective and quantitative than subjective and qualitative measurement of the impact of having faculty be selected to serve on committees of prominent national organizations and funding agencies. This situation brings to mind a famous quote attributed to Albert Einstein: "Not everything that can be counted counts, and not everything that counts can be counted." An astute leader is more inclusive and holistic in what they value, especially when they assess the quality of performance reports, rather than simply counting dollar figures.

It is important for a leader to develop a vision for the future and be able to predict changes based on well-studied and calibrated trajectories. Here are examples of questions a good leader contemplates about what the academic environment will look like in ten to fifteen years: How different will the student body be? How should colleges prepare to accommodate their needs? How will teaching be delivered? How will faculty be trained to keep up with new methods and technologies in teaching, such as artificial intelligence and virtual reality? What type of faculty should be recruited to meet these changes? Anticipatory thinkers are capable of connecting the dots between and across various trends and predictions. They are able to differentiate between real signals and aberrant noise. This capacity allows them to envision and act on opportunities earlier than others, therefore gaining a valuable head start. Less visionary leaders are essentially followers of trends initiated by others. As expected, "me too's" never do as well.

A successful leader should be able to distinguish challenges that can be circumvented from those that, for whatever reason, are hopelessly incurable. Acknowledging that a challenge is untreatable for the moment does not imply that the leader is incompetent or a defeatist; it actually means they are pragmatic. Leaders should also be capable of reasonably gauging the optimal magnitude and timeline of a change they plan to enact. There is a limit to how much sudden change one may invoke before disequilibrium and chaos ensue. I was taught a valuable lesson by a former president at my institution: Leading in academia is like driving a train that runs on tracks built many decades ago. These tracks represent the academic culture that shapes what and when change should be wisely introduced to achieve buy-in from stakeholders. Unrealistic leaders incorrectly believe they are driving a car or a plane, in which they can make turns at will. This belief results in frequent discouragement and disappointment.

Academic leadership requires resilience and tolerance of failure. Good leaders are good learners. They analyze and reflect on the outcome of initiatives they started and, more important, those started by past leaders. They pay more attention to initiatives that did not bear fruit and find out why. This careful analysis enables them to avoid past errors in the estimation of challenges and positions them to figure out better remedial plans the next time around. Good leaders surround themselves with a trusted team of people to consult with and are humble enough to seek guidance from various stakeholders. They look for counselors who are candid critics, rather than cheerleaders. A favorite example is the concept of the "Team of Rivals" that President Abraham Lincoln willingly adopted to get sound feedback on and rebuttal of his ideas and plans. This approach proved its merit in guiding Lincoln to lead the country through very difficult times and experiences.

Challenges to Academic Leadership

Academic institutions are currently facing more challenges than ever. Research funding and state support are scarce. New colleges and institutions sprout regularly and become competitors in recruiting students and faculty. Online education steals away many students from university campuses. Together, this scenario makes approaches to solutions as complex as the challenges. An astute academic leader, therefore, must excel at looking at the entire picture through many layers of optics. They should be aware of how different challenges are connected and avoid deciding on a solution that solves one problem but creates another.

If you are considering leadership as a career move, you must also learn about life constraints imposed on those in leadership positions. A dean, for example, will be required to attend evening events to welcome distinguished visitors or faculty job candidates. They must be willing and ready to respond to emergencies at any time. Some serious emergencies may even necessitate interrupting the leader's annual vacation and having them get back to campus to attend to the crisis.

Becoming an academic leader also dramatically changes one's relationship with colleagues, students and staff, as one is considered to have gone over to the "dark side" of academia. Some may wonder about the real motives behind your career move to administration. Are you seeking power or control? Do you have hidden agendas that may cause them problems? They may initially size you up to learn about your leadership style and ensure that you can be trusted. Some (perhaps many) may think they could do a better job than you. You may be blamed for the failures of others while not receiving fair credit for your contribution to their successes. You may have colleagues in the department or college who have been there for quite a long time—sometimes longer than you have—who may prefer the status quo and staying within their comfort zone over dealing with the discomfort that change usually brings. They believe in the motto "sometimes it's better to deal with the devil you know than with the angel you don't."

I must confess that I have been there and done that in encountering a negative kneejerk reaction to proposed changes by academic leaders in my institution. The faculty, students and staff sometimes look at the introduction of new, supposedly improved tools for university accounting, for example, with suspicion. Their reaction is mainly based on past experiences in which some of these changes made operations more cumbersome rather than easier. It also took time to get personnel to master the new systems, at which time another major change was introduced by the university. A common feature of these rapid changes is the desire by the leadership to be fashionable and follow in the footsteps of other universities, without considering whether the new tools fit the unique local culture and needs of their institution. However, there have been numerous cases in which the fears about change expressed by those who are being led prove to be totally unsubstantiated. It is the leader's responsibility to carefully study and debate the pros and cons of making changes, especially major ones that impact many people. They should involve representatives of those who will be impacted by the change in these deliberations. There should be clear communication with all those impacted by a given change about the basis of the decision and what improvements it is expected to introduce. More important, they should be apprised of the timeline for attaining anticipated benefits of the change and how to give feedback on problems or suggestions for effecting improvements.

Setting Boundaries

Setting boundaries is a very important feature of a healthy organization. Boundaries go both ways. Employees and colleagues should not feel free to suddenly encroach on a leader's time and space without considering how busy their calendar may be. The leader, in turn, should avoid unnecessarily interrupting others' work and should keep a reasonable distance from those they are leading to allow them a chance for personal growth and avoid micromanagement, but leaders should also be available to contribute to troubleshooting whenever needed. In addition, leaders should maintain a congenial relationship with others while properly exercising their authority without the interference of personal relationships or conflicts of interest. A good leader should avoid adopting one or a few employees as favorite pets to spend more time with, both in and outside the office. Friendship between a boss and their employees almost always creates problems in the workplace, since such intimate relationships may influence one's judgment when evaluating friend employees. Even for a very fair leader who manages to dissociate personal relationships from candid and unbiased evaluation, a friendship may create a perception of potential bias. Life has taught me that perceptions should be acknowledged and respected as they are, no matter whether they are based on reality. The only option one has is to change their actions to correct a given perception. A leader should make it clear to those who were close personal friends prior to assuming the leadership position that they will be expected to perform their duties at the highest level and abide by established deadlines and policies like all others. A leader should do the same for those with whom they had personal conflicts, assuring them that they will be treated and evaluated fairly.

Making Difficult Decisions

Successful academic leaders base their decisions and actions on evidence and data. They invest time and effort in doing research to gather needed background information. However, leaders are often faced with emerging situations in which they must make fast decisions without having all the facts at hand. One should carefully assess the risk of not acting in a timely manner. In these urgent situations, good leaders make decisions based on gut feeling using available information, in spite of being incomplete. They consult with others to figure out the potential costs and benefits of various options. A good leader must be willing to make tough decisions in such circumstances, but they should use extreme caution and consider potential long-term consequences of short-term solutions to a big and complicated problem. They must also take ownership of their decision in case it proves to be the wrong one.

Good leaders are aware that the safest or most obvious solutions may not be the best in the long run. Whenever possible, a leader should break solutions and actions into stages that follow a defined timeline and milestones. This strategy will allow them to gauge the plan's effectiveness by looking at the trajectory of success and making adjustments as needed. Effective leaders are not crowd pleasers. They make decisions based on what is good for the whole organization. Hopefully their decisions benefit the majority of their constituents, but there is always a likelihood of hurting (and therefore displeasing) a few. Leaders have to be realistic and transparent about possible damages a decision may cause and share that information with others. This level of transparency is essential for maintaining credibility. Trying to sugarcoat things may backfire and create suspicion of a leader's future decisions or actions. If a tough decision results in more harm to certain groups of constituents than others, the leader must recognize such sacrifices made for the sake of the common good and plan to offer adequate compensation to the afflicted population once the storm is over.

Setting Organization Values

Each organization, including academic institutions, must define its own set of values. Values represent core ethics and behaviors that guide all aspects of an organization's strategies and operations (i.e., organizational culture). They aim to create a better working community that provides the highest quality of service to its clients and therefore have a major influence on satisfying every member of an academic institution. Commonly expressed values include integrity, teamwork, excellence and innovation. As an academic leader, do not seek the easy path by simply adopting such a generic set of values. You must be thoughtful and inclusive in contemplating values that best fit your department, college or institution. Invite faculty, students and staff into discussions to determine the most important values and their hierarchy. It is best to select a set of values that your department or college already lives by and another aspirational list that you would like to integrate into the workplace culture.

I have observed that it is often easier to declare values of an academic institution than to practice them. There is often a disconnect between faculty, staff and students knowing what these prescribed values are and fully realizing what actions and behaviors do or do not conform to each value. Maintaining a collegial environment depends on applying the values established by the group in every action and decision. There is nothing more discouraging for people than seeing banners and posters around the workplace that tout respect and collegiality, for example, while witnessing rampant behaviors to the contrary. A leader should reward those who exhibit exemplary behavior and stop problematic team members who make life miserable for others. Academic life is full of "star" faculty who feel entitled to special privileges and liberties since they bring significant funding or stature to the institution. Of course, it is appropriate to give these stars special rewards, but it is unwise to allow them to bully or demean others. (See more details on how to handle these difficult team members in chapter 3.)

Forming a Collegial Community

One of a leader's most important roles is introducing and maintaining harmony in the group of people they are leading. Making people feel they belong to a cohesive team is a foundational pillar for happiness and enhanced productivity. This cohesiveness is based on making the entire team aware of each member's roles and responsibilities, so that everybody's contributions are acknowledged, valued and celebrated. Collaborations between individuals and units toward the common good should be encouraged and rewarded. Such team spirit emphasizes that an individual's success is a triumph for all and vice versa. Imagine a soccer team in which each player is assigned a position and a role on the field. While scoring goals is the main target or endpoint in achieving victory in a game, the player who assists by passing the ball to the goal scorer is also acknowledged as being equally important. The goalkeeper and defenders of the team are recognized for preventing the opposing team from scoring goals. A good coach cultivates a culture in which collaboration toward the commonly shared endpoint is necessary for the success of both individuals and the entire team. They discourage and actually reprimand behaviors that prove detrimental to the final outcome of a game—for example, having a player exhibit selfish behavior and not pass the ball to another who has a better chance of scoring a goal.

Handling Complaints

When you are in an administrative position, there is no escape from hearing frequent complaints about others. Make sure to listen carefully and never jump to conclusions based solely on what you hear from the complainer. Half a story is never the real story. People report on problems according to their own perception. Some may have selective memory or hearing, which tends to create an inaccurate scenario. People also tend to use innate self-defense mechanisms to place the full blame on others and expect you to take their side. Hear from the accused party and others if necessary. Request additional information from all if needed to explore the reality of the situation. Be transparent with both sides about the inquiry steps you have taken or will be taking. Be neutral and nonjudgmental, as you will simultaneously be playing the roles of a prosecutor and a defense attorney. Your main goal is to make a sound judgment in assigning the blame while keeping a civil spirit in the relationship between the plaintiff and the accused. Apply the conflict resolution tactics detailed in chapter 3.

Complaints vary in how serious the issues are. Trust your gut feeling if you sense that handling a certain conflict requires skills or authority you do not have. In these circumstances, refer the case to somebody else in your unit or to an office in your college or institution that specializes in handling similar problems. Some complaints require a formal process to achieve justice and avoid possible litigation against you or against the institution. Examples of such sensitive and complicated matters include accusations of harassment, substance abuse, scientific misconduct, physical threats or any behaviors you may deem criminal in nature. Soon after you assume your administrative position, familiarize yourself with policies and procedures for properly handling such complicated issues.

Building a Strategic Plan

Strategic planning is an important part of the mission and responsibilities of academic administrators at all levels. Having such a plan also ensures that resources are aligned with plans and vice versa. This rule applies to both financial and human resources. Being a strategic academic leader is all about utilizing available resources and attracting additional ones to elevate the status of research, teaching and service to the community. Last but not least, a well-crafted strategic plan cultivates trust among various stakeholders in the potential of the college or institution leadership's plans to achieve their goals and therefore improves the institution's chances of attracting funds from states and private donors.

Strategic leaders excel at long-range planning, in which their vision and plans are based on analysis, evaluation and monitoring. These tactics enable them to set up frameworks, design interventions and ensure allocation of resources according to priorities set by the master guiding plan. Stakeholders value leaders who get things done, particularly when it comes to achieving the goals of their strategic plans. There is nothing less strategic than having a leader declare lofty vision and goals but failing to lead the way there due to their lack of necessary leadership skills or the unrealistic nature of their vision in relation to available resources. Strategic plans must also be realistic in considering the institution's dominant culture with regard to being open to adopting change. In his book *Good to Great: Why Some Companies Make the Leap … and Others Don't*, Jim Collins states, "Greatness is not a function of circumstance. Greatness, it turns out, is largely a matter of conscious choice, and discipline." Here is another relevant quote from the same book: "Great vision without great people is irrelevant."

Innovation is one of the most important qualities of a strategic leader. Such a leader is always on the lookout for ways to bring the organization to higher levels by improving the quality of service and the culture of the workplace. Their leadership often uses shared organizational values as a foundation for plans and actions. A good strategic leader is able to rally faculty and staff to believe in the cause, own it, and work hard toward achieving it.

Strategic leaders intentionally shift their attention from dealing with today's problems to envisioning the possibilities of the future. They are clever in delegating crisis containment to those with better managerial skills. In other words, good leaders may not necessarily be good managers. One of my favorite books is titled *Free the Idea Monkey*, by G. Michael Maddock and Raphael Louis Viton. The main take-home message of this book is that any successful organization needs two drastically different types of people. The first group is called "the idea monkeys." They are endowed with high creativity and imagination. They jump around from one tree branch to another, fancying possibilities. They come up with many ideas but may not be good at prioritizing them or taking proper actions to bring the ideas to fruition. The second indispensable employee type is called "the circus ring leaders." They excel at comparing ideas brought up by the monkeys and at running operations to bring the best of these ideas to reality. According to Maddock and Viton, an organization's success requires the collaborative efforts of both groups. It also mandates a good balance between the two groups. One could easily imagine a workplace full of ideas generated by the monkeys that do not progress any further, or another environment that is dominated by managers who excel at making things happen but lack imagination and vision.

A strategic plan should conform to the established vision and values, and it should be paired with metrics and milestones for assessing progress. Ideally, there should be alignment between strategic plans of a department, college and institution. A good administrator shepherds and facilitates the execution of the strategic plan. They are there to help circumvent obstacles and resolve conflicts. In creating a strategic plan, the most successful leaders are well attuned to internal and external pressures that may influence the overall direction of their profession. They structure their plan based on educated calculations and predictions of future possibilities. This proactive approach is what visionary leadership is all about. It connects goals with what is possible in terms of available resources, therefore maintaining the right mix of realism and optimism.

Every academic leader naturally aspires to elevate the status of their college or institution in research and education. While some may dream of having their institution be on the top ten list of one or both of these academic missions, only a few make it to that level of distinction by carefully designing how to get there. Quite often leaders spend more time on perfecting statements of aspirations and goals in their strategic plan than on delineating strategies and tactics required to achieve them, including timelines and metrics for gauging progress. Lack of living with reality, planning and execution is the Achilles' heel that explains why many academic leaders do not see their vision materialize. It is also the reason why collegiate or institutional task forces responsible for crafting new strategic plans come up with documents that are similar (or sometimes identical) to the ones produced a few years back by other task forces without examining why the goals of the previous plan were not achieved. This is most certainly a prescription for repeated history.

An astute leader is willing to learn from the outcomes of past strategic plans. They start by asking vital questions: Why haven't certain goals of the previous strategic plan been accomplished? What were the obstacles? Was there something wrong with the tactics? Were the goals too grand compared to available resources? Answering these questions will guide success on a second try. Good leaders also benefit from studying successful strategic plans in other academic institutions and finding out how others went about achieving their declared goals.

A strategic leader, while focusing on long-term vision, is also able to change routes in response to a rapidly changing environment. In creating their strategic plan, they consider many "what if" questions at numerous junctures. They contemplate alternative solutions in case primary approaches do not work. They always have their finger on the academic environment's pulse to predict upcoming changes and be ready to adapt to them.

The following is a summary of the main elements of effective strategic planning.

- **Vision**: Inspirational statement of where the institution would like to be in the future

- ***Mission***: Core purpose and contribution to the profession and the society at large
- Short-term, mid-range and long-term ***goals***
- General ***strategies*** to achieve goals
- Specific ***tactics*** for acting on each strategy
- ***Objectives***: Defined desired achievements by the end of the plan
- ***Key performance indicators***
- ***Timeline***

A leader should start the process of creating a strategic plan by involving a small group of consultants and then expand the conversation to a wider audience. An engagement plan should be developed ahead of time to ensure the inclusion of representatives of all bodies that serve a particular mission of the university. Inclusive participation of all faculty starting from early stages of planning, for example, will allow them to develop ownership and motivation to execute the plan. Faculty are often resistant to top-down decisions. Leaders may also consider including student and staff representatives. Transparency is important for encouraging participation in the plan's design and execution. Sometimes it is helpful to engage a professional consulting agency in moderating discussions, making suggestions about process and sharing examples of strategic plans adopted by other universities. However, a good leader must not be tempted to imitate plans of other colleges or institutions, especially those with high national rankings. They should instead ensure that the main elements of the strategic plan are organic in nature and aligned with the culture and resources of their institution. This approach makes the plans realistic and achievable.

Structuring Meetings Toward Attaining Goals and Efficient Use of Time

Meetings in an academic environment serve many important functions. Their main goal is to exchange information in an efficient manner, share the collective wisdom and vision of the group, and provide transparency. Meetings also serve to update and refine plans, in addition to assigning roles, responsibilities and level of authority for their execution. Some meetings are held to discuss strategies for implementing a decision made at a higher level. This section is intended to provide discussion of features of productive meetings and practical aspects of implementing them. This information is important for senior faculty who currently chair various local and national committees, task forces, or review panels, as well as those who are preparing to become academic leaders. The information may also be helpful to all faculty in conducting efficient meetings with individuals or groups of their research or teaching teams.

Meetings must be properly planned and conducted to be effective. There are many questions to ask before one decides to hold a face-to-face meeting, especially one that includes a large number of people. First and foremost, is there really a need to schedule a meeting? Could the issue be resolved by convening a small number of wise and trusted representatives of concerned groups? Could a phone or virtual conversation serve the same purpose? If the meeting is simply meant to share information, could this be done by email? Might deferring a matter to a committee or a task force be a way to diffuse responsibilities or delay decisions you are not ready to make? What would be the likely setbacks if a given meeting is not held?

Unfortunately, only a few leaders are talented at or have had training in running efficient and productive meetings that end up fulfilling their purpose. This common flaw in the academic culture wastes so much time and energy. It also reduces confidence in the merit of the process and makes faculty drag their feet on their way to any of the numerous meetings they must attend almost every day. Academics often strive for perfection. They easily (and sometimes unnecessarily) get into the weeds too quickly while discussing an issue at a meeting. Moreover, more energy and time are invested in reaching consensus than in paying attention to designing action plans and safeguards to ensure that recommendations by the convening group are implemented in a timely manner. In my experience, academics seem to derive joy from discussions that rehash old "supposedly finished" business without investing time in learning from past experiences regarding why such issues are still visible on the horizon, sometimes quite frequently. There is often no adequate exploration of whether past task forces or committees, within or outside the institution, may have tackled similar issues and actually drafted reports that were filed away and forgotten without implementation. In the next section, I will use chairing an academic committee as an example for good practices.

Before a Committee Meeting

The chair of a committee should invite agenda items ahead of time, as well as at the end of each meeting. A couple of days before the meeting, they should send out the agenda, minutes of the previous meeting and supporting documents. Doing so will save time and will also help members of the group think of issues and formulate questions, ideas and positions.

Each item on the agenda should have a start and end time for discussion. Items should also be differentiated as "for information," "for discussion" or "for action." An important function of "for information" items is to briefly report to the group decisions made by related committees that some members of the group serve on. Presentation of "for information" items should be very brief. Otherwise, this exchange should be done via email. Items that fall under the category of "for discussion" include new policies and general strategies related to upcoming opportunities and challenges. Some of these agenda items will most likely be labeled "for action" in future meetings. This is when proposed strategies will be discussed in depth, tactics will be developed, and responsibilities for implementation will be assigned. Each agenda item that is for discussion or action must be allowed its fair time for deliberation. Cursory discussion of an important issue does not do it any justice. Jam-packed agendas result in useless meetings since they do not allow for deep discussion of any of the individual items.

Much work could and should be done between meetings to prepare for the group's next gathering. This includes exchanging progress on tasks and sharing new, related information. A committee chair may form a small group of committee members to deeply investigate an issue and bring their findings to the entire team. Together, these strategies will result in short but efficient meetings. Meetings should not be planned for more than ninety minutes. If you decide to run longer meetings, be prepared to witness yawning, glazed eyes and scrolling down cell phone screens.

It is important to decide on the order of agenda items. Some experts advocate for starting meetings with urgent matters that require timely decisions. Items that require mental energy should also be scheduled early in the meeting when participants are fully attentive and energized. A leader may want to prioritize matters on which he or she expects agreement, as this practice helps set a calm tone necessary for productive discussion of contentious items later in the meeting. Others prefer the opposite sequence: they start with contentious issues to allow ample time for vetting and hearing different points of view. Find out for yourself what works best for you and members of the committees you lead.

During the Meeting

A chair must start meetings on time, even if some members are still trickling in. They should not repeat what has already been said to inform latecomers of what they have missed. Being firm will establish a pattern and eventually result in more compliance with arriving to meetings on time. As each agenda item is brought up, the chair should clearly state the goal of discussion. Is it to start a preliminary conversation or to make firm recommendations? A common pattern for discussing agenda items that require action is to begin by stating the underlying challenges or opportunities and their impact, in both the short and the long term, followed by discussion of causes and cost-benefit analysis of various potential solutions. The discussion should end with deciding on actions and assigning individuals as leads to make sure things get done in a timely manner. Selection of the leads should be based on their individual skills. At the end of discussion for each agenda item, the chairperson should invite additional questions before briefly reiterating decisions and action plans. This summary serves as material for the meeting minutes and enforces the group's feeling that the meeting has accomplished its goal.

Discussion of an agenda item should be ended if more facts are needed or more people should be invited to the table. Certain complicated issues that require additional time for contemplation should be deferred to a future meeting rather than being dealt with in a hurry. Similarly, a matter should be deferred when it becomes clear that it is more productive to assign it to a subgroup that will proceed with further discussion and bring back recommendations to the entire committee.

A perennial challenge that faces group leaders at meetings is dealing with agenda items on which they have a strong opinion. How do they lead a democratic and open conversation without imposing their beliefs on others? One solution is to be upfront and declare this fact, and then ask somebody else to lead the discussion of this particular issue. It is advisable for a leader to reserve their contribution to the discussion until after listening to all others to avoid the appearance of imposing a personal opinion or preference on the group. Moreover, listening to the discussion may lead open-minded leaders to change their initial stance.

A prudent meeting chair watches for those who jump too far ahead—for example, providing solutions before hearing the background and causes of a problem or starting a discussion before a motion is seconded. Safeguards should be in place to prevent some from talking at length without getting to a specific point or recommendation or repeating things that have already been said. How many times have we all heard someone say, "I agree with all that has been said," and then take five or more minutes to tell us, again, what it is they are agreeing with without adding any new information? Worse yet, some rehash discussion after a vote has been taken. A good leader should put a stop to such time-wasting practices. A chair of a national committee I served on used a creative approach to ensure that no individual would dominate the discussion by talking endlessly without adding significant value. In such scenarios she would lift her coffee mug that said, "SUMMARIZE"!

Participation and engagement are essential qualities of productive meetings. Disagreement about certain amorphous issues should be encouraged. However, respect for differing points of view must be cultivated and maintained. It becomes a major detriment when the person chairing a meeting occupies the stage without allowing sufficient time to hear others express their point of view. A meeting chair should fully realize that they are there to be a servant to the group rather than its master. Their role is to stimulate conversation, provide interpretation and clarification, and moderate a healthy dialogue toward reaching a resolution. Meetings are most effective when everybody at the table feels welcome to contribute to the exchange. A good chair should invite, but never force, those who are silent if she or he believes they may have specific information or expertise to share with the group but needs encouragement to speak up. They should also protect the person they called on against possible uncivil reactions by some of the participants. Such protection is particularly important if the person invited to speak is a junior faculty member who happens not to support the prevailing point of view of their senior colleagues. In fact, it is better to ask junior faculty to express their opinions first before inviting contributions from senior colleagues. This practice will save a junior faculty member the angst of having to disagree with or contradict others.

Some agenda items may require a vote. The majority, however, require consensus without necessarily taking a vote. An effective leader should be tactful in guiding the group toward consensus, knowing very well that reaching unanimity on certain issues is likely not feasible. It is important to recognize that consensus is different from unanimity. Consensus implies overwhelming settlement in which the majority agree they can live with a decision or a proposal that has been fairly vetted by the group. Such decisions are often based on benefiting the majority of stakeholders while minimizing setbacks to others. Unanimity, in contrast, is achieved only when all members of the group vote on an issue in the same direction.

Summary

There are many qualities a good leader must have, many of which exist in ying-yang pairs. He or she must be thoughtful and consultative but also decisive, forgiving while maintaining accountability, compassionate but fair, firm but flexible, friendly but not a friend. Leaders should also have impeccable integrity to gain the trust of their constituents and should maintain a reasonable balance of lofty vision and existing reality. A good academic leader cares about service quality and guiding the department, college or institution, sometimes at the expense of some financial gains. To succeed, leaders must surround themselves with thoughtful and creative people who are loyal to the institution and candid in giving necessary feedback. They should also excel at garnering a variety of financial and intellectual resources necessary to achieve their goals.

Self-Reflection Exercises

- Think of your most and least favorite academic leaders in your department, college or university. What personal qualities have contributed to their selection as best and worst?
- Contemplate the pros and cons of becoming an academic administrator in the future in relation to your professional, family and personal goals.
- At the current stage of your career, what are the drives that would sway you toward or away from becoming an academic leader?
- What academic leadership positions fit you best? Think of the short and long term.
- What experience have you gained thus far that prepares you for a successful administrative role? Which experiences or training do you need to add to your portfolio?
- What personal qualities do you have that would make you a good leader? Which qualities would stand in your way?

11

Challenges to Academia

In the past couple of decades, academic institutions have faced different kinds of curve balls. Some of these ordeals have been financial, while others have been related to significant changes in student and faculty populations. Furthermore, fierce competition for obtaining research funding and recruiting outstanding faculty and students has compounded the problem. Institutions with astute "leaders" have learned from these painful experiences and have designed proactive strategies to avoid having history repeat itself. Unfortunate universities led by "managers" who continue to be reactive are not expected to weather so many blows. Rather, they will likely soon become dinosaurs.

Financial Challenges

Academic institutions are mainly supported by research funds, tuition and private donations. Recently, they have experienced significant financial challenges coming from many directions. Research funding has become more scarce and incredibly competitive. New institutions that offer similar curricula have drained what used to be a stable pipeline of highly qualified students. Many of those entities offer online education that provides the flexibility needed by adult learners who have day jobs and families. Alumni loyalty has plummeted, along with their donations to their alma maters.

Public institutions have suffered the additional drop in state funds in support of both operations and infrastructure. To put it satirically, some have been transformed from being "state funded" to becoming "state located"! To add more fuel to the fire, the public has gradually grown apathetic in protesting cuts of state funding to public universities. This position stands in sharp contrast to the usual outcry and barrage of appeals made when a state does not approve enough finances to build a new football stadium, for example. The reasons are clear in my mind: Many citizens are not fully aware of the complete range of what academics do—especially what academics do for them. State residents get their knowledge through newspapers that almost always favor going after scandals and various types of misconduct at academic institutions rather than touting faculty accomplishments and the caliber and placement of university graduates.

Universities must therefore become actively engaged in educating the public about their mission and the role they play in people's lives and the lives of their children. They should do the same with state legislators who have a say in determining how much money is dedicated to supporting higher education. I have seen some creative approaches used to convey this message. Some universities rent booths at annual state fairs, not only to advertise education opportunities but also to have representative professors speak to the public about the type of research they do and explain its potential benefits to them. Others invite the public and legislators to participate in brief educational experiences (for example, week-long mini-engineering or mini-medical schools that provide a general sense of how higher education institutions accomplish their tripartite mission to serve society).

Faculty of the Department of Neuroscience at the University of Minnesota came up with a brilliant concept many years ago—namely, the "Brain Awareness Week." Each year during this week department faculty, graduate students and postdoctoral fellows visit local schools and community colleges to introduce students at all levels to how the body's nervous system works. They bring along clever and interesting props to attract students' attention. One person used a preserved human brain, for example, to demonstrate the role of different brain regions in controlling speech, vision, emotions, thoughts, movement and gait. Lo and behold, some students at the schools they visited ended up applying for admission to the neuroscience graduate program at the university many years later. The faculty of this department even convinced the university president at that time to take similar props when he visited the state capital to submit his annual request for state funding. After brief opening remarks about what the university does for state citizens, he moved on to discuss ongoing research endeavors. Suddenly he grabbed two human brains hidden behind the podium and exclaimed, "This is your brain, and this is the brain of a person who died of Alzheimer's disease." The difference in the size of the two brains was stark due to marked degeneration of almost entire brain regions as a result of Alzheimer's disease. The president then went on to explain the research activities at the university that aimed to decipher the mechanisms of neurodegeneration in this disease and efforts to design medications for treatment or prevention, as well as biomarkers to be used for early diagnosis. The legislators were quite impressed and granted one of the most generous budgets in the recent history of the university. Connections with the community are also made through providing high school and college students in the region with a chance to get research experience at the university.

The effects of the gradual drop in financial resources for educational institutions have been magnified by increased costs of meeting the demands of steadily emerging compliance regulations. Universities have had to expand their administrative teams of executive faculty and staff who draft guidelines, provide necessary training and enforce compliance. Naturally, this change came at the expense of hiring faculty to contribute to research, teaching and service, especially at a time when the cost of recruiting star faculty has rocketed in terms of salary and sophisticated research instruments. The large web of administrators in most institutions often causes dysfunction, added bureaucracy and waste of resources: too many cooks in the kitchen! There is usually a lack of effective communication and collaboration between similar offices in colleges and universities at large, which results in duplicating efforts and occasional conflicting messages. While I strongly oppose adapting a corporate model in handling the priorities of investment in higher education institutions with bottom-line monetary gains as the main target, I clearly see there is much for universities to learn from the business world, especially when it comes to exemplary management and leadership styles that result in enhanced operational efficiency. Learning good project management from the private sector comes as a close second.

Additionally, universities have recently been a popular target for cyberattacks. These attacks generally aim to steal sensitive information (such as valuable intellectual property or personal information) or to threaten individuals by installing ransom software on their computer terminals. What makes universities particularly vulnerable to such attacks is their open and sharing nature, qualities that are usually foreign to the corporate world. The alarming frequency of such threats has diverted significant financial and intellectual resources to fortify the infrastructure of cyber defense walls.

As a result of dwindling resources combined with escalating costs, universities have been forced to seriously consider "what not to do" to save unnecessary costs of operations associated with medium or low benefits. For example, many have replaced employees with electronic programs, such as "chatbots" that respond to questions raised by current students and those who are interested in applying. There has also been a national trend in not hiring replacements for faculty who leave or retire. Furthermore, some universities have sold their hospitals to private parties, even though one of the main functions of these hospitals is to educate medical students and residents. It has become common to hear about naming a teaching or research building after a generous donor. I actually know of institutions at which the price tag for name rights to various buildings is public knowledge.

Ideally, academic institutions should focus on providing higher education to citizens and creating solutions to social challenges through research and service. This philosophy has led universities to stay as far away as possible from business models in which maximizing profits dictates plans and actions. Unfortunately, recent financial challenges have forced academic institutions to take measures that deviate from these idealistic principles in order to remain afloat. Corporate mentality has driven institutions to favor initiatives and programs that generate money over ones aimed at improving the quality of education and research. Examples include cutting services and programs that are in demand by the public but do not generate enough revenue to justify their survival.

Some of the financial choices made by university administrators puzzle many citizens. They do not comprehend why universities keep expanding their administrative cabinet at a time of financial constraints. One of my neighbors told me sarcastically that he believes the goal of universities is to ultimately have one administrator for each faculty member! One cannot blame the public for this perception since, as I mentioned earlier, the specific roles of many academic administrators and offices are not clear even to faculty, students and staff. Another example is how much emphasis institutions place on athletics. A large percentage of university budgets is dedicated to supporting these activities. Ordinary citizens are shocked and dismayed when they learn that a basketball coach in a university makes quadruple the income of most senior faculty, including the university president!

Changes in Student Demographics and Attitudes

College education, especially in professional colleges, has become quite expensive. The higher price tag has resulted in students carrying enormous loan debts upon graduation. An alarm was triggered recently when, for the first time in history, the amount of loans for students in some professional colleges exceeded an average graduate's first-year salary. These mathematical facts have discouraged many students from seeking further education upon obtaining their bachelor's degrees. The high cost of higher education has also driven many students to seek part-time employment while they are attending college. While this practice provides valuable experience and skills, it takes away from precious time dedicated to studying.

There has also been a steady decline in enrollment of international students in American universities, mainly due to the significantly lower cost of education and improved quality of academic programs in their home or neighboring countries. Recent government policies that have been hostile to international students also played an important role in discouraging foreign students to come to the United States for their education. One memorable example was the government policy during the COVID-19 crisis of rescinding visas for international students who received education online by necessity. Luckily, such decisions were reversed in time before they caused too much damage.

The majority of students decide to enroll in a given institution based on its elite status, quality of education and placement of graduates. However, universities must consider other relevant factors that play an important role in luring students. It always amazes me to hear stories from friends regarding why their children decided to go to a certain university. Reasons include choosing a university that has a strong basketball team, electronically modern dorms, large gyms, or even a location in a party town or a state where recreational marijuana is legal! Safety is also an important factor for both students and parents. Such variations in the basis of students' decisions on where to be educated has created a race among universities to create many of the elements that are attractive to students. This race is quite costly and drains resources that should be spent on recruiting top-tier faculty or modernizing research facilities.

Other approaches to increase enrollment that have been adopted by some institutions include lowering standards for admission, such as eliminating requirements for national standardized tests. Naturally, this decision results in students being unprepared to learn. I have witnessed a steady decline over the past few years in student knowledge of subjects that represent an essential foundation to the material I teach. Another trend aimed at attracting students is having universities engage in a race for higher graduation rates, which have become bragging rights among educational institutions. I get quite irritated when I see new students who have just arrived on campus wearing university T-shirts showing their anticipated graduation year instead of their year of admission (as was customary until recently). I believe this practice makes students believe that graduation is a right rather than a privilege for those who work hard. While some institutions achieved high graduation rates by improving education quality and providing a positive culture, a few sacrificed their integrity by demanding that faculty craft easier exams. Some colleges in my institution even stipulated an open-book policy for exams during the COVID-19 crisis. Faculty were not allowed the necessary time to transform their questions to make them more challenging and therefore more appropriate for open-book-style examinations.

Other measures to attract more students include creating three-year bachelor's programs that admit students who are academically prepared to handle content of the curriculum or designing undergraduate programs that prepare a pipeline of students who will pursue various types of professional education. Creating unique hybrid degrees is another solution. There are many examples of dual bachelor's degrees in related disciplines, such as international relations/foreign language, psychology/criminal justice, economics/ political science or economics/mathematics. There are also hybrid degrees in unrelated subject matters (for example, liberal arts/engineering, biology/foreign language or psychology/foreign language). Similarly, there are numerous examples of dual graduate or professional degrees. Dual degrees are a good approach to producing graduates with very unique combinations of sets of knowledge that make them more competent in pursuing certain specialized professions. The trick here is determining that there is a good balance between supply and demand.

Universities must keep investing in modernizing and updating their educational programs to accommodate significant changes in social demographics. Universities must adapt their offerings to provide continuing education to adults at various stages of their careers and lives. Practical opportunities must be created to accommodate adults who seek additional education while holding full-time jobs (for example, by providing night classes or virtual learning programs).

Academic institutions also need to cater to students from different ethnicities, first-generation college students, and students of modest financial means. Such diversity necessitates using a variety of teaching modalities to match students' preferences for different ways of learning information, in which, for example, some students may be more visual or auditory learners while others learn better by problem solving. Research indicates, for example, that Mexican American students are comfortable with cognitive generalities and patterns. They are therefore more comfortable with broad concepts than component facts and specifics. They also value connections with others, which explains why they often seek personal relationships with teachers. African American students usually value oral experiences, physical activity, and loyalty in interpersonal relationships. These traits call for classroom activities that include discussion, active projects, and collaborative work. There is also a body of literature that indicates a preference among Native American students for connecting pieces of information to the global picture and being allowed quiet time to think and analyze new information. White American students, by contrast, value learning experiences that focus on competition, very specific information, tests and grades, and linear logic. These are the patterns are prevalent in most

American schools and colleges, which naturally do not appeal to non-white American students.

There is major controversy, however, regarding the validity of the linkage between culture and learning styles. First, generalizations about groups of people have often led to misleading inferences about individual persons within these groups due to the proven existence of diversity within diversity. A second source of controversy is the dangerous creation of another layer of ethnic and racial profiling. This trend may easily be misconstrued as an explanation for differences in achievement between minority and nonminority students.

Professors have been encouraged to apply active learning techniques proven to result in deeper understanding of the material being taught. This practice includes breaking students into small groups for discussion, holding debates about controversial issues among students or giving reading assignments to students prior to class and have them rotate in presenting the material. Unfortunately, many faculty members (particularly senior faculty) have been adamant in resisting change. They still deliver lectures from the podium like the good old days. Worse yet, a few continue to literally read from crowded PowerPoint slides that are difficult to decipher. It is a big mistake for an instructor to apply these outdated practices without adding new information or delivering the material in a more attractive format than the presentation file they provide to students to use as a source for studying. This practice leads to students skipping classes and not reading the posted lecture material.

By peeking into classrooms in my college, it is quite easy for me to deduce the lecturing style of a given faculty. Some classrooms are jam packed, while others have only a few students monitoring their cell phones instead of paying attention to the instructor. This divergence is also reflected in student evaluation of teaching. Those professors who engage students consistently often receive high marks, while those who resist change are deemed ineffective. Evaluations of the latter group of instructors usually become even worse when they reach for the wrong solution to address poor student attendance—namely, penalizing those who skip lectures. I have actually seen comments by students asking that certain faculty be removed from a course teaching team. Students can also be merciless in letting a faculty member realize they are not thought highly of. A long time ago, the son of a colleague of mine was admitted to the same college where his father was teaching. One day, the father was assigned to give a lecture in a course his son was enrolled in, but his son was not in attendance. He handed the slide carousel (yes, I am talking of the old days of 35 mm slides!) to the teaching assistant responsible for managing audiovisual setup in the classroom. When he clicked on the first slide, he was astonished to see the statement "Do you know where your son is?" He was totally devastated by the second slide: "Your son, like many others, did not want to sit through one of your most boring lectures!" Obviously these slides were placed in the deck by students as a way for them to speak their mind.

Every now and then, one of the instructors in courses I direct complains about low student attendance. I have found it best to hold off on giving an answer until I attend some of the lectures given by that faculty member. I sometimes ask peers to join me in evaluating their teaching. Quite often I find that the style of teaching is the reason why students are not motivated to attend lectures. I then try to deliver this message to the instructor in the most constructive way, making suggestions for improvement and referring the faculty member to helpful resources. Sometimes I hear counterarguments and accusations that I am handling students with kid gloves and that I should stop succumbing to their whims. I usually respond using the common motto "the customer is always right." After all, students are our customers. They pay the bill for their education and deserve to be offered the best learning opportunity possible.

Another threat to academia is the gradually increasing reluctance of bright college graduates to pursue additional education. They prefer getting lucrative jobs with high pay to spending more years in achieving further higher education. They are also deterred from applying to graduate school by hearing gloom-and-doom stories about how hard their professors work, often with few perks and no life outside work. Furthermore, international graduate students get recruited back to their home countries with lucrative offers of funding and up-to-date research facilities. Together, these alarming trends result in drainage of the faculty pipeline.

Graduate students in some institutions belong to collective bargaining units, the goal being to protect their rights and prevent their exploitation by the faculty and the institutional administration. Unions also fight for equitable financial compensation for graduate teaching and research assistants and for improving their benefits (for example, health insurance and vacation). Some unions call for restricting the working hours of graduate students to forty hours per week on a 9:00 a.m.–5:00 p.m. basis. If I were a graduate student, however, I would not have wished for such limitation on my working hours, since working extra hours to complete certain types of experiments is absolutely necessary in many lines of research. Most graduate students recognize that the harder they work, the sooner they will get their degree. Working additional hours is therefore mostly their own decision. Such union-related regulations that do not suit the nature of graduate education are likely related to the fact that graduate students in many institutions are organized by the United Auto Workers union. Obviously, the needs of graduate students and auto workers are vastly different.

Changes to the Faculty Body

Serious financial challenges have forced universities to take drastic steps. Some gradually replaced tenure-track faculty with adjunct instructors who teach the majority of courses. Adjunct faculty (most of whom are exceptional teachers) are paid less and are usually hired at a percentage effort that does not qualify them to accrue healthcare or retirement benefits. Graduate student teaching assistants also increasingly substitute for regular faculty in the classroom, to the dismay of students and their families, who pay high tuition to be educated by seasoned professors. Other institutions have simply increased the teaching load of tenure-track and tenured faculty without recruiting additional help. Naturally, their service duties have also increased proportionally since contingent faculty normally do not contribute to this particular academic mission. Furthermore, non-tenure-track research-oriented faculty have become favorite hires, in contrast to tenure-track faculty. They are (and will likely remain) highly productive and tenacious in gaining research funding to support their research programs since renewal of their appointment is contingent upon maintaining financial research support. More important, their salaries are often totally derived from external grants. They therefore represent a very attractive low-risk, high-gain option for colleges and universities.

Academic institutions are regularly challenged by having their faculty leave for other universities, therefore losing valuable home-grown individuals who are familiar with the local culture and values. They get lured by other institutions in exchange for higher pay and perks, probably the most significant of which is being given an endowed chair that supports their full salary and provides funds for research supplies for life. It makes me sad that, in most cases, being loyal to a single institution does not pay off financially. Lately, annual faculty salary raises in academia have hardly kept up with inflation. It is also painful and demeaning for productive faculty to discover that some colleagues who have been enjoying life away from work without showing much professional productivity or contributing to the mission of the department or college got a raise that is within the margin of error of what they got by burning the midnight oil. Stagnating salaries and the escalating market value of talented junior faculty have jointly resulted in having newly recruited assistant professors get paid close to (or sometimes even more than) what some seasoned associate or full professors receive.

Of course, finances are not the only factor that leads faculty members to consider moving somewhere else. Some faculty move to industry to gain access to proprietary databases or technologies they need for their research, or they get fed up with academic bureaucracy and inefficiency.

However, many faculty would forgo a lucrative job offer from another institution that does not provide career development support of the same quality as their current institution. Faculty also tend to spend the entirety of their career in an institution with values that result in a tightly knit, respectful, encouraging and supporting professional community. Lack of such an environment has been instrumental in having minority faculty in particular leave institutions. I firmly believe that many universities invest disproportionately in recruiting faculty from underrepresented populations rather than grooming them and providing them with a friendly and supportive environment. A particular challenge faces colleges that employ faculty with professional degrees (for example, medical, veterinary, pharmacy, law, physical therapy, architecture, nursing or engineering). These faculty often leave to practice their profession if they discover that the service-heavy nature of their academic position does not provide them with the necessary time to accomplish their dreams of contributing to discovery through research.

Loss of vitality in some tenured and mid-career and senior faculty is another serious problem for academia. This malaise results mainly from a lack of carrots and sticks combined with benign neglect. A grave mistake that many academic administrators make is assuming that tenured faculty will without any doubt continue their journey toward stardom. Therefore, they believe that tenured faculty no longer need mentoring. The simple fact is that they do. Some mid-career faculty suffer from significant burnout at the end of their agonizing journey to achieve tenure. Others fail to keep up with recent advances in research technologies and methodologies. Their research becomes stale and outdated and loses its appeal to granting agencies. Having received several consecutive rejections of grant applications may create a downward spiral of self-defeat and surrender.

Faculty in some institutions (mainly public ones) have also been unionized—that is, they belong to organized collective bargaining units. Unions play an important role in protecting the rights of faculty, especially the adjuncts, and serve as watchdogs to ensure academic freedom, tenure and shared governance. However, regulations imposed by faculty unions complicate the academic process of approving new initiatives. Moreover, bargaining units negotiate annual salary raises or timed salary agreements that apply uniformly to all faculty, regardless of the quality of their work and contributions to the mission of their institution. This situation results in universities losing highly productive faculty who object to such an indiscriminating rewards system. Unions also make it very difficult for universities to fire tenured faculty who have consistently demonstrated poor performance (or even to remove an unproductive assistant professor by denying them tenure and terminating their employment).

Challenges to the Tenure System

The American Association for University Professors defines *tenure* as "a means to certain ends; specifically: (1) freedom of teaching and research and of extramural activities, and (2) a sufficient degree of economic security to make the profession attractive to men and women of ability." The concept of tenure was therefore established to provide faculty with academic freedom of speech, thought and action. It has been the foundation of intellectual advancement in our universities and society at large. Furthermore, tenured faculty represent members of a stable community who have shared experiences and have contributed together to advancing the mission and status of their institutions.

However, faculty tenure has been under scrutiny by members of the public who question its basis and value. They wonder why a certain group of elite citizens are endowed with such a lifelong benefit, even though some do not continue to live up to what is expected of them. More seriously, some tenured faculty commit sins that, according to university policies, should result in revoking their tenure. Such measures, however, are rarely applied. Every now and then, newspapers report on a senior faculty member who has been convicted of serious immoral conduct or violation of institutional or federal policies or laws who only received a slap on the wrist as punishment. As mentioned previously, post-tenure reviews designed to maintain senior faculty vitality by keeping only the best are often not associated with any serious consequences. This situation contributes to having the public envision tenure as undeserved entitlement for a group of people who are sometimes immoral or deadwood individuals who get paid generously for doing very little. Scrutiny of the tenure system has escalated to calls for its elimination. In fact, new laws have been introduced in some states to allow institutions more leverage in firing tenured faculty.

One must also carefully consider the practical applications of the concept of academic freedom to understand some of its limitations. While faculty have total freedom in choosing the type of research they pursue, their proposed projects must be blessed by grant reviewers who decide which research applications get money to support them. In other words, granting agencies have the power to determine which research projects are worth carrying out, simply by deciding which ones to fund. In turn, the government has control over research budgets allocated to federal granting agencies and has the leverage to earmark certain pots of funding for research on specific topics. As for teaching, what a faculty member teaches must be contained (within reason) within the boundaries of the approved curriculum. They are likewise limited in how much they challenge students in the learning experience since poor student reviews have negative consequences.

Are tenured faculty truly free to express their views without any threats of retaliation? Not really. Department heads are appointed at the pleasure of their dean. Speaking against the dean may result in an email announcement that Dr. X "has *decided* to step down as department chair!" A tenured faculty member who strongly opposes the views of the department chair, particularly in public, may lose their corner office and get minimal annual raises in spite of being highly productive.

Another tenuous aspect of the current tenure system is the lack of correlation between tenuring an academic position and guaranteeing a full salary. The financial challenges imposed by the COVID-19 pandemic, for example, led most academic institutions to reduce faculty salaries, tenured and untenured alike. There is also a trend in how salaries of new tenure-track faculty are calculated, in which only a certain percentage of the salary is guaranteed, while the rest depends on continuation of revenue generated by the faculty member from research grants, clinical service, and so forth.

The COVID-19 Pandemic Crisis

The COVID-19 pandemic has created significant challenges for higher education institutions, mainly in having to adapt quickly to meet the needs of education and research. This problem was associated with significant financial costs, especially in updating technology to meet the sudden demand for online instruction. Institutions also needed to build up psychological and psychiatric therapy services for students, faculty and staff. Being locked down away from social circles and knowing people who have caught COVID-19 (or even died from it) has caused major stress in many individuals. Altogether, these elements created a perfect storm threatening the stability of mental health.

Revenue from student tuition plummeted as admission numbers went down precipitously. There was also a significant increase in the number of dropouts, due to either psychological factors or devaluing the online teaching modality applied by most institutions. Many students decided to take a gap year as a result of losing part-time employment (or due to the major income earner in their family losing their job) or having to take care of family members who were afflicted with COVID-19. Some worried about the threat to their health posed by traveling to or being on campus (in the case of institutions that offered hybrid models of education). This effect was naturally more noticeable for out-of-state students, which resulted in losing the extra revenue from this tuition. International students could not enroll for some time due to temporary travel restrictions. To make matters worse, students in many universities demanded partial or full refunds of tuition and fees, claiming that virtual education was not optimal for their learning needs. A few institutions succumbed to their demands, in part or in total, to avoid costly lawsuits. Most institutions decided to refund service fees to students since many services were not available during the pandemic lockdown (for example, exercise facilities and libraries).

Loss of tuition and fee revenue was not the only cause of the COVID-induced financial crisis in academic institutions. There was much loss in clinical income in university hospitals. Many clinics had to shut down completely and numerous services were eliminated, such as elective surgeries. Patients delayed scheduling appointments, even when some clinics started to open up, due to worries about getting infected during their visits. There was also loss of revenue associated with ticketed university events such as athletic games, concerts and other artistic experiences that were shut down during the pandemic. Student housing and dining revenue dropped, due to lower enrollment and students choosing to rent off-campus housing and cook their own meals to avoid the higher risk of infection by living in a shared room in a dormitory or eating with others in a crowded university dining hall.

Institutions used their financial reserves (if they had any) to keep most of their faculty and staff while hoping the storm would soon pass. Others had to lay off many employees of various classifications. The first ones to go were staff who were declared nonessential. The financial crisis forced some universities to declare financial stringency that threatened the continued employment of tenured faculty.

Another serious blow caused by the COVID-19 pandemic was the suspension of onsite research operations. This decision slowed down the pace of research and led to the loss of precious research samples that had a limited shelf life. Fortunately, many universities allowed tenure-track faculty to extend their tenure clock by at least a year to make up for time lost during the pandemic. Halting research also provided an opportunity for faculty, graduate students and postdoctoral fellows to write manuscripts using the data they already had in hand. I know many faculty who were quite prolific in publishing during the shutdowns. They resurrected drafts of old work that were residing in a desk drawer or on a computer terminal for many years due to a lack of time to finish writing them. Many graduate students used the hiatus in research to draft chapters of their dissertations. Most important, some researchers decided to experiment with mining and analyzing large existing databases, which enabled them to ask very pertinent research questions without the need for additional experiments.

To plan for similar future interruptions in research due to pandemic or other causes, I highly recommend that institutions train their scientists in informatics through data mining—that is, analyzing existing databases. There is already a huge body of data out there collected for a specific purpose that could serve as a source for answering many other questions. This approach will also be helpful in case research funding is lost and one is unable to support generating new research data.

Emergence of Virtual Education

The COVID-19 crisis has resulted in many changes in the way we administer higher education, some of which ended up being positive following the inevitable growing pains. When campuses closed because of the pandemic, faculty had to switch their teaching modalities to an online format. They did their best to adapt and improve on lecture design using platforms such as Zoom and Google Conferencing. Faculty discovered unique features of these modern tools, such as polling students to get a sense of what they had just learned in real time. Another benefit is the ease of dividing students into groups for active-learning exercises. I, among many of my colleagues, believe this is the way to teach in the future. Why go back to highly technical classrooms that are quite expensive to construct and maintain? What is wrong with having students learn while feeling comfortable in their pajamas or petting their dogs or cats? Another advantage of virtual learning is that this option expands the geographic reach of an institution's educational programs.

Institutions have homework to do in getting buy-in from both the faculty and the students in adopting this approach. They should engage faculty and students in a dialogue to address their concerns and some individuals' resistance to change. Many faculty lack sufficient knowledge of the unique features such virtual platforms offer. Their past experience in using these modern tools has been largely limited to participating in meetings with colleagues, in which the technology was applied only to hear voices and see faces. Therefore, institutions should educate their faculty (particularly senior faculty) in effective means of using online teaching platforms. They should create a safe environment that encourages faculty to experiment with and share creative approaches to virtual learning. Those who are resistant to learning new tricks should be encouraged to rely on the skills of the younger generations (for example, teaching assistants) to optimally set up the system to perform various functions.

As a result of the success of the virtual learning experience during the pandemic, fully returning to the way things used to be does not seem to be a viable option. There are new norms at play. Remote learning has offered much flexibility for staff and faculty to work from home and avoid the time and cost spent in commuting to work to either teach or attend meetings. Ideally, what started as jumping to online teaching without being fully prepared for it should morph into thoughtful and intentional planning of rigorous partial or full online offerings. In the absence of ensuring high-quality online learning in well-established academic institutions, many students will be tempted to enroll in veteran online universities (for example, the University of Phoenix) while paying significantly lower tuition. These institutions have the advantage of having optimized their remote teaching technology, methodology and content over a couple of decades. It is rather ironic that many academics used to make jokes and snobby remarks about online universities during their early stages of existence and development. It was common to hear questions like "who in their right mind would want to pay money to be taught by a computer or a remote instructor?" Such universities were considered kids leagues. There are stories of job seekers who opted not to list a degree from one of these virtual institutions in their application for fear of imparting a negative image on their education portfolio. Now, years later, most universities are currently thinking of introducing elements of remote education that were proven effective during the COVID-19 pandemic.

There are, however, serious challenges to online learning that must be considered and faced head on. Internet blackouts have become common because of so many people being online at the same time, most of the time. This problem is magnified when several family members in the same household who use the same internet bandwidth simultaneously sign on using different computer terminals or other electronic devices. Internet instability poses a serious problem during online examinations or quizzes. It is also difficult for students with young children to find a quiet place to take online classes and examinations while the kids are at home. During the peak of the COVID-19 crisis, students who could not afford the cost of high-speed internet lost access to free Wi-Fi services available on campus or at coffeehouses and restaurants that were no longer available due to the shutdown.

Online instruction has also made it quite difficult to administer traditional closed-book exams, even in the presence of intensive proctoring. A student may be looking for answers to questions in a notebook or on a second device, or they may be receiving hints from peers via email or chat applications. I have been ecstatic to see the transition to administering open-book exams designed to test students' ability to analyze and assimilate information, in contrast to the practice of memorization and regurgitation involved in good, old-fashioned multiple-choice questions. Being allowed to use lecture notes, books and internet resources to answer a challenging question more closely mimics real-life situations while on the job. One could go a step further and allow collaborations and conversations between individuals to come up with the correct solution to a difficult problem. Naturally, this process involves structuring questions that test for deeper knowledge of the subject and even synthesis of knowledge gained from multiple classes and courses. This is what one hopes a successful student will do when pursuing their career following graduation—namely, consult the literature and seek the opinion of others when they cannot solve a tough problem on their own.

Summary

The academic landscape has recently undergone marked changes. Most of these have been in response to financial pressures. Competition for students has been at a record high due to the emergence of so many new, small, private colleges. Research funding has become scarce. State funding for public universities has plummeted. The COVID-19 pandemic has magnified the financial crisis. Universities had to respond quickly to the closure of campuses by adopting online teaching. Many research operations were halted. Other challenges that academic institutions face are the result of the student and faculty bodies becoming more diverse than ever, so that it is necessary to cater to their specific needs in order to retain them and ensure their success and career advancement. Such pressures, in addition to public scrutiny of the value of higher education institutions, their administration-heavy structure and the presence of unproductive tenured faculty, have resulted in outcries to modify the tenure system or cancel it altogether. Only institutions that adapt to these changes and pressures wisely and in a timely fashion are expected to survive.

Self-Reflection Exercises

- What type of financial pressures on your college or institution have you witnessed lately?
- If you had all the power and authority, what would you change in response to these pressures?
- What challenges to academia do you foresee in the next ten to fifteen years? What do you think university administrators should do in anticipation of these challenges?

Bibliography

Adams, M. *Change Your Questions, Change Your Life: 12 Powerful Tools for Leadership, Coaching and Life*. Oakland, CA: Berrett-Koehler, 2015.

Baker, V. *Charting Your Path to Full: A Guide for Women Associate Professors*. New Brunswick, NJ: Rutgers University Press, 2020.

Bakken, J., and C. Simpson. *A Survival Guide for New Faculty Members: Outlining the Keys to Success for Promotion and Tenure*. Springfield, IL: Charles C. Thomas, 2011.

Barker, K. *At the Helm: A Laboratory Navigator*. Cold Spring, NY: Cold Spring Harbor Laboratories Press, 2002.

Biswas-Diener, R. *Practicing Positive Psychology Coaching: Assessment, Activities and Strategies for Success*. Hoboken, NJ: Wiley, 2010.

Bland, C., A. Taylor, A.L. Shollen, A.M. Weber-Main, and P. Mulcahy. *Faculty Success through Mentoring: A Guide for Mentors, Mentees and Leaders*. Lanham, MD: Rowman & Littlefield, 2009.

Bland, C., A.M. Weber-Main, S. Lund, and D. Finstad. *The Research-Productive Department: Strategies from Departments That Excel*. Hoboken, NJ: Wiley, 2005.

Bloomfield., V., and E.E. El-Fakahany. *The Chicago Guide to Your Career in Science: A Toolkit for Students and Postdoctorals*. Chicago: University of Chicago Press, 2008.

Bonner, B., A. Marbley, F. Tuitt, P. Robinson, R. Banda, and R. Hughes. *Black Faculty in the Academy: Narratives for Negotiating Identity and Achieving Career Success*. New York: Routledge, 2015.

Brounstein, M. *Coaching and Mentoring for Dummies*. Hoboken, NJ: Wiley, 2000.

Burge, G. *Mapping Your Academic Career: Charting the Course of a Professor's Life*. Downers Grove, IL: IVP Academic, 2015.

Byars-Winston, A., and M.L. Dahlberg, eds. *The Science of Effective Mentorship in STEMM*. Washington, DC: National Academies Press, 2019.

Collins, J. *Good to Great: Why Some Companies Make the Leap ... and Others Don't*. London: HarperCollins, 2001.

Doyle, M., and D. Straus. *How to Make Meetings Work*. New York: Jove Books, 1983.

Dweck, C. *Mindset: The New Psychology of Success—How We Can Learn to Fulfill Our Potential*. New York: Ballantine Books, 2016.

Fisher, R., and W. Ury. *Getting to Yes: Negotiating Agreement without Giving In*. Auckland, New Zealand: Penguin Books, 1993.

Franko, M., and M. Ionescu-Pioggia. *Making the Right Moves: A Practical Guide to Scientific Management for Postdocs and New Faculty*. Research Triangle Park, NC: Burroughs Wellcome Fund; Chevy Chase, MD: Howard Hughes Medical Institute, 2004.

Goleman, D. *HBR's 10 Must Reads: On Managing People*. Boston: Harvard Business Review Press, 2011.

Goleman, D., A. McKee, and S. Achor. *Everyday Emotional Intelligence: Big Ideas and Practical Advice on How to Be Human at Work*. Boston: Harvard Business Review Press, 2018.

Gonzaga, A.M., E. Ufomata, E. Bonifacino, and S. Zimmer. "Microaggressions: What Are They? How Can We Avoid? How Can We Respond?" 2019. https://www.chp.edu/-/media/

chp/healthcare-professionals/documents/-faculty-development/microaggressions.pdf?la=en.

Griffin, J. *How to Say It at Work: Putting Yourself Across with Power Words, Phrases, Body Language and Communication Secrets.* Paramus, NJ: Prentice Hall, 1998.

Guild, P. "The Culture/Learning Style Connection." *Educational Leadership* 51 (April 1994): 16–21.

Gunsalus, G.K. *The College Administrator's Survival Guide.* Cambridge, MA: Harvard University Press, 2006.

Hoppe, T.A., A. Litovitz, K.A. Willis, et al. "Topic Choice Contributes to the Lower Rate of NIH Awards to African-American/Black Scientists." *Science Advances* 5, no. 10 (2019): eaaw7238. doi:10.1126/sciadv.aaw7238.

Huston, T.A. "Race and Gender Bias in Higher Education: Could Faculty Course Evaluations Impede Further Progress toward Parity?" *Seattle Journal for Social Justice* 4, issue 2 (2005): 591–608.

James, R. *Tenure Hacks: The 12 Secrets of Making Tenure—A Brutally Machiavellian Guidebook for the Current and Aspiring Assistant Professor.* CreateSpace Independent Publishing Platform, 2014.

Jay, A. "How to Run a Meeting." *Harvard Business Review*, March 1974. https://hbr.org/1976/03/how-to-run-a-meeting.

Johnson, W.B. *On Being a Mentor: A Guide for Higher Education Faculty.* New York: Routledge, 2016.

Kanigel, R. *Apprentice to Genius: The Making of a Scientific Dynasty.* Baltimore, MD: John Hopkins University Press, 1993.

Kaplan, B. *Winning People Over.* Paramus, NJ: Prentice Hall, 1996.

Kennedy, D. *Academic Duty.* Cambridge, MA: Harvard University Press, 1997.

Kimsey-House, K., H. Kimsey-House, P. Sandhal, and L. Whitworth. *Co-Active Coaching, Fourth Edition: The Proven Framework for Transformative Conversations at Work and in Life.* Yarmouth, ME: Nicholas Brealey, 2018.

Knight, S. *The Life-Changing Magic of Not Giving a F*ck: How to Stop Spending Time You Don't Have with People You Don't Like, Doing Things You Don't Want to Do.* New York: Little, Brown, 2015.

Long, J. Scott, ed. *From Scarcity to Visibility: Gender Differences in the Careers of Doctoral Scientists and Engineers.* Committee on Women in Science and Engineering, National Research Council. Washington, DC: National Academy Press, 2001.

Mack, D., E. Watson, and M. Camacho, eds. *Mentoring Faculty of Color: Essays on Professional Development and Advancement in Colleges and Universities.* Jefferson, NC: McFarland, 2013.

Maddock, G.M., and R.L. Viton. *Free the Idea Monkey: To Focus on What Matters Most.* Brentwood, TN: Franklin Green, 2011.

Mallinger, A., and J. De Wyze. *Too Perfect: When Being in Control Gets Out of Control.* New York: Fawcett Columbine, 1992.

McCabe, L., and E. McCabe. *How to Succeed in Academics.* San Diego: Academic Press, 1999.

Morgenstern, J. *Time Management from the Inside Out: The Foolproof System for Taking Control of Your Schedule—and Your Life.* New York: St. Martin's Griffin, 2004.

Mrig, A., and P. Sanaghan. *The Skills Future Higher-Ed Leaders Need to Succeed.* Academic Impressions, 2017. https://www.academicimpressions.com/PDF/future-skillset.pdf.

National Academy of Sciences, Committee on Maximizing the Potential of Women in Academic Science and Engineering and Committee on Science, Engineering, and Public Policy. *Beyond Bias and Barriers: Fulfilling the Potential of Women in Academic Science and Engineering.* Washington, DC: National Academies Press, 2007.

Newman, S. *Higher Education Administration: 50 Case-Based Vignettes.* Charlotte, NC: Information Age Publishing, 2015.

Parks, S.D. *Leadership Can Be Taught: A Bold Approach for a Complex World.* Boston: Harvard Business Review Press, 2005.

Perlmutter, D. *Promotion and Tenure Confidential.* Cambridge, MA: Harvard University Press, 2010.

Pfund, C., S. House, P. Asquith, K. Spencer, K. Silet, and C. Sorkness. *Mentor Training for Clinical and Translational Researchers.* New York: W.H. Freeman, 2012.

Philipsen, M., and T. Bostic. *Helping Faculty Find Work-Life Balance: The Path toward Family-Friendly Institutions.* San Francisco: Jossey-Bass, 2010.

Phillips, S., and S. Dennison. *Faculty Mentoring: A Practical Manual for Mentors, Mentees, Administrators and Faculty Developers.* Sterling, VA: Stylus, 2015.

Rath, T. *Strengths Finder 2.0.* New York: Gallup Press, 2017.

Rath, T., and J. Harter. *Wellbeing: The Five Essential Elements.* New York: Gallup Press, 2014.

Ringer, J. *Turn Enemies into Allies: The Art of Peace in the Workplace—Conflict Resolution for Leaders, Managers, and Anyone Stuck in the Middle.* Newburyport, MA: Career Press, 2019.

Rockquemore, K., and T. Laszloffy. *The Black Academic's Guide to Winning Tenure—Without Losing Your Soul.* Boulder, CO: Lynne Rienner, 2008.

Skinner, T. *Effective Team Meetings: How to Run a Team Meeting [Even on Zoom].* Rhythm Systems, 2021. https://www.rhythmsystems.com/blog/5-tips-for-running-effective-team-meetings.

Solomon, M. *Working with Difficult People.* Englewood Cliffs, NJ: Prentice Hall, 1990.

Sue, D.W., C.M. Capodilupo, G.C. Torino, J.M. Bucceri, A.M.B. Holder, K.L. Nadal, and M. Esquilin. "Racial Microaggressions in Everyday Life: Implications for Clinical Practice." *American Psychologist* 62, no. 4 (May–June 2007): 271–86.

Sutton, R. *The No Asshole Rule: Building a Civilized Workplace and Surviving One That Isn't.* New York: Grand Central Publishing, 2010.

Turner, C., and J. Gonzalez. *Modeling Mentoring across Race/Ethnicity and Gender: Practices to Cultivate the Next Generation of Diverse Faculty.* Sterling, VA: Stylus, 2015.

Ury, W. *Getting Past No: Negotiating Your Way from Confrontation to Cooperation.* New York: Bantam Books, 1993.

Witt and Kieffer. *Leadership Traits and Success in Higher Education: How College and University Leaders Compare with Corporate Executives.* 2013. https://aascu.org/corporatepartnership/WittKieffer/Leadership.pdf.

Index

academic environment 2–4, 21–24, 183
adjunct faculty 23, 187, 216
advising 81–106
aligning expectations 86–87

boundary setting 88–89

career development 86, 113, 147–149
coaching 119
communication skills 49–50
conflict resolution 50–52

delegation 72–73
difficult people 54–60
discrimination 58–60
diversity 94–103

energy management 65–68

feedback 89–90
firing 123–124
funding 157–158

governance 15–20
group mentoring 133

harassment 58–60
hiring 106–108

individual development plan 68

leadership 105–111

meetings 202–206
mentoring 24–25, 38–43, 81–104, 126–137, 169, 180
minority faculty 35–39
motivation 118

negotiation skills 52–54

peer mentoring 134
post–tenure review 116
project management 71–74
promotion 17–21, 139–161
publishing 154–157

resilience 181–182
Robert's rules 15

self assessment 116
self promotion 30
senior faculty 168–188
soft skills 24
strategic plan 199

team management 105–125
time management 62–80

values 197
vitality 162–165

women faculty 27–33, 169
work-life balance 77–78, 159